SAUDI ARABIA
UNVEILED

By Douglas Graham

KENDALL/HUNT PUBLISHING COMPANY
2460 Kerper Boulevard P.O. Box 539 Dubuque, Iowa 52004-0539

This edition has been printed directly from camera-ready copy.

Copyright © 1991 by Douglas F. Graham

ISBN 0–8403–6461–X

Printed in the United States of America
10 9 8 7 6 5 4 3 2 1

SAUDIA ARABIA UNVEILED

TABLE OF CONTENTS

INTRODUCTION
    Saudi strategies were demolished by the Kuwait invasion.   Page 1

1. HISTORY
    Why is the Kingdom so important? . . . . Page 3

2. POLITICS
    The Royal Family Buys the People Off with Oil Money.
    Desert Democracy functions in the Majlis System. . . . . Page 17

3. FOREIGN POLICY
    Checkbook Diplomacy has bounced. . . . . Page 31

4. MILITARY AND SECURITY
    The Price is no Object where Military Expenditures
    are concerned. . . . . Page 39

5. RELIGION
    The Regime is Finding that Old-Time Religion. . . . . . Page 53

6. SOCIETY
    We are the World (that counts). The Kingdom's people
    cope with change. . . . . Page 71

7. WOMEN
    Sexual Apartheid Holds Back Development . . . . Page 85

8. LABOR
    Merchants of Visas . . . . Page 95

9. PETROLEUM
    The Kingdom Lost the Oil Price Wars, but doesn't mind . Page 111

10. INDUSTRY
    A Dangerous Dependency . . . . Page 119

11. INFRASTRUCTURE
    Human and Physical Infrastructure A Wise Buy . . . . . Page 127

12 . FINANCE
    Islam's Prohibition of Interest No Asset To Banking . . . Page 141

13 . AGRICULTURE AND WATER
    A Harvest of Troubles. The Water's Running Dry,
    and The Kingdom Can't Afford the Cost of Subsidies. . . Page 151

FOOTNOTES   . . . . Page 161
TABLE OF SONS OF ABDULAZIZ . . . . Page 164
BIBLIOGRAPHY   . . . . Page 165
INDEX   . . . . Page 166

PREFACE and DEDICATION

I set a longevity record for Western journalists in Saudi Arabia, but only by accident. A classmate from Texas A&M suggested I leave my poorly paid job with the *Huntsville Item*, in Texas, to seek fame and fortune in the Kingdom. The lure of a decent living wage and a chance to freelance was irresistable, and I arrived in the Kingdom in 1983, determined to serve only two years. Midway through my second year, I decided to write a book; before I knew it, six-and-a-half years passed.

The first night I landed in Jeddah, I was struck by the fact that its new buildings looked no more exotic than those in Midland, Texas, and that Arab families were picnicking on the Airport's grass. That was my clue that, despite massive modernization, the Kingdom's life revolved around the family and religion. As time went by, I covered various stories in the Kingdom and spoke with Saudi officials, businessmen, and doctors. I even met a few Saudi women. I camped in the desert, scuba dived in the Red Sea, acquainted myself with the wonderful, but maligned, camel and traveled to different provinces. I always came back to the idea that tradition, embodied in the family, and religion, were the key to understanding the Kingdom.

I did not want to write another "I was there" book, but a work that would try to lay the Kingdom open for the reader and help him or her understand a bit more about the secretive desert nation and its people. The West needs to know more about Saudi Arabia, particularly when American and European troops are encamped upon its deserts. The Kingdom is too important to think of in terms of camels, Cadillacs, oil wells, and sand.

Now, on to the nice part of acknowledging those who assisted me wittingly, or unwittingly, in one way or another, with this effort. I would like to mention my colleagues on *Saudi Business Magazine* and the *Arab News*. Philip Shehadi, Habib Rahman, Alfred Taban, Fidell Price, and Jerry Brown were on *Saudi Business*. *Arab News'* Editor-in-Chief Khaled Al-Maeena, Patrick Werr, Khaled N., Farouk, Ram, and Dr. Walid, were my comrades in Jeddah. Sir Sidahmed, Abdulatif, Amr, Saleh, and the indefatigable Javid, were stalwart co-workers in Riyadh. They were all completely unaware I worked on this book. Other friends in the Kingdom included Saad Al-D., Donna and Guian, Barbie Tomlin, Ali, the Pattersons, Mike and Tatiana, Rick Snedeker, Spud, T. Lavell, Dick Newcomer, the Sharabesh family, Claude, Cathy K., Cathy F., Susan S., Berhan, Mike M., Chuckles, J. Pratt, and many others.

I worked with many good reporters. Colleagues like Philip and Patrick, both now with Reuters, alone refute a claim by Sandra Mackey that she was the only serious journalist working in the Kingdom. I could add the urbane, witty Peter Theroux, formerly of the *Saudi Gazette,* and now a published author as well as Scott Pendleton, now with the *Christian Science Monitor*, and Kevin Meurhing, now with the *Institutional Investor*, who both slightly pre-dated me. All of these writers worked in the Kingdom during Ms Mackey's sojourn in the Kingdom.

Here I must thank those who assisted in this book. Michael Field, who introduced me to the *Financial Times*, is a good friend and knowledgable writer, and was always a welcome visitor to the Kingdom. He gave important encouragement and help. Peter Theroux read and re-read chapters, giving guidance and suggestions. He spent more time on this than he ever wanted to. Peter Wilson, my arch-competitor on the *Saudi Gazette*, helped edit, critique, trade information, and shared meals in Riyadh's *Mexican Connection* restaurant. A true friend indeed. I also thank Daniel Graham, my brother, for providing the computers for writing this book, and Laurie Graham, my sister, who produced the artwork for the cover. The gracious Dr. Michelle Munoz deserves my gratitude for getting me re-started on this project. Then there's Scott Monte Pendleton, whose advice sent me overseas, and makes him responsible, after a fashion, for this book you see before you. Lastly, this book is dedicated to my parents, especially my mother, Ruth M. Graham. I wish she were here to see it.

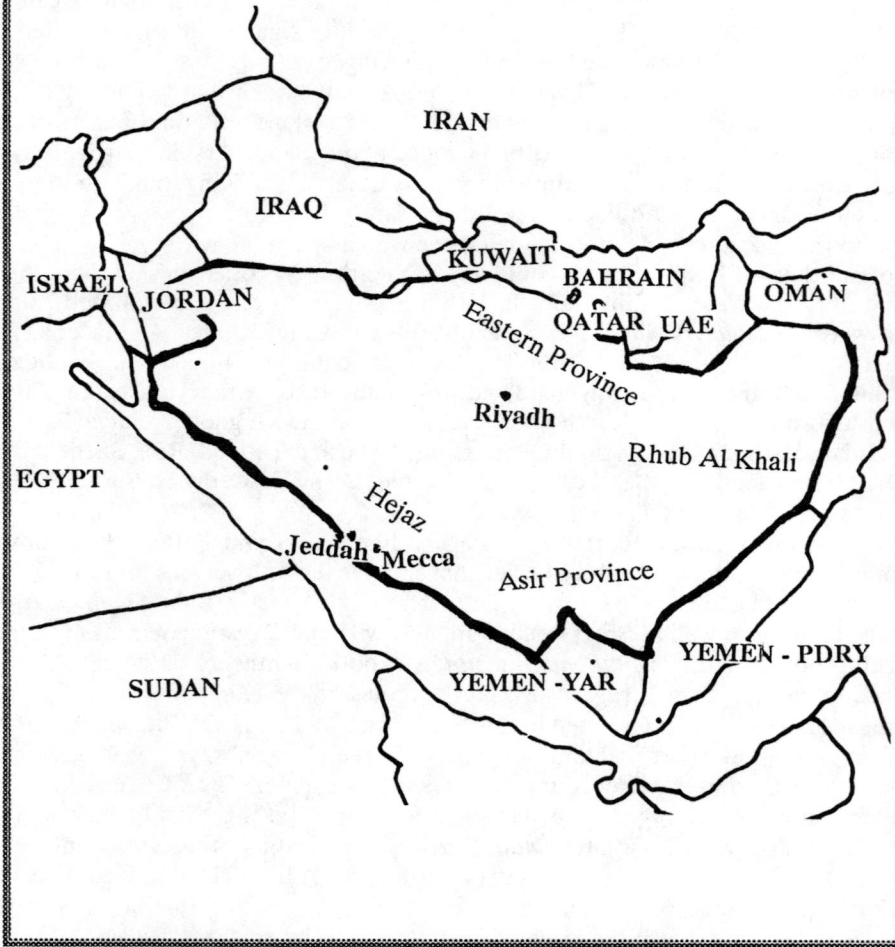

INTRODUCTION

The mood was tense in Taif's luxurious Conference Palace. The cool mountain city was quiet, but many miles away, 100,000 heavily-armed Iraqi troops idled their tanks on Kuwait's border. Diplomats of the two countries met and drank Arabic coffee as guests of Saudi Arabia's King Fahad. The traditionally-robed Kuwaitis had been instructed to yield to President Saddam Hussein's demands. Yes, Kuwait would agree to curtail oil production. Yes, she would grant a long-term lease to a small strategic island, and, yes, the Emir, Al-Sabah, would consider writing off nearly $15 billion loaned to help Iraq fight Iran. The Saudis thought they had successfully defused a fratricidal conflict between Arab nations, when the Western-attired Iraqis suddenly demanded nearly half of Kuwait. The stunned Kuwaitis stammeringly replied they would have to contact their government for further instructions. The Iraqis stormed out, but promised to attend another meeting later that night.

Instead, Iraqi armored units rumbled across Kuwait's borders at 2 a.m., and within 24 hours, had smashed the tiny nation. The Saudis, so paralyzed by the invasion that they refused to tell their people about it for an entire day, saw in the smoking wreckage the destruction of decades of checkbook diplomacy. Their carefully crafted Gulf Cooperation Council proved unable to save one of its six members from destruction. Multi-billion dollar arms purchases, constant promotion of Pan-Islamic causes, and holding the Americans at arm's length, didn't spare the Saudis the indignity of calling on the non-Muslim United States to save them from a brother Arab Muslim country.

The invasion, like so many of the predicaments facing the Kingdom, was partly the result of policy (the Saudis bankrolled and encouraged Saddam's invasion of Iran) and partly oil-related; Hussein justified his armored invasion in part on Kuwaiti over-production. Many decisions made during the kinder, gentler days of unlimited oil wealth have proven mis-steps in the harsh light of lower oil revenues.

None foresaw the steep decline of Saudi fortunes. In the Seventies, "experts" predicted oil prices would hit $100 a barrel. The Saudis, with nearly a quarter of the world's reserves, had no worries about running dry. They put spending plans into high gear.

Even with a massive development program, a weapons buying spree, exorbitant commissions and some old-fashioned corruption, the Saudis could not spend the $250 million a day pouring into their coffers. By the time the oil boom ended, the Kingdom built up financial reserves of over $180 billion. The Saudis' moderate government, stability, free enterprise economic system, and nearly limitless oil money ignited a development explosion. The population, pampered with free education, free medical care, and numerous generous subsidies, was reasonably content. The desert bloomed, thanks to irrigation, and people drank water extracted from the sea. Arms purchases gave the monarchy a modern arsenal. The Saudi checkbook won friends and influenced enemies. Writers frequently referred to the Saudi "Miracle."

The oil glut hit in 1983, but the people of the Kingdom learned of it only in 1986, when their monarch dolefully addressed them on television. "I am today directing this speech to you at a most delicate moment for all of us..." King Fahad bin Abdulaziz said, as he announced the postponement of the 1986 budget. Up until then, the government tried to hide problems with bland assurances. Now, Fahad tearfully informed his subjects, the oil boom was history and they would have to adjust.

The monarch spelled it out clearly. The oil market was glutted. Saudi production had dropped from a high of over 10 mbd to, at times, less than 2 mbd. The price of oil fell from more than $34 a barrel, to less than $15 a barrel.

After listing the Kingdom's achievements in industrial, infrastructural, and agricultural fields, he declared that the country would continue without a budget, and simply pay to maintain subsidies and benefits for citizens. The government would muddle along on an ad hoc basis, as it had already done so far, budgets and five-year plans notwithstanding.

The boom, for which Fahad's speech was an overdue eulogy, had been killed by OPEC oil policy. Against Saudi advice, OPEC raised oil prices and inadvertently encouraged conservation, alternate fuels, and discovery of new oil fields. Soon the Saudis found their total production shrinking while prices continued to slide. The resulting lower oil revenues affected every aspect of the Kingdom.

Checkbook diplomacy was forced to become smarter and tougher, especially since the Saudis were committed to underwriting Iraq's war. Domestic spending remained high. The government tried to cut costs and discourage waste by trimming subsidies, but was thwarted by popular sentiment. Attempts to raise electricity, gasoline, and water rates were stoutly resisted.

Religious conservatives have grown restive since the government's largesse has shrunk. Doubt about the wisdom of Westernization and modernization has begun now that the boom is over. This is reflected in a tilt toward fundamentalist Islam. The government tries to placate religious conservatives by allowing them to place further restrictions on women and non- muslim foreigners. Yet the demands of the Iraqi threat may still force the government to allow women a larger role in the economy.

Saudi Industrial development was revealed as a creature of government expenditure. Easy low-cost government loans and operating subsidies created overcapacity just when the economic downturn reduced demand. Now, many firms cannot compete without assistance. Those that can export are running into protectionist measures.

The Saudis imported vast numbers of foreigners to build and operate its new infrastructure during the boom. The increasing number of young Saudi jobseekers cannot find work, because employers prefer less expensive and more tractable expatriates. Further, financial and physical abuse of these employees has increased.

American and European financiers loved cash-rich Saudi Arabia during the boom. As they booked profitable loans, few bankers considered the contradiction of operating a Western interest-based system in a country where Islam forbids interest. After oil prices went bust, many Saudi investors successfully used the religious courts to avoid repayment of debt.

The Kingdom is proud of its agriculture program, but it was built on an expensive subsidy program. Farmers now grow excess wheat the government does not need, using money it cannot no longer afford, and consume precious water that cannot be replaced.

After the expenditure of one-third to a half of each budget for the past two decades on the military, the Saudis were still forced to turn to foreign troops for defense against Iraq.

The oil bust and the Saudi reaction to it reveals a lot about the Kingdom and its people. This book looks at the people, government, and culture of Saudi Arabia, and their ad-hoc approach to the problems which beset them. It seeks to educate the intelligent layman or interested Middle Eastern expert about the Kingdom, how it works, and why it works the way it does.

1

HISTORY

"The Angel Gabriel asked about the signs of the end of the World. The Prophet (peace be upon him) said: That the slave girl will give birth to her mistress and that you will see the barefooted, naked, destitute herdsmen competing in constructing lofty buildings." — A Hadith.

A space traveler would be excused for passing over the Arabian peninsula. It is monotonous, dry and sparsely inhabited. The first clue of its intrinsic interest would come from aerial observation of the Muslim world. Five times each day, the world's 900 million Muslims bow toward Mecca, the birthplace of their religion. If the spaceman needed to refuel his craft, he would learn another reason why humans are interested in the Arabian Peninsula; underneath the arid surface lie the largest petroleum reserves in the world.

These two factors are keys to the importance of Saudi Arabia, a large, empty land one-third the size of the continental United States. Saudi Arabia covers 62.1 percent of the peninsula's approximate 1,200,324 square miles (3,119,636 square km.). Around its periphery are newly-united North Yemen (Yemen Arab Republic) and South Yemen (The People's Democratic Republic of Yemen), the Sultanate of Oman, the United Arab Emirates (UAE), Qatar, the island of Bahrain, and Kuwait. To the north are Jordan and Iraq.

Saudi Arabia rests on "Al Jazira Arabia," which means the "Arabian Peninsula." Surrounded on three sides by water, and on the north by a sea of desert, it is almost an island, cut off from foreign influences. If physical barriers were not enough, the grinding poverty of the arid country further discouraged outsiders from meddling with its fiercely independent inhabitants, the Arabs.

GEOLOGY

These inhabitants have played on a stage made of a great pre-Cambrian shield of rock that imperceptibly moves away from Africa, widening the Red Sea and slowly, slowly, pinching shut the Straits of Hormuz on the Gulf. At the southern edge of the peninsula is a belt of mountains, which form the borders of the two Yemens and Oman. Along the Western edge of the plate are more mountains, which drop rapidly to the coastal Tihama plain.

Shallow prehistoric seas covered the peninsula and were filled with primitive molluscs, brachiopods and microscopic animals. They died and sank into the ooze and muck on the sea floor. The seas dried up, and the muck was compressed at high temperatures under layers of sedimentary rock to form oil and gas. Thus, millions of years ago, wealth was stored for the eventual inheritors of the peninsula.

The land rose, and Arabia, became, until 18,000 years ago, a savannah grasslands. Nomads hunted large game and left rock paintings, some of which still exist. Some African animals still live in the Kingdom. Baboons wander in the mountainous Asir region, as do the almost extinct Arabian Hyena, and various other mammals. Others, such as the ostrich, were recently exterminated by man.

After the last ice age, the Peninsula, like the Sahara, suffered prolonged drought. Satellite photos show extinct rivers that disappeared. All that remains are dry riverbeds, called "wadis," and large aquifers of water which are, like oil, non-replenishable.

The drying created three major deserts. The Nufud covers a large northern area with dunes of red or white sand. The Al-Dahna "Red land" stretches south from the Nufud to the Rhub Al-Khali, a desert so barren that its name means "The Empty Quarter." These deserts receive some scattered rain which results in growth of plants and brilliant flowers prized by bedouin herders.

CULTURE

The mention of bedouin brings the student of the Arabian peninsula to its inhabitants, the Arabs. Much of the Arab's past was known only through oral tradition, but lately, archeological excavations have begun shedding light on early Arabian cultures. Several civilizations arose along the Gulf, the earliest of which was Dilmun, which thrived on Bahrain as early as 2,000 b.c. and was known to the Sumerians. King Solomon excavated for Gold in Western Arabia. The center of the peninsula remained thinly populated and traversed by nomads and their one-humped Arabian dromedary, commonly called the camel. Centuries rolled past; little changed. The highlands of Yemen produced Frankincense, an aromatic resin beloved by the Romans and the Egyptians for religious ceremonies. After sea travel declined, camel caravans plodded to and from Yemen, passing the cities of Medina, Mecca, and Jeddah. The locals traded with, provisioned, and robbed or extorted from the merchants. Legends say that Yemen declined after the ancient Marib Dam burst, but archaeologists say the deathknell was sounded when Christianity became dominant in the Roman Empire. Christians made little use of Frankincense, and Arabia Felix, "Happy Arabia" as the Romans called Yemen, grew poorer.

Before the advent of Islam, the Kindites ruled central Arabia. Ironically, this central Arabian empire's rulers were the only non-foreign Arab kings to be called Malik. It was not until the arrival of the House of Saud (also from the center of the peninsula) that Arab kings were to reuse that honorific. Philip Hitti writes that the Kindites were the first to unite tribes under one chief, and their experiment proved a model for the Prophet Mohammed when he came on the scene. The Hellenized Nabateans left behind tombs and buildings carved in solid rock. Petra in Jordan and Madain Saleh in Saudi Arabia stand as silent monuments to these people. The Arab queen, Zenobia, of Palmyra, withstood the Roman legions until, finally, her armies were crushed and she was taken to Rome in gold chains.

Throughout history, the central part of the Peninsula was never dominated by foreigners. The only serious Roman invasion occurred in 24 B.C., when Aelius Gallus, prefect of Egypt, invaded with 10,000 men. He may have reached as far south as Najran, but had to return to Egypt with a decimated army.[1]

Caravans to Yemen often stopped in the small town of Mecca, which, even in the period of Jahiliya, "the time of ignorance" before Islam, was the peninsula's religious center. The tribes converged yearly at Okaz, outside nearby Taif, for an annual poetry festival. Warfare was banned during this period, and necessary trade was conducted. Most of Mecca's religious activity surrounded the Kaaba, which Arab tradition held was built by Abraham with the help of Ishmael.

The bedouin had already left their stamp on the Arabian psyche. Traits essential to desert survival are found in their concepts of manliness, honor, stoic endurance, and generosity to those, like themselves, who were at the mercy of the elements. The bedouin's vengefulness gave him a reputation as a tough customer.

These ethics are mirrored in Arabic society to this day. This is common in other cultures. A Houston banker may mock unsophisticated cowboys, but he still thinks of himself as having the qualities of the Old West, such as self-reliance, pride, and a belief in workin' and playin' hard.

The nomadic bedouin never developed the plastic arts such as painting or sculpture. Instead, they took their most portable tool, the only weapon they had against boredom, the Arabic tounge, and turned it into a work of art. Beautifully spoken classical Arabic can sway its listeners, even though they might not understand all of it. Poets by nature, the Arabs love their language.

Since extra food and treasure cannot be stored in the desert, and disasters strike anyone at any time, the most durable thing of value is a good reputation. Thus, most actions are done with an eye toward enhancing one's prestige. A reputation as a hospitable man is important. When guests arrive at a bedouin tent, they expect the host to serve them before himself. Thesiger wrote that during a hungry portion of his trip through the Rhub Al-Khali, he and his companions shot a rabbit. While they were cooking it, guests appeared out of nowhere. He and his companions proved perfect hosts and sadly watched the guests devour the entire scrawny animal.

The bedouin formerly spent much of their time stealing each others' camels. Ghazw, or raiding, redistributed wealth and proved one's manhood. "In desert land, where the fighting mood is a chronic mental condition, raiding is one of the few manly occupations," wrote Philip Hitti.[2]

Although the camel made bedouin life possible, their the ultimate weapon was the Arabian horse. Camels were ridden to the site of the battle. There, riders switched to their steeds for the final melee. It was said that a man would let his children go thirsty to give his Arabian horse a drink.

Interestingly, the bedouin never formed a majority. Most Arabs lived in the small towns near reliable sources of water. These settled Arabs traded badly-needed agricultural products with the bedouin, and supplied the few manufactured items, such as metal goods, that the bedouin could not make themselves. The bedouin exchanged animals and animal products with the townspeople. This uneasy balance between the bedouin and the towns held sway through the institution of Islam, until the appearance of the House of Saud at the beginning of this century.

Although the Arabian Peninsula and its bedouin tribes imparted important cultural traits to the Arabs, it was relatively unimportant until the rise of Islam. For the most part, Arabia was only a path through which caravans passed. But in 610 A.D., this changed when Islam or "submission to God" was born.

ISLAM

Islam was revealed to the world through Mohammed, who was born A.D. 570 A.D, to the Al-Quraish tribe of Mecca. He began to receive revelations from God at age 25, and attacked the prevalent polytheism of Mecca. Mohammed performed no miracles along the lines of Jesus. In fact, he had to retract the famous "Satanic Verses" allowing worship of some popular goddesses, claiming that Satan slipped him those revelations. Muslims consider the compilation of his revelations, called the Koran, such perfect Arabic that the book itself is his major miracle.

In the beginning, Mohammed said that Muslims should bow and pray toward Jerusalem, but after he was completely rejected by the Jewish tribes, he received a revelation which reoriented the direction of prayer toward Mecca. His message of the one-ness of God was rejected by the Meccans, and he fled with his followers to Medina, some 400 kilometers to the north, at 622 A.D. Later, this event was used as the start of the Moslem calendar. In 630 A.D., Mohammed reconquered Mecca, and the Islamic empire was started. In the space of a few centuries, Islam conquered the entire Middle East. Islam proved the only replacement for blood ties as a basis for society among the bedouin, and was used by Mohammed to forge them into a weapon that conquered the Peninsula. This lesson was not forgotten centuries later by the Al-Saud.

Four of Mohammed's companions succeeded him as the ruler, or Caliph. These "Four Righteous Caliphs" were: Abu-Bakr; Umar, who while being considered exceptionally pious, also broke all existing treaties with the "people of the Book," i.e. the Jewish and Christian tribes; Uthman, under whom strict religious observance began to weaken; and Ali, who was Mohammed's cousin, and husband of Mohammed's only surviving child, his daughter Fatima. A member of the Quraish tribe eventually usurped the throne. His generals killed Ali and later massacred his son, Hussein. This dispute over the succession of the leadership resulted in schism. The Shia claimed that the caliphate should have passed down through the descendants of Mohammed, i.e., through the line of Ali. Most Moslems, (86 percent) are Sunni, who follow the "sunna" or collected practices of the Prophet. They accepted the usurpers, and have remained at odds with the Shia, who mainly live in Iran, ever since.

Mohammed's death did not slow Islamic military expansion. Egypt, Syria, Persia, and Spain fell to Islam. Soon, the capital was moved. Mecca and Medina remained Islam's two holiest cities, but the Arabian Peninsula became a backwater. An interesting episode in Saudi history, denied or deliberately downplayed by many Saudis, was the birth of the Islamic sect called the Qarmations. These revolutionaries preached communal wives and property and called themselves brothers, or Ikhwan, a term later adopted by the soldiers of the Al-Saud. They even conquered Mecca and carried off the holy Black Stone. It was later returned, and the Qarmations destroyed, leaving behind Eastern Province Shia.

Except for the Qarmation episode, the Peninsula remained in a slumber. The bedouin gradually reverted to animistic beliefs interwoven with tribal tradition and Islam. They raided each other, preyed on commercial and Pilgrim caravans, and in general, carried on as they had centuries before. The Ottoman Turks eventually seized the Caliphate, but exercised only nominal control over barren Central Arabia.

THE AL-SAUD

It was here that the Al-Saud family arose. Their ascendancy coincided with the emergence of an earnest Islamic preacher, Muhammed Bin Abd Al-Wahhab. Muhammed was a man on a mission to purify Islam from all its corruptions. Muhammed came from a family of Islamic judges from the Central Arabia Nejd region.

Wahhabism, known to its adherents as "Unitarianism," made a distinction between state and religion that was not made in classical Islam. He ruled that a government derives its religious legitimacy by implementing Islamic sharia law. This lay in enforcing the Wahhabi Dawa, or "call" that emphasizes the Tawhid, or "unity" of God. Anything which draws attention away from God, whether it is wealth, statues, or veneration of saints or tombs, is Shirk "polytheism" since it worships something other than Allah. To implement these revolutionary ideas the Wahhabi preacher needed secular strength. His first two towns expelled him. He finally found an ally in the ruler of Diriyya, Prince Muhammed Bin Saud. The alliance between the Al-Saud and the Wahhab (later known as the Al-Sheikh) families began.

The alliance produced three distinct periods of Al-Saud rule. The first was a time of vigorous expansion, as the Nejdis subjugated most of peninsula. The holy cities of Mecca and Medina were captured. The Gulf states were reduced, Oman was raided, and Iraq was attacked. Their excesses after capturing Mecca in 1805 resulted in destruction of the first Saudi empire.[3] They went on a purifying rampage, smashing shrines, overly ornate mosques, musical instruments, and other aids

important businessmen and administrators got their start with Aramco. Multi-billionaire businessman Suleiman Olayan, a company employee, got his start with a loan from Aramco.

Despite increased oil revenue, the Royal family's profligate spending kept the Kingdom wallowing in an economic crisis. Abdulaziz, old and feeble, died, without leaving much of a government in place. He had introduced important new technology, often against the opposition of religious conservatives. Aircraft, motorcars, and radio were all initially opposed by the Ulema. Abdulaziz conquered their resistance to radio by reading the Koran over the airwaves.

Though Abdulaziz appointed his eldest son, Saud, as Crown Prince, and established the Majlis Al-Wuzara (Council of the Wazirs or Ministers), the government was that of a tribal sheikh. Any subject in the land could call on the King in his Majlis chamber and ask for help, or judgement on a complaint. The national treasury was treated as the monarch's private purse. There was not much of a standing army, and little in the way of organization.

When Abdulaziz died on Nov. 9, 1953, the succession took place smoothly, with Saud appointing Faisal the Crown Prince. The reign of Saud from 1953-1964, was a disaster. Although the well- intentioned man established the first universities, his main activities wee reserved for the marriage bed.

Saud had a tremendous sexual appetite, which, to the disgust of the blood-conscious Arabians, included many African women. Like many princes, Saud had a first, favorite wife, but ran through others. He was also offered a young "wife for the night" when he visited small towns, a practice still followed today. Saud fathered 290 children. The Royal Court used to post a secretary at the door to write the name of the woman and the time he slept with her, so that if she claimed she had been made pregnant by him, they could check to see if her claim were true."

Saud's generosity and good intentions inflated royal expenditures. By 1958, the Kingdom earned $340 million per year from oil, but had spent itself into a debt of $480 million. On the foreign policy side, things were not much better. In the late Fifties and the Sixties, the Saudis found themselves part of a shrinking number of conservative Arab governments. Iraq's royal family was butchered. Yemen's Imam was overthrown. Syria went "socialist." Egypt's King Farouk sailed off to exile and Col. Gamal Abdul Nasser rose up to electrify the Arab world and threatened to destroy the Saudi monarchy.

The Royal Family grew concerned at the danger resulting from Saud's incompetency. Older brother Mohammed, future Kings Khaled and Fahad, future Crown Prince Abdullah, and Fahad's six full brothers, pressed Crown Prince Faisal to take over the Kingdom. Faisal demurred for a while. Civil war began in Yemen during 1962, and relations with Egypt worsened again, over the Kiswa, the ornate gold-trimmed black cloth that covers the Kaaba. For generations, the Egyptians supplied the Kiswa, bringing it to Mecca on a special caravan. The Saudis claimed it was substandard, and built a special Kiswa factory that produces them to this day. Saud's attempt to bribe the Syrians to assassinate Nasser was exposed. Meanwhile, the liberal Prince Talal, Minister of Finance and National Economy in of Saud's cabinet, was rebuffed by Saud, the Ulema, and Faisal in his efforts to establish a constitutional monarchy. He and a few other princes left the country and were were exploited by Nasser's propaganda machine. The group returned to the Kingdom chastened, by 1963.

Saud never adjusted to Faisal's role as power behind the throne, and rebelled after several years. He tried to reclaim power, but was finally quietly deposed with the backing of the Ulema. Saud, to most Saudis, was a humiliating failure. For years, he was never mentioned in books or the press. King Saud University was renamed the University of Riyadh. Saud was modestly rehabilitated during the reign of Fahad. His photograph began appearing with those of his brothers, and his university regained its former name.

The reign of Faisal, from 1964 to 1975, was a remarkable turnaround in fortunes. Faisal was not as likable as Saud, but his piety, hard work, and shrewdness enabled him to propel the Kingdom on a path toward modern development. For one thing, he actually had a vague plan of what to do once he assumed office. In 1962, he had issued his ten principles:

1. Rule by Sharia.
2. Local administration in different regions.
3. Establish a Ministry of Justice, Supreme council of jurists, independent judiciary.
4. Establish Council for Fatwa (a religious council for rulings on Islam).
5. Spread Islam.
6. Good morality to be practiced.
7. Improve living standards by offering free medical care, subsidize food, provide free education, establish social insurance.
8. Organize social and economic progress.
9. Build roads, dams, explore for water, build industries, and establish Petromin.
10. Abolish slavery.

The list contains the general prescription the Royal family has tried to follow in ruling the Kingdom. Four of the 10 have to do with implementing Islam. Three have to do with economic development, and made subsidized services and food a pillar of government policy before the oil boom. Talal had offered citizens shared power through some sort of democracy, Faisal offered them money. Money won.

Faisal sternly led his people into the twentieth century. Many credit the rather humorless monarch with taking the first steps in creating a modern police state. He was the first to hold numerous political prisoners, most of whom were freed by King Khaled.

He outfoxed and outlasted Nasser in Yemen., who introduced troops into Yemen in 1961, during Saud's reign. Nasser overthrew Yemen's ruler, and became bogged down in a civil war. Characteristically, the Saudis backed the Royalist side, but attempted to keep a low profile. This proved impossible after Egyptian bombers attacked Najran and later, Jizan. The Kingdom provided arms and funds to the Royalists. Many observers say that the Saudis actually reined in the Royalists when it they were on the verge of winning. Faisal countered Nassarism and other pan-Arabic trends, by initiating a Pan-Islamic Movement.

THE BOOM

Faisal was a charter member of the Organization of Petroleum Exporting Countries (OPEC) which helped boost oil income from 3.79 mbd in 1970, to 4.76 mbd in 1971, and 7 mbd by 1973. Revenue rose from $1.15 billion in 1970 to $1.99 billion in 1972.[9] His new oil Minister, Ahmed Zaki Yamani, pushed for gradual nationalization of Aramco.

On Oct. 6, 1973, Egypt's Anwar Sadat, with Faisal's backing, launched the October War, known by the Israelis and the West as the "Yom Kippur War." Faisal announced the oil embargo after U.S. President Richard M. Nixon sent an emergency request of $2.2 billion for Israel to Congress. The embargo sent prices rocketing upwards. Americans waited in lines at gasoline stations. The second Oil Shock, coinciding with the fall of the Shah in 1979, pushed oil prices to around $36 a bbl. Saudi production was close to 10 mbd. Some $300 million per day flowed into the treasury. With $180 billion in its coffers, and one-quarter of the world's oil reserves, the Kingdom became a world heavy weight whose investment strategy affected stock markets and currency values.

Yamani, backed by Faisal, dominated OPEC. Its oil production levels determined world energy prices and rocked industrial economies. In the process of enriching OPEC countries, the rest of the world suffered. Economic growth ground to a halt or declined in much of the Third World. The industrialized economies were hammered.

During the period of oil shortages, all the pundits, except Yamani, predicted that oil prices would rise continuously. He warned that such phenomenal oil prices would result in conservation, switches to alternate energy sources, and exploration for more oil. This created the conditions for the Oil Glut of the early 1980s.

Faisal never implemented some of his 10 points, but did introduce "innovations" over the fierce opposition of religious conservatives. He opened the first schools for girls and the first television station. In 1959, he began a push to boost literacy up from the meager 5-10 percent level.

Television eventually cost Faisal his life. In 1965, young Prince Khaled bin Musaid was shot dead by a policeman as he and others tried to storm the television station in Riyadh. His brother, Faisal bin Musaid, attended one of the Majlis, or council sessions, where citizens present petitions to the King. As Kuwaiti Oil Minister Abdul Mutaleb Kazimi was being introduced to Faisal, the prince sprang from behind the Kuwaiti, and fired three shots at the King with a .38 pistol. Faisal died from a bullet wound to the throat, and his Crown Prince, Khaled, was approved by the Ulema within three hours of the assassination.

Khaled reigned from 1975-1982. "He was a man who could go to sleep on both ears," was an Arabic saying about the well-loved monarch. His health was poor, and the intelligent pro-Western Crown Prince, Fahad, was considered the power behind the throne. Khaled freed most of Faisal's political prisoners and presided over an economic boom.

During Khaled's reign, the Kingdom entered its golden age. From the austerity of 1970, the kingdom suddenly found itself with a surplus. The GDP rose from $11.3 billion to $42.2 billion by mid-1975.[10] Contracts were let to build anything and everything. The Americans won gigantic defense contracts for naval bases, anti-aircraft missiles and F-5 fighters. The French won orders for Frigates. Highway contracts were awarded. Telecommunications systems were installed. The rush was stupendous.

The ports soon proved wholly inadequate to the task of development. Ships waited months outside of Jeddah, and some companies resorted to hiring helicopters to unload cargoes of cement. The ports problem was relieved by a rush construction program.

Most contract bids were made with padding for unknown contingencies such as port, bureaucratic, and Act of God delays. In those halcyon days, the Saudi government paid 20 percent down upon award of a contract, which permitted a contractor to finance an entire job off of the down-payment.

This was the era of Kemal Adham, Gaith Pharoun, and Adnan Khashoggi, the mega-commissioners who parlayed their connections and familiarity with the West into gigantic commissions and immense wealth. Khashoggi, in particular, was involved in the weapons trade. Most Saudis (government employees included) had small companies on the side, and received low-cost loans to build homes, erect rental property, or start factories or farms.

The most riveting event of Khaled's reign took place during the month of Hajj on Nov. 20, 1979. A band Moslem fundamentalists seized the holy Mosque of Mecca. The bank included Saudis, some of whom were National Guardsmen, and Muslims from other countries. They seized the mosque and held off Saudi soldiers for several weeks. Coming on the heels of overthrow of Iran's Shah Reza Pahlavi, the seizure shook the Kingdom to its foundations. The greatest shock to the Saudi authorities was that the seizure was mounted not by foreign agents, but by Saudis themselves.

The Mecca incident highlighted the Kingdom's concern with nearby Iran. They had resented the Shah's domineering role in the Gulf, but he was not the danger Ayatollah Khomeini proved to be. The Ayatollah's revolutionary Islamic Shia regime challenged the Kingdom on its fundamental claim to power: Islamic legitimacy. This fear, which overcame Saudi nervousness over its aggressive neighbor, Iraq, led Khaled to connive in Saddam Hussein's attack on Iran.

The Iran-Iraq War allowed the Kingdom to forge the military and economic organization called the Gulf Cooperation Council (GCC). The organization, based in Riyadh, consists of the Kingdom, Kuwait, Qatar, Oman, Bahrain, and the United Arab Emirates (UAE). Iraq and Iran were both preoccupied, and gave the Kingdom a free hand in the Gulf.

The situation was growing tense when King Khaled's frail heart finally stopped beating in 1982. Crown Prince Fahad was named King, and the Commander of the National Guard, Abdullah Bin Abdulaziz, was named Crown Prince.

Fahad held several important posts before he became crown prince. He was first appointed Minister of Education by Saud, Minister of Interior in by Faisal, and Crown Prince by Khaled.

THE DECLINE

Fahad's regime has been marked by a decline in Saudi fortunes. The Kingdom held reserves of $180 billion in 1983, and over $300 million a day flowed into their coffers according to the SAMA 1984 Annual Report. Yet signs of weakening already existed. Oil production fell 43.4 percent in 1982. By 1983, oil income slumped 31.1 percent. to SR128.1 Billion. For the first time in nearly a decade, the Saudis had to dip into their reserves. The next year was worse, because the budget was based on overoptimistic oil projections. In 1985 production fell lower than 2 mbd. In 1986, King Fahad announced the delay of the budget, tearfully announcing that the oil boom was over.

PAYMENT DELAYS

The government's response was to claim nothing was changed, while it stopped paying its bills. Contractors and suppliers took out loans to stay afloat, and involuntarily financed Riyadh. They waited desperately for each new budget, when a flurry of bills were paid. But payments fell further behind. Ministries used minute defects to waste time haggling with contractors and delay payments. Only companies, such as Saudi Oger, owned by Fahad's friend, Rafiq Harriri, had the "Wafta" connections to get paid on time.

Bouygues-Blount, builder of the giant $3.4 billion King Saud University campus near Riyadh, waited 6 months or more for several payments of $150 million. Delays on three projects forced Jeddah's Fahad and Ali Shobokshi to reschedule $400 million in debts. Other companies, such as Ghaith Pharoun's REDEC, also had problems. Korean contractors were owed billions, but were kept afloat by their government, which valued their hard currency earnings and the market they provided for Korean steel and goods. Carlson Al-Saudia, a joint venture between Carlson of Massachusetts, Saud bin Fahad, a son of the King, and other Saudis, went bankrupt, and stranded three thousand Filipino workers in the desert. Laing Wimpey Alireza, a Saudi-British joint venture, despaired of delays and finally cut its losses and fled. While completing three hospitals for the Ministry of Health, top management prepared for a stealthy exit. In staggered groups, executives and senior officers went to different parts of the Kingdom and departed on exit-re-entry visas for "vacation." On the last day, the remaining core of officials fled the country. In a story in London's *Financial Times*, they blamed their losses on late payments. Saudi officials were furious, but powerless. Laing and Wimpey were satisfied; they got their people out without having them taken as commercial hostages. (See the Labor chapter).

Minister of Finance and National Economy Mohammed Abalkhail told the Saudi Press Agency that everyone was being paid on time, adding that the existing problems were being dealt with. Contractors and bankers read the story with disbelief. By the time the next budget rolled around, experts estimated that the government owed more than $3-5 billion to contractors. In a classified study of Riyadh, the government learned that almost 90 percent of construction firms reported that they experienced difficulties in collecting payments.

It was only in 1987 that the government quietly confronted the late payment problem. Payments lumped in the budget under government services shot up as billions of dollars of back payments were made. Yet, by 1989, payments were late again.

PROJECTS

The Kingdom could have cut spending on projects, but did this very reluctantly. Dammam's existing airport may be unimpressive, but it is adequate. No matter. The government announced plans to build the King Fahad International Airport for the Eastern Province. Only a few projects were scrapped. Petromin cancelled two new oil refineries, and a new lubricant base oil refinery. A new desalination and power generation plant for the Asir region was retendered 4 times, and scaled down each time around. Rather than admit cost was a problem, the government said the bids were flawed. The institution of open bidding saved a lot of money since secret negotiated contracts were an invitation to payoffs. Minister of Commerce Soliman Al-Solaim said in 1984 that costs of projects were reduced by 50 percent as a result of open bidding. [11]

SALARIES

If trimming project expenditures proved painful, then cutting manpower expenses was agony for the Saudi authorities. Government salaries accounted for up to one-third of the budget and were growing. As many as one third of the Kingdom's 1.2 million working Saudis work for the government. In 1986, the payroll alone was SR22 billion.

This was after salaries were cut by as much as 35 percent in 1985, and a hiring and promotion freeze was partially implemented. Most of the savings came through restriction of perks, overtime, and expenses. The men of the armed services suffered no such indignities.

THE PROBLEM OF SUBSIDIES

Agriculture production subsidies were no longer affordable. Wheat producers were guaranteed a price of SR3.5 a kilo (approximately $1,000 a ton). In 1987, even with the subsidy cut to SR2 per kilo, wheat alone cost the government nearly SR4.6 billion ($1.23 Billion). Barley imports soared to five million tons, at a cost to the government (with a SR300 per ton import subsidy) of $400 million.

Costs continued to grow in other fields. As electric power was extended to more distant areas, consumption per Saudi grew. Electricity subsidies rose to $1.5 billion a year. Water use jumped. In the five years up to 1986, Riyadh's water consumption reached the point where Riyadh uses more water per citizen than any other city in the world.

THE ATTEMPTS TO CUT SUBSIDIES

"Well, illhamdu lillah (praise to God) we have cut almost all of the subsidies," Minister of Commerce Soliman Al-Solaim told me at a bank reception. The Kingdom simply took advantage of falling commodity prices to do so. When the United States and the European Community (EC) launched their trade wars over agricultural exports, the beneficiaries (other than American and European farmers) were world consumers. The subsidies were removed when world prices declined enough to mask the cut on sugar, chilled meat, corn, oils, and milk.

"We don't want to tell the people about this," Dr. Solaim confided. "That way, the government still gets credit for the low prices." The indirect approach was used, because an earlier frontal assault on agriculture subsidies, Solaim explained, had been torpedoed by publicity.

Efforts to trim other subsidies have run into problems. If a subsidy is related to an item used by the common man, such as gasoline, bottled gas, water and electricity, then public outcry can be fierce. Public reaction forced modification of the first attempt to trim the fuel subsidy in April, 1984. Prices for fuel and other refined petroleum products were raised. Gasoline prices were hiked 70 percent.[12] Yamani told the Arab News on April 8, that Petromin had lost SR4 billion the previous year because of the fuel subsidy. The hike, however, was actually a tax, since he said the additional money went to the treasury, not Petromin.

The full price hike was rolled back. Premium gasoline was supposed to nearly double but was only increased to SR35 h per liter after the complaints. The government again raised gasoline prices three years later from 35h per liter for premium, to 51h per liter in 1987. This supposedly permits Petromin to break even.

Minister of Industry and Electricity Abdulaziz Al-Zamil announced new electric power rates in 1984. He argued that Saudis were wasting energy. Strings of lights burning all night, hordes of window-mounted air conditioners and homes with zero insulation. The response was not restraint but complaint. It costs the Kingdom 20.5h per kilowatt-hour (kwh) in large cities and 50h per kwh in small cities, so even the highest new rate, of 15h per kwh, requires sizable government subsidies are sizable. The new rates charged only 7h per kwh for the first 1,000 kwh of consumption, and scaled it up to 15h per kwh. Industries and agriculture still pay only SR5 per kwh. Although only 35 percent of the people were affected by the changes, the government revised rates back down in 1985.

Government attempts to cut water subsidies have run into even tougher resistance. Government attempts to curb wastage have tended to center on heavy penalties for over-use of water. Most houses have rooftop tanks, and many owners run their refill pumps until the tanks overflow into the streets. Those that do so face stiff fines, but this has had little effect on overall consumption.

The government is still trying to grapple with agriculture subsidies. This is covered in more detail in the Agriculture chapter, but essentially, the government is paying money it can't afford for wheat it does not need. It has slowly ratcheted down the agricultural subsidies, most of which benefit wealthy individuals and princes rather than small farmers. Fahad doesn't have much leeway to trim subsidies since they regarded as a citizen's right, ever since Faisal put them in his 10-point Plan.

ATTEMPTS TO RAISE REVENUE

The government tried to raise revenue using tactics that hit expatriates as much as, or more than, the Saudis. Wherever possible, it instituted higher fees to make government organizations self-supporting. The Saudi Sea Ports Authority raised fees, although it cut them them for Saudi exporters. The goal was to make the Ports Authority self-sustaining.

The five government credit agencies that provide low-cost loans for everything from houses to industries all cut back on activity. These were the Real Estate Development Fund (REDF), the Saudi Industrial Development Fund (SIDF), the Public Investment Fund (PIF), the Saudi Agriculture Bank (SAAB), and the Saudi Credit Bank (SCB). Officials now make new loans only out of money repaid on previous loans. This new policy created huge delays for loan applicants. During the boom, most loans were approved within a month. Now, a loan for a house can take more than a year.

Public transportation hiked rates back in 1985. Fares were doubled to SR2 per in-city ride. The Saudi Public Transportation Co. (SAPTCO) receives a subsidy in much the same way the electric companies do. The government guarantees shareholders a specific profit per share, regardless of losses. SAPTCO loses a lot of money.

The 1988 budget included several interesting proposals. An airport departure tax of SR10 for internal flights and SR50 for international flights was proposed. So was a monthly SR10 electricity tax. Water bills were to be assessed monthly SR10 taxes as well. Each time a patient visited a public hospital, a SR10 medical fee was to be collected. All of the fees were to be deposited in the Ministry of Finance's account. The government also sought to assess a real estate transaction fee of 5 percent and a SR200 annual road tax on vehicles. The expatriates-only income tax was proposed and then dropped. Interestingly, when the proposal left the desk of Deputy Minister of Finance Saleh Al-Omair, the tax was supposed to peak at 12 percent. By the time it reached the King for his signature, the top tax rate had ballooned to 30 percent. Omair, say sources, privately blames ministers hostile to his boss for the increase. After the tax was announced, and Expatriates prepared to leave en masse, the King rapidly backed down. The tax is covered more thoroughly in the Labor chapter.

Telephone and telex charges were raised. For instance, telephone connections once cost SR60 ($16). They were raised to SR600 ($160). Usage rates were increased across the board. Drivers license fees were raised from $30 to $133. Car registration renewals rose to SR500 ($133). Exit-re-entry visas, required by expatriates, were raised to SR100. Foreign work permits, called Iqamas, were increased to SR1,000.

Many of the 1988 proposals were cut back. By Jan. 4, the income tax was dropped. The airport departure taxes, water, electricity, and health service taxes were scrapped on Jan. 18, by the King who promised that Saudia airfare and electricity rates would not be hiked.

Newer government services have been establishment on a self- sustaining basis. In 1987, the Ministry of Communications established a network of car safety inspection stations. These stations are operated by a private firm that makes a profit off of the government fees.

Riyadh Municipality opened its zoo under a management contract. The firm expected to make a profit, but is in trouble because religious police banned family days at the zoo.

COST OF LIVING

The average Saudi family, while buffeted by the oil downturn, benefited from a cost of living that has been declining since 1983. This was the year the oil boom went bust, and housing costs began to fall. Housing costs nearly doubled from 1974, the start of the boom, to 1975 and nearly doubled again by 1977. They have been halved because foreign wages have fallen by nearly 50 percent since 1983, the number of foreigners has declined, and because Saudis overbuilt housing..

In Riyadh alone, 32.5 percent of apartments were empty, while 24.2 percent of the other housing was vacant.[13] The construction was mostly funded by the no-cost loans of the REDF. The REDF dished out loans so sloppily in the beginning, that a few years later, advertisements were placed in local newspapers that asked those who took out loans to come in and tell the REDF how much they had borrowed. By 1987, the waiting period for a REDF loan lengthened from a month or so, to a year, or longer.

PRIVATE SECTOR ADJUSTMENT

The private sector suffered terribly because it is so dependent upon government contracts and because Saudi businessmen tend to share the government's lackadaisical approach to paying bills. Many owners do not differentiate between personal money and business cash flow. In a typical firm, Saudi Media Systems, the owner, Ahmed Al-Jaaferi, continued to build his luxury villa while his Filipino workers went months without pay.

This widespread approach to debt and responsibility created chaos. If clients were not already bankrupted by government payment delays, they might, after getting paid on a contract, forget their suppliers and , retire unrelated debts first. Banks that tried to collect on loans ran into roadblocks. The courts ruled that, since interest is forbidden by Islam, the loans were illegal. Many banks were stiffed by wealthy men who had the money to retire their loans. By 1987, when the government finally paid off most of its arrears, damage had already been done. Yet, the beneficial aspect of the payments crises was that it forced surviving companies to exercise more financial responsibility and control.

The problem of payments did not mean Saudis were impoverished. Individual Saudis continued to place their money abroad, and built up reserves probably equal to the government's. This reservoir of private capital is a resource the government would love to mobilize. The Kingdom has always emphasized the desire to get the private Saudi investor involved in the Kingdom's economy but the banks cannot loan for fear of defaulting borrowers. Also, when the Iraqi invasion took place, the outflow of capital was nothing short of astonishing.

The invasion was the humiliating outcome of the Kingdom's ad hoc approach throughout the Eighties. Although it poured billions of dollars into AWACS jets, Tornado fighter-bombers and F-15 Eagles, the Saudis turned to the United States to save them. Further, it is the most stunning demonstration of the failure of checkbook diplomacy. No nation ever received more aid from the Saudis than Iraq did, yet, just two years after the end of the Iran-Iraq War, Saddam Hussein's troops overran Kuwait, and gathered ominously on the Saudi border.

When this crisis is over, they will have some serious thinking to do on the wisdom of their previous choices, and on where they want the country to go in the future.

2
POLITICS

*"If you didn't become a Saudi in the days of King Abdulaziz,
you will never be a Saudi.
If you didn't become rich during the days of King Khaled,
you will never be rich.
If you didn't become poor during the days of King Fahad,
you will never be poor."*
—a modern Saudi saying

King Abdulaziz, founder of Saudi Arabia, knew the value of gifts. The year was 1927, and his fanatical Ikhwan warriors were ready to revolt. They hated the presence of infidels in the Kingdom, distrusted Satanic Western technical innovations, and chafed under his restrictions against raiding Jordan and Iraq. Their fierce leaders accused Abdulaziz of apostasy.

Abdulaziz responded in classic Saudi fashion. He called the men together in a big conference, reaffirmed his Islamic credentials, called them brothers, and offered them a few concessions. Next, He bribed those whom he could, and sowed discord amongst the rest. Savran writes, "Ibn Saud arrived at the conference with chests full of treasure acquired in the Hejaz, which he distributed differentially among the assembled chiefs to mollify and divide them." When they finally revolted, Abdulaziz was prepared, and crushed them with modern weaponry.

Abdulaziz's ad-hoc approach has been followed ever since. In 1989, King Fahad announced the first government borrowing in in nearly 20 years, but justified it: "In order to enable the citizens to lead a comfortable and luxurious life, the state might find itself obliged to cover the deficit..."

Providing a "luxurious life" is part of the unwritten Saudi political compact: the Royal Family can exercise power provided it pays off the people. Desert Sheikhs always ruled by a combination of force and consensus reinforced by gifts. Abdulaziz threw gold coins; his sons use oil wealth to pamper the Saudi citizen. The government grants low cost loans for homes, rental property, farms and factories. University students get free tuition, housing and a salary while they attend. The people consume subsidized gasoline, electricity, water, and, up until recently, subsidized staple foods. All medical care is free. In the 1983-84 budget, classified estimates showed that 14.7 of the Saudi budget went toward direct subsidies. Payments for social welfare, healthcare, education, and housing loans, added another 11.4 percent, for a total of SR43.4 billion ($11.57 Billion). Further, even with Iraqi troops on the border, Saudis are not conscripted into the military, and pay no income tax. They do pay the 2.5 percent religious "Zakat" tax, which goes to the poor.

This wealth was bestowed by Allah, most Saudis believe, because they were poor, pious Muslims. Conversely, present difficulties are often attributed to divine displeasure over the drift from Islam and their traditions. This feeds the society's strong xenophobic tendency. Saudi culture is based on kinship, and makes a strong distinction between those who are in or out of the group. Islam's division of the world into believers and infidels reinforces this.

Competition for jobs between 4 million guest workers and growing numbers of young Saudis has strained traditional Saudi hospitality. Public resentment means that citizenship is awarded stingily, compared to the free-handed days of Abdulaziz. Saudis also claim foreigners are stealing their jobs.

Resentment erupted after the Kingdom beat Iran in the the Asia Cup soccer championship. Several expatriates were attacked during after-game street celebrations. Later, the American team at the 1989 World Youth championship was hectored before, during and after play. Since soccer games are the only authorized non-religious mass activity, they provide the best glimpse of the "Shabbob," or common man's, attitudes. The treatment of the team implies that American soldiers should not expect gratitude for shielding the Kingdom from Iraq.

These attitudes are fostered by poisonous anti-Western articles in the Saudi press. Occasionally, the Ministry of Information muzzles it, such as during the Rushdie Affair, or after the USS Vincennes shot down an Iranian Airbus. The Al-Saud think that this policy distances them from the Americans, but in the eyes of many Saudis and most Arabs, Fahad in particular, is hopelessly compromised. Many Saudis complain, wrongly, that the CIA has too much influence in Riyadh. The press policy only helps to enflame anger without educating the populace.

Riyadh has long been difficult to navigate, mainly because, up until 1988, few streets had names. New names do not help the mainly expatriate truck, taxi, and bus drivers, because Riyadh's governor, Pr. Salman, placated conservatives by ordering new signs printed only in Arabic.

The resentment against foreigners has increased because of the oil bust. Before the downturn, the government provided every graduate a civil service job. Ambitious young men secured top jobs in private industry, or founded their own companies. Lower revenues brought on a government hiring freeze, and a recession that limited business opportunities. Older Saudis say the recession was needed to bring bring expectations down to Earth, but many young men are forced to compete with lower-paid foreigners and don't like it. Traditional arrogance, plus resentment, creates dangerous passions.

Iraq's attack on Kuwait and confrontation with the West plays to these passions. Fahad's statements, if properly sifted, do nothing than restate his earlier positions on women and general welfare, in a fashion calculated to appeal to Western ears. Western insistence on changes in the treatment of Saudi women, for instance, will further discredit a regime that has lost face because of its scramble for Western assistance. Further, Saddam Hussein's appeals to the common Arab emphasize the gulf between the average Saudi and the Royal Family.

ROYALS AND COMMONERS

The increased competition for jobs heightens the contrast between commoners and princes. Abdullah's son, Miteb, beat Olayan and Alireza, two of the most important merchants in the Kingdom, for the Ford agency, in what is a harbinger of things to come. The business community, till now, has been the royal family's strongest backers, but princes are becoming more voracious just when lower oil revenues are shrinking the Saudi pie. The burgeoning number of young Royals puts pressure on the technocrats. Many are taking the best jobs in government and industry. Some abuse their insider status to force their way into deals.

The public tolerates a certain amount of corruption. In family-oriented Saudi Arabia, the concept of "conflict of interest" is foreign. Most people would consider it odd if even an honest Minister did not steer at least a few contracts in the direction of friends or relatives. Of course, some Ministries are more notorious than others for kickbacks and bribes, called "baksheesh." Saudis and their Arab entourages weren't the only dabblers in corruption. Some British advisors at the MODA Hospital in Riyadh were known for demanding payments from suppliers. The highest bribe attempt exposed by the government involved the Ministry of Defense. An executive of the Korean contractor Hyundai, was arrested while paying $2.5 million in cash. Hyundai,

THE SAUDI ROYAL FAMILY

"The Royal family is more than a family, it is a tribe," says an important prince. "It is not organized, especially compared to other Gulf royal families who have central funds, joint investments, and other institutions. We are independent."

Tribe is the best description for a family that now numbers nearly 20,000 men and women. There are additional families with near-royal status through long service and frequent inter-marriage with the Al-Saud. The Sudairies, many of whom serve as governors of provinces, are the best known. A Sudairy woman was the mother of King Fahad and his six brothers. Bin Jiluwi fought alongside Abdualziz since the storming of Musmak Fortress in Riyadh. His family was rewarded with the hereditary governorship of the Eastern Province, they were replaced by one of Fahad's sons. Another related semi-royal family, the Al-Sheikh, consists of descendants of the Islamic reformer Muhammed bin Wahhab.

The Al-Saud consists of not only the 39 surviving sons and similar number of daughters born to Abdulaziz, but the sons, daughters and descendants of Abdulaziz's brothers as wel.l. Royal fecundity is a result of Islamic marriage law. The Prophet Mohammed allowed a man four wives, who can be divorced easily. The kings usually kept one favorite wife, but had others on a rotating basis.

Many wives lead to many half-brothers, who establish blocs within the family. This is only natural in a society where blood relationships are so important. The full brothers of Fahad are known abroad as "The Sudairy Seven" because of their mother, but by Saudis as "The Al-Fahad." The late King Faisal's boys are called the "Al-Faisal." The numerous offspring of the deposed King Saud shared his collective disgrace as well. Abdullah, the Crown Prince, suffers from a lack of blood-allies in the Royal Family since he was the only son of his mother.

The family is dominated by the Al-Fahad, Abdullah, and 200 other senior princes. All members of the family receive a government stipend, which varies according to age, sex, and number of children. For the average second or third generation prince, the amount is enough to live comfortably, but not sufficient for a jet set lifestyle. The rate ranges from SR2,000 to SR30,000 a month. Other families, such as the Sudairies and the Al-Sheikh, also receive allowances. The same office handles payments to everyone who helped Abdulaziz conquer Kingdom. That includes stipends to former slaves. Further, senior princes get crude oil entitlements, which they market through various channels. The state oil company, Petromin, gained its first oil sales experience marketing princely crude.

Though the family is loosely organized, a board was established by Faisal to regulate family disputes. The Higher Committee of Princes is a seven-man board consisting of senior princes. The family convenes rarely, and even then, on an informal basis. This usually takes place for some extraordinary reason. "The word spreads, and then they have the family gatherings," says an informed source.

The word spread quickly after Iraq rolled into Kuwait. Most princes found it hard to believe Saddam Hussein would actually invade. Though Fahad's collegiate style of decision-making is usually slow, it took little time for the senior princes to agree on inviting American forces in. Sultan and Abdullah, both of whom command armed forces, immediately pressed a hesitant Fahad to act. Naif and the other senior princes were unanimous that the first thing was to prevent Iraq from wheeling south to capture the oil-rich Eastern Province.

At other times, acrimony reigns. King Hassan II of Morrocco had to mediate after Fahad demanded Abdullah surrender the National Guard after being named Crown Prince in 1977. Fahd and Abdullah flew to the London bedside of the ailing Khaled to promise to respect the succession. The family also split on whether or not to accept the Camp David Accords between Israel and Egypt. Abdullah led the hard-core rejectionists. Fahad's accomodationist stance was so soundly defeated that he left on vacation to sulk. However, he later energized himself to generate support for the Fahad Peace Plan, which was never given a chance to work due to Arab and Israeli intransigence. When decisions are made within the family, age is fairly important. Prince Mohammed was voluntarily passed over for succession, but was terribly influential prince until he died.. The dynamics of the family are not easy for outsiders to figure out. The safest thing to say is that, while Royal decision-making is not always crystal clear, the goal is easy to discern. The princes will always try to reach a decision that preserves the family business -- the Kingdom of Saudi Arabia.

through a combination of bribery, and low bidding, proved so formidable that contractors said its competitors set up the arrest. Cynics say bribes are exposed by ministries when officials think too little is being offered.

"As long as we could afford it, this commission-taking served as an incentive to get things done," one Saudi businessman said in an interesting analysis. He argues that the prospect of gain

KING FAHAD

King Fahad may be chummy with his brothers, but publicly, he is aloof. Few bedouin have the nerve to call out "Ya Fahad" in his Majlis, the way they did to Khaled. His petitioners display an unIslamic amount of obsequiousness during his Majlis sessions, and addressed him by titles conjured by his Minister of Information, Ali Al-Shaer. Fahad was called "father of the Arabs," "Light of the Kingdom" and and "Al-Mufaddah" or "Object of one's self-sacrifice."

Iranian ridicule prompted him to to drop every title but "Custodian of the Two Holy Harams (Mecca and Medina)", which emphasizes his Islamic qualities. Hundreds of books and brochures were re-written with the new title. The Al-Jomaih family exhibited their famous parsimony when their brochure for a new plant dedication was patched up with adhesive stickers printed with, "Custodian of the Two Holy Harams."

A common jest was that the national emblem of a palm tree with crossed swords, was now a mop bucket with crossed brooms. Some Arabs awarded him a punning title, changing "Khadem" or custodian, to "Hadem" or "Destroyer" of the Two Holy Harams. The nickname is due in part, to the ambitious development schemes which have entailed destruction of the historic cores of the two holy cities.

Fahad falls short not only in humility, but in good fortune. Traditional rulers or sheikhs in the Arabian Peninsula are expected to have a quality called Hazz or "luck." A lucky leader brings good rains, successful raids, and good pasture. Fahad's successors presided over increasing oil income; he has not. That is not "Hazz."

Fahad is in poor health, mostly because of obesity that required the British to reinforce an ancient horse carriage carrying him during his 1986 visit. An untreated hereditary problem has left one of his eyes askew. When doctors planned surgery to correct the condition on a son, Fahad first sent a daughter to the King Khaled Eye Specialist Hospital. Once the operation proved a success, he sent the boy.

He is habitually late, whether it is for the camel race at Janadiriyyah, or a meeting with a foreign leader. In 1986, Egypt's President Hosni Mubarak waited over an hour while the King talked with U.S. Secretary of Defense Caspar Weinberger. Did Fahad discuss arms deals? No. He lectured Weinberger about how effectively the Kingdom's legal system prevents crime. One can only imagine what crimes Mubarak wanted to commit as he waited. Holland's Defense Minister arrived in early 1988 to push Dutch submarines and minesweepers, but was subjected to a monologue about how Saudi Arabia spent oil money more wisely than other countries.

prompted otherwise slothful officials to promote more projects and more efficient work.

Princes, who treat the country's oil wealth as their private income, have further tarnished the House of Saud's image. Bankers once welcomed Royal borrowers, but today shun them. A bank has an outside chance of collecting from a commoner, but none at all from a stubborn prince. Prince Abdullah Bin Faisal reached an agreement with Saudi Investment Bank on rescheduling a loan for the Saudi Arabian Agriculture and Dairy Co. (SAADCO) but immediately reneged. In 1987, Royals owed SR30 million alone to the Riyadh Intercontinental Hotel, and sometimes beat employees sent to collect money. A high level source from the Ministry of Posts, Telegraphs, and Telephones, (MoPTT) confided that over 90 percent of the unpaid phone bills owed to Saudi Telecom come from Princes. Prince Salman eventually had to place a moratorium on installation of new phone lines for young princes.

"The technocrats are very critical," one keen Arab observer said. "As long as they have been getting a share, they have accepted the present system. But now, as far as the King goes, they respect the position, but they don't respect the person."

The King, in theory an absolute monarch, does have checks on his power. He cannot move against Islam without losing his legitimacy. Further, he must either dominate or persuade fellow family members. Faisal was the last King to have sufficient self-confidence to rule single-handedly. Khaled, and now Fahad, make decisions on a consensus basis which robs the government of dynamism in foreign and domestic policy. Non-princely Ministers avoid decisions for fear they may antagonize some prince. Faisal sometimes backed Yamani against Fahad and other senior princes, but this would never happen today. The Kingdom's government arrives at decisions in the ad hoc fashion of a school-boy gang, except that the group is composed of senior princes, not

FAHAD'S LUXURIES

Fahad loves palaces, and has erected them in Jeddah, Dammam, Riyadh, Taif. Geneva, and Marbella, Spain. Most were constructed by Saudi Oger, owned by his Lebanese-Saudi friend, Rafiq Harriri. The Riyadh Palace sits on acres of ground surrounded by 30-foot tall walls broken only by gigantic black steel doors beneath massive square arches.

Fahad's Jeddah palace, also walled, occupies an entire peninsula. Near it is a fountain, built to be higher than the fountain jet at Geneva. King Fahad's yacht, larger than some small Caribbean cruise ships, is anchored nearby. One Saudi Oger source said the palace has a submarine pen to permit the King to slip away secretly if necessary, but that may simply be embellishment. Across the shallow lagoon stands an empty hotel building meant to house the Jeddah Intercontinental. Since the hotel overlooked the palace, the government purchased the building.

The Dammam Palace, also huge and expensive, is on its third set of walls. For some reason, perhaps the proximity of 250,000 Saudi Shia, Fahad has not been content with one wall. So, like a modernistic fortification, it is hemmed in by concentric concrete barriers. The rationale behind this multi-billion dollar expenditure is that the new palaces will be permanent royal residences, the way Buckingham Palace is.

That way, Fahad's palaces won't resemble the unfinished seaside palace of King Saud, about 40 kilometers north of Jeddah. It decays by the shore, with a pier reaching out like a broken bridge across the Red Sea. Designed to house a king, it is now the haunt of sexually ambiguous youths who leave it covered with graffiti and littered with plastic water bottles and sheep bones.

Fahad's palaces accompany him on his annual desert trip. Some 50 tractor trailer rigs, mounted with mobile homes on flatbeds, form his camp. These "Desert Palaces" have gold bathroom fixtures, stereos, video machines, and overstuffed furniture. Several link up to form an operating hospital. Two carry huge satellite dishes for communications. One of the Kingdom's flying C-130 mobile hospitals is parked nearby. Generators growl through the night, and lights blaze. Most of the desert camping equipment was accumulated by Khaled who loved the bedouin and falconing. His pampered falcons perched amidst crystal. Fahad prefers Jeddah, but goes to the desert for politics' sake.

A flying palace was created for Fahad when he bought the world's first private 747. The interior designer used computers to create the ambience of a small gothic-style British manor complete with a fountain. The aircraft has a small second hump which contains a radar and satellite communications system. This allows a television link between the Cleveland Clinic staff and the plane's open heart operating room. An elevator lifts the King from the pavement to his flying throne room.[1]

When the plane was first delivered in Riyadh, Fahad went to inspect the plane with Jeddah businessman, Salem Bin Laden, who helped put together the deal. "And the best thing is this elevator your majesty...." he said as he pushed a button and nothing happened. He later told a friend he felt the most excruciating humiliation.

Fahad lavishes attention on his youngest son, Abdulaziz. Fahad's Jeddah-based fortune-teller predicted that the King would die in Riyadh without his favorite son. Abdulaziz now accompanies him everywhere. Sultan Qaboos of Oman angered Fahad once by demanding that the boy be evicted from a state meeting.

Abdulaziz's mother's family, the Al-Ibrahim, have benefited from Fahad's love. They cut themselves in on many deals, and get a commission for every jet engine used in the Tornado fighter program. They founded a company, Saudi Arabian Automobile Services Co. (SAASCO) which was awarded a monopoly on gasoline stations on the main highways between the cities.

Fahad also appears to like monuments to himself. One can hardly avoid Fahad-named landmarks. The Saudi-Bahrain Causeway is named after the King. So are any number of hospitals. Riyadh's largest stadium is named after King Fahad. So is the Eastern Province's new airport. The Brazilians hopoed to score a tank sale by calling it the Fahad. Perhaps the reason why Fahad was so eager to buy Germany's Leopard II tank, is because his name is Arabic for "Leopard."

boys. The gang sits together, hashes issues over, and then lets its leader, Fahad, make the final decisions. At the elbows of the inner circle, or gang, are other princes or advisors, but power emanates from the center, much as it did in the European courts of old. The decline of oil money has strengthened these senior princes. During the boom, any number of princes could guarantee a contract, or assistance. Today, Saudis go straight to those princes, in other words, Fahad, his full brothers, and their sons, whom they KNOW can deliver the goods.

FAHAD'S BROTHERS

SULTAN

Sultan, the second of the Al-Fahad, is called "Bul-Bul" the nightingale, because of his appetite for work. Like his brothers, he is, well, chubby. Intelligent, hard-working, and charming, he is Minister of Defense and Aviation, and is next in line for the throne after Abdullah. "Mr. Five Percent," as he is known, controls the Ministry of Defense and the national airline, Saudia. It is no surprise, then, that he represents, through various agents, the French arms sales company, Sofresa.

He masterminded a $1 billion barter deal for 10 Boeing 747 Jumbo jets, which were "given" to Saudia, to the detriment of the airline, which had no funds for maintaining them.

NAIF

Prince Naif is arguably the most powerful man in the Kingdom, with more men under arms than Prince Sultan. Some observers estimate that about half of the government is involved in the Ministry of Interior in some fashion or another. Details of Naif's forces are discussed in the chapter on military.

AHMED

Prince Ahmed, Naif's deputy, is more open-minded than his boss and older brother. After the Shia rioted in Qatif in 1979, he toured the area, admitted the Shia were poorly treated, and was conciliatory.

ABDUL RAHMAN

Prince Abdulrahman is Sultan's deputy.

SALMAN

Prince Salman Bin Abdulaziz, the governor of Riyadh, is respected and liked, both by conservatives and progressives. His Majlis is well-run and well-attended. Salman's cool head and thoughtful decisions have earned him a place in the councils of the King. He could be a compromise candidate for King if a deadlock ever arose.

TURKI

Prince Turki fell from power after marrying the sister of Mohammed Fassi, the Arab whose escapades made all the tabloids. When he bought a Beverly Hills mansion and painted pubic hair on the nude statues, neighbors were thankful that the place burned down.

A former U.S. State Department official, Walter Reed Martindale III, on trial for smuggling a machinegun, told the court he was paid by Prince Naif to either murder or kidnap Dr. Sheikh Shamsuddin Al-Fassi, then living in London. The London Observer's story provoked an angry denial by the Saudi Press Agency (SPA). SPA denied the story and circulated accounts of Pr. Turki's charity in an attempt to rehabilitate him. Until he divorces his Al-Fassi wife, though, he will be unlikely to regain power.

Surrounding the central core, or "gang" are the families that grew with the Al-Saud. The merchant families, the Alirezas, Bin Ladens, Kakis, Mahfouz, Al-Gosaibis and Al-Zamils, all dealt with Abdulaziz, and their sons have dealt with his sons. This relationship has endured in the Kingdom's tribal society, in which personal and blood relationships are all-important.

All this means that the Council of Ministers is a little irrelevant. In "Political Adaptation in Sa'udi Arabia: A Study of the Council of Ministers," Summer Scott Huyette makes a case that the Council of Ministers has evolved into a separate power base that can influence the actions of the Kingdom.[2] She also sets great store on "votes" in the Council. Sure, the King casts his vote in the event of a tie, but sane Ministers first try to persuade him, or see what he favors and then vote for that.

Huyette adds, "No longer the exclusive province of the Al-Sa'ud, commoners comprise four-fifths of the council membership."[3] Yet, the Al-Sheikh are not exactly "commoners" and hold several key portfolios. Since she wrote her book, the Kingdom's two most important non-Royal ministers, Yamani and Al-Gosaibi, have been sacked.

Ghazi Al-Gosaibi, former Minister of Health, was the exemplar of a Saudi commoner. Fahad liked him and he hailed from a big Eastern Province merchant family. He is polite, charming, highly intelligent, hardworking, honest, and even a respected poet. He straightened out the

SONS OF THE SUDAIRY SEVEN

"Sons of the Sudairy Seven" sounds like a mindless Hollywood Grade B monster movie sequel. Except in this case, a Kingdom, not a metropolis is being devoured; the Sons are snapping up important jobs and lucrative contracts. By 1984, King Fahad had already appointed his oldest son, Faisal bin Fahad, as head of the General Presidency of Youth Welfare, the group responsible for spending money on the sports establishments of the Kingdom. One of the Presidency's jobs is to guide the youth away from temptations, an ironic task, considering Prince Faisal's rumored fondness for forbidden substances.

Faisal can take credit for getting Coca-Cola off the Arab Boycott where it had languished since it set up an Israeli bottling plant in 1966. Saudis are Soccer-mad, and Faisal wanted to host the 1989 FIFA World Youth Cup in the Kingdom. As part of the deal, the Kingdom had to honor all of FIFA's legal commitments. Coca-Cola sponsors FIFA. Consequently, Fahad approved pulling Coke off the boycott, even though the official Arab Boycott Office, in Damascus, had not released the soft drink manufacturer. The Saudis then "allowed" Oman and the United Arab Emirates to begin bottling Coke first, to avoid the onus of breaking the boycott. Faisal's strangest project has been construction of a huge opera house near Fahad's palace in Riyadh, ostensibly for folk art performances. Conservatives are deeply suspicious of it.

Prince Mohammed, another son, was given the important governorship of the oil-rich Eastern Province. Since the founding of the Kingdom, the harsh Bin Jiluwi clan held the governorship as a hereditary reward for services rendered. After Prince Abdul Mohsen Jiluwi grew old and ineffective, he was replaced in early 1985. Mohammed's previous claim to fame was garnering one of the largest commissions in history, perhaps $500 million cash, for winning the huge telephone network contract for the Dutch-Swedish consortium Philips-Ericsson.[4] Fahad, as crown prince, stalled a Royal order limiting the size of commissions until his son completed the phone deal. In Mohammed's defense, he has proven an able and energetic governor who has improved the lot of the Shia, mainly by restricting the activities of Sunni religious police in their towns. Mohammed appears to have won a good measure of popularity in the region.

Other jobs have fallen to the Al-Fahadlings. The Ambassador to the United States, Bandar bin Sultan, son of Pr. Sultan, has become the preferred emissary of King Fahad, bypassing Pr. Saud Al-Faisal, a member of the conservative Abdullah bloc. He was involved in the Chinese Missile deal, a short-lived peace in Lebanon, and in U.S. arms sales to the Kingdom. The personable ambassador argued the Kingdom's case to the American public after the Iraqi invasion of Kuwait.

In December, of 1984, another son, Saud Bin Fahad resigned as head of the huge but money-losing advertising company, Tihama, to become Deputy Director of Intelligence. Turki Al-Faisal now has an Al-Fahad to look over his shoulder. Turki isn't the only official who has a young Fahadling as an understudy for his job. The new Petroleum Minister, Hisham Nazer has Prince Abdulaziz bin Salman in his office. In some cases, Fahadlings have Fahadlings as their deputies. Faisal Bin Fahad's deputy at the General Presidency of Youth Welfare is Saud ibn Naif.

When the first Saudi went into space, he was not a commoner, or even a common prince. He was Sultan bin Salman, son of the Riyadh Governor. He flew into space aboard the American Space Shuttle, the Discovery and was honored as the "First Muslim Arab Astronaut" especially because he beat a Jew into space. One of the crew was Sally Ride, and her presence drew an unusual outburst by a Saudi woman when Sultan and the Discovery's crew later toured the Kingdom. "You can fly into space with a woman, and I can't even drive a car in Riyadh," she cried.

In July, 1988, one of the actual sons of Abdulaziz was edged out of a job by a junior prince. Prince Mamdouh ibn Abdulaziz, 37th son of Abdulaziz, was edged out of his job as Governor of the strategic northern city of Tabouk. SPA said he requested a transfer to the newly created, and eminently unimportant, Strategic Studies Bureau (SBB). His friends say he was simply bored with being in a backwater town. Nonetheless, His place was taken by Prince Fahad bin Sultan, son of the Defense Minister. The Fahadlings may be the first to break Abdulaziz's system of succession, in which his sons would each inherit the crown, from oldest to youngest. The King is selected by the royal family, which swears an oath of loyalty after he is blessed by the Ulema. When will the new generation of princes elbow the remaining sons of Abdulaziz aside and claim the throne themselves?

Ministry of Industry and Electricity and was then assigned to clean up the Ministry of Health where his anti-corruption measures won him princely enemies. Al-Gosaibi tried to bring all hospitals under control of the Ministry of Health, but the head of Riyadh's King Faisal Specialist Hospital, a friend of Sultan, thwarted him. Al-Gosaibi wrote a poem based on the plaint of a

Tenth century poet to his royal benefactor, in which he attacked Fahad's reliance on flatterers.[5] The poem was published on the front page of Al-Jazira newspaper. Al-Gosaibi and the editor were sacked. The fall of Ahmed Zaki Yamani, longest-serving minister in the free world, confirmed the ultimate impotence of commoners in the face of the Royal Family.

OPPOSITION

Those who actively oppose the government do so for reasons that are religious, secular, or a combination of the two. Secular opposition began with the Aramco Strikes of 1953, when workers, angered at the better pay and benefits of American expatriates, demonstrated. The government arrested worker spokesmen, and precipitated a larger strike which was broken by force and King Saud's guarantee of better living conditions. After a second strike in 1956, a new law was promulgated threatening imprisonment for strikers. Leaders of a 1959 strike were jailed.

One of the strikers was Nasser Said, who helped form the Kingdom's tiny communist party after the strikes were over. Said fled into exile, and harassed the regime with exposes of corruption and immoral behavior. Finally, the Saudi secret service paid off the Lebanese, captured Said in Beirut, and brought him back to Riyadh, where he disappeared.

Other secular opposition groups are also minuscule. A Saudi Baath, or "renaissance" party, fashioned along the line of Iraq and Syria's Baath parties, follows Baghdad instead of Damascus, but is negligible. The brutality of those regimes has robbed Baathism of its allure.

The secularists are not nearly as threatening as the religious fundamentalists. Although the religious establishment is co-opted into the government, it is by no means passive. Even less reliable are the newly fundamentalist bourgeoise who feel the sting of the economic downturn.

Even while things were good, religious conservatives forced the regime to tread softly. Saudis rioted at the opening of a Girls school in Riyadh in 1960 and at the opening of a TV station in 1965. The seizure of the Grand Mosque in 1979 was the latest manifestation of this attitude.

This last action frightened the Royal Family because many participants were members of the supposedly reliable National Guard. The House of Saud knows that most Arab leaders have fallen not to foreign armies, but their own. The Saudi armed forces are compartmentalized to prevent widespread coups from being organized. The National Guard is the main counterweight to the Army, and is considered politically reliable. The Royal Saudi Air Force (RSAF), whose members are exposed to more foreign influence, is least reliable. Princes give "Stipends" or rewards to soldiers to supplement their regular pay. A National Guardsman is paid by the Guard, and receives bonuses from Prince Abdullah, the regional governor, and other princes as well. This makes it unlikely the military as a whole will prove dangerous to the regime.

Officers are a specialized sort of technocrat, and are therefore part of the disenfranchised middle class. The middle class, to which they belong, presently favors the status quo, but there are indications that after the Iraqi threat has diminished, they will want more say. Those who favor Western-style democracy, or, rarely, communism and socialism, are in the minority. Cowed by the Iranian example of militant Islam, they have become reluctant allies of Fahad against conservatism.

"When Faisal was king, we had to hide, but now we have no power, and they don't care if we talk, talk, talk. The problem (for the regime) is the religious ones," one liberal confided. This is because many Saudis think less Westernization, and more Islamization should take place. A return to "true" Islam as espoused by Ibn Wahhab was what created the nation of Saudi Arabia in the first place.

CROWN PRINCE ABDULLAH

Abdullah Crown Prince and Commander of the National Guard, interrupts the Al-Fahad's hold on power. His mother was the widow of one of Abdulaziz's enemies. Today, he is the leader, especially after the passing of the elder Prince Mohammed, of the conservative wing of the Royal family. He looks robust, strong and intelligent. He has a stammering speech defect, but this has diminished as he has gained self-confidence. Abdullah, whose entourage is laced with Syrians, appears to prefer Europe to America and would pursue a non-aligned foreign policy.

He is likely get the Kingship when Fahad dies, but that is not guaranteed. The succession must still be ratified by the family. Sultan is highly ambitious and may fear that he won't outlive Abdullah. But the Crown Prince's health is not as sound as was believed. He had a minor heart attack in 1986, while in Morocco. The SPA said he was suffering from a cold, and then spent hours each night recounting the foreign and domestic dignitaries who visited him to wish a quick recovery from his "cold."

Some consider Abdullah an unsophisticated bedouin, but a nurse in the King Faisal Specialist Hospital's heart ward learned Abdullah had an Arabic translation of Geothe read to him at bedtime. This may be why many Westernized Saudis have more confidence in him than in Fahad. "I think he will do more for women than Fahad has done," said one businessman. "He is from the bedouin, whose women drive and work. He can do more for them because he is a stronger man than Fahad."

Abdullah's strengths in the event of disputed succession are his reputation and his popularity. The religious authorities are comfortable with him. The average Saudi seems to like Abdullah. Further, his National Guard troops are considered tougher than the regular army. On the other hand, the bedouin tend to go to the highest bidder, and could prove a weak reed in the event of a real dust up. The best guarantee that Abdullah will succeed Fahad is that the Royal Family does not want a repeat of the fratricidal strife that decimated the family and led to the loss of the second Al- Saud dynasty.

This does not guarantee that Sultan will not try to make a power play. After all, things have gotten rough before. In 1934, Muhammed B. Abdulrahman, Abdulaziz's brother, tried to invalidate Saud's succession, because his own son, Khaled bin Muhammed, was the logical candidate for succession. Khaled was even accused of trying to kill Saud in 1927, and in 1930. Abdulaziz tried to buy Muhammed off on the succession problem with several thousand riyals. Muhammed resisted, but Abdulaziz was patient. In 1 April, 1938, Khaled "passed away" according to the Royal Gazette, the Umm Al-Qura. Some think he was assassinated. Mansur bin Abdulaziz, one of Abdulaziz' favorites, died under mysterious circumstances in 1951 after forming special army units loyal to himself, which proves that the path to the Saudi throne is not always a safe one. [6]

Increased Islamic militancy worries Fahad and his brothers. Abdullah told his British hosts during a state visit that he worries most about the rise of Islamic fundamentalism in the youth. The unlikely alliance of youth with reaction is forged in the Islamic universities or Islamic and Arabic studies departments of the secular schools. Fahad placates the zealots by femphasizing the Islamic legitimacy of his monarchy and allowing them to harass foreigners and restrict the activities of women.

Those who are not content with pay-offs or concessions face the Ministry of Interior's secret service, called the "Mubaheth." "The Mubaheth is the black beast," one source said. "And now it has been reinforced more and more and more, because of Fahad's weakness. He has lack of management, and lack of leadership. So now he must manage by fear. It depends upon how much power you give to the police, and how much you respond to their reports. If everything they report frightens you, and causes you to hit out, then you let the police run you. This is what has happened with Fahad. He doesn't trust his people."

Those arrested by the Mubaheth go to one of two types of political prisons, according to Saudi sources. One, called the "Loudmouth" prison is relatively mild, more like a compound than a prison. The inmates are "sentenced" for periods up to 8 months, and are "re-educated." They are shown films, and taught about other Third World countries, showing that compared to countries such as Nigeria, Syria, Iraq, and others, that the Kingdom is not such a bad place after all. They are then shown the good achieved by the present regime. At the end of the sentence, the inmates are given money and government contracts and are invited to become productive citizens. One dentist, a student activist in the United States, was picked up upon his return to the Kingdom. He now he runs a large dental clinic, founded using the money he received after getting out of prison.

Those who go into the second tier of Political Prisons simply "disappear." Once a Saudi enters, the guards let him know in no uncertain terms that he is dispensable, but few are killed. Torture does take place, according to Amnesty International. Shias from the Eastern Province have the most to fear from these prisons.

Faisal created the prisons to hold political enemies. Many were not freed until after he died, but they were well-paid. After an attempted Air Force coupe, Gen. Hashim S. Hashim was arrested for no particular reason. Today he is a successful businessmen.[7] This is a marked contrast with most of the Middle East. Iran, Libya, Iraq and Syria routinely exterminate enemies.

THE PARLIAMENT

One might wonder why Fahad won't try the democratic option. He often speaks of it, but for for foreign, not domestic, consumption. The answer is that he does not want to share power. His predecessors, from Abdulaziz to Faisal, also talked of parliaments when crises arose. Abdulaziz talked of a parliament to mollify the world's Muslims after he conquered Mecca. Faisal spoke of elections when the Kingdom was rocked by Arab Nationalism during the time of Egypt's Nasser. Fahad, on a 1986 state trip to Britain, said democracy was on the way. He even signed a multi-billion contract to build a Majlis As-Shoura, or Council of the People, in Riyadh. This was interesting news, since Fahad supported the squelching of both the Bahraini and Kuwaiti elected assemblies.

So far, the closest the government is coming to democracy is a plan presented by businessmen to attach citizen's advisory councils to each ministry that will help assess public sentiment. The only authorized Saudi democracy occurs in shareholder meetings of companies.

Many technocrats are unenthusiastic about elections. "We are not ready for democracy," more than one Saudi has said. "If we had the vote, then each bedouin would vote for his own tribe, and the country would fall apart. Maybe the Royal family is not too good, but when we look around and see where Arab Socialism or democracy has gotten Iraq, Egypt, or Syria, we think we are doing pretty well."

KING FAHAD'S MAJLIS

Most Saudis rely on "Desert Democracy," the Majlis system. Every Tuesday, commoners enter a huge, carpeted room lit by chandeliers, and filled with the ornate overstuffed furniture of the peculiar style termed "Louis Farouk." The old and young stand in line to meet Fahad, kiss his shoulder, nose, or hand, and present him petitions. A relative must have an operation, a new pickup truck is needed, the Real Estate Development Fund is stalling on a loan application, or a son requires several thousand riyals to pay a wedding dowry. Sometimes, a prince or official has committed an injustice that the King can rectify. Some Saudis simply come to meet their King and sit with him to dinner. The King's head of protocol writes down the requests, and records the King's comments. Saudi television shows Fahad greeting his subjects with a strained and bored smile as he accepts the petitions.

"Do you always want to hear people's problems? A lot of the money ends up coming out of your own pockets. Still, if you want any influence, you have to hold them," one prince confided.

A generous Majlis creates grateful citizens, and a useful powerbase. Saudis rather like the institution of the Majlis. To an extent impossible in most countries, an aggrieved Saudi can voice his criticism to the top people. The Majlis provides continuous feedback, but is limited when it comes to assessing reaction to future policy.

A few Saudis dislike the Majlis. "He is a generous thief," one Saudi banker said of a senior prince. "But wouldn't it be better if we had no thieves at all?" The cynicism expressed by the Saudi banker comes from the fact most of the money distributed in the princely Majlis sessions ultimately comes from the Kingdom's oil revenues. The Royal Family takes the oil revenue, skims off its hefty commission, plows a lot into internal development, and personally dispenses a portion to a grateful population. Harder times are putting more demands on the Majlis system, while the princes have less money to give. Many better educated Saudis want some political power as well.

PROGRESSIVES AND CONSERVATIVES

Since the people have no direct say, they tend to line up behind those members of the Royal Family who share their views. The divergence of views within the family provide political stability and an outlet for opposing views. The family has lined up into "conservative" and "progressive" blocs, though the terms are misleading.

Crown Prince Abdullah and the conservatives, prefer traditional Saudi ways of doing things, such as working through the tribes. This bloc tries to pursue a non-aligned foreign policy, and would have liked to lessen dependence upon the United States. They solidly supported Fahad on calling for American help during the Iraq crises, but worked for a greater United Nations presence.

Fahad, leader of the progressive wing, was, strangely, the most hesitant of the princes about asking the Americans in. His bloc shares the conservatives' commitment to preserving royal power, but is more West-oriented and more willing to introduce changes in society, particularly to weaken the tribes and religious authorities. Fahad and Abdullah clashed in 1982 over a plan to disarm the tribes. It was never implemented.

Both groups distrust urban elites, in particular, those of the Western, "Hejaz" province, which contains Jeddah, Mecca and Medina. Thus, the conservatives are happy to see Fahad trimming the influence of the Hejazis in favor of men from the central, Nejdi region. They also support Fahad's plan for developing rural areas. If health care, electricity and jobs are available in the country, then people won't flood into the big cities and create unstable urban populations.

The two groups also united to quash the challenge of Prince Talal, one of the brightest of Abdulaziz's sons. He advocated limited democracy and then mortified the Royal Family by publicly freeing slaves and fleeing to Cairo during the reign of Saud. His political future was ruined, so he concentrated on business. Afterwards, he rehabilitated himself by serving as the Kingdom's special Envoy to Unicef, and founding the Arab Gulf Fund for United Nations Development organizations (Agfund) to channel Gulf donations to Unicef and other U.N. organizations.

Talal is down-to-earth. After announcing his resignation from AGFUND in 1985, the Arab reporters began making speeches that are usually, mercifully, untranslated. After a half hour of painfully obsequious opening statements, a huge Egyptian correspondent for a Kuwaiti publication barreled into the room, slicked his hair down, and proceeded to speak.

"Oh Prince Talal, when you called the press conference, I had a feeling this doleful news would be announced, and I was so distressed about it, that I came this half hour late," he began. He then began to implore Prince Talal, on behalf of mothers and children everywhere (who must of course be weeping when they learned of his resignation) to reconsider the act. His Highness' greatness and mercy plus his well-known feelings of tenderness for the affairs of the world's mothers and children, should surely incline him to rescind his sad and regrettable decision...." he droned on. One reporter turned to a comrade, made a gesture as if he would vomit, and then saw, with horror, Talal's gaze. Talal shrugged and smiled as the paean continued, and quietly commented, "We are Arabs." Talal's agenda was not terribly radical for the Third World. He proposed government control over industry, oil, and mines, all steps the government eventually took. He erred in recommending a reduction in Royal family allowances and creation of a constitutional monarchy with an elected assembly of 120 members.

Savran makes a good case that Talal and Faisal had two different approaches to modernization. Talal sought a controlled move into democracy. Faisal opted for the more traditional tribal model in which the government "bought off" the people with oil wealth in return for quiescence in politics. So far, Faisal's approach has been followed and has been successful.

The economic downturn has strained the relationship between the House of Saud and its subjects, but the title of "prince" retains magic, says former British Ambassador Sir James Craig. He claims that only an eccentric bedouin would fail to address King Fahad by his proper titles. That's probably because the bedouin have a saying, "Every man is a prince," and don't believe in humbling themselves to other men.

THE BEDOUIN TRIBES

For the princes of the House of Saud, these princes of the desert can be a nuisance. An early Al-Saud ruler, Faisal bin Turki Al-Saud, claimed "If only rain would fall, agriculture would be possible, and the tribes might be rendered sedentary."[8]

"Draw the sword in their face and they will obey; sheathe the sword and they will ask for more pay," Abdulaziz told the British.[9]

Since the tribe, not the nation, claims a bedouin's loyalty, bedouin are notoriously fickle. Ibrahim Pasha was assisted in destroying the first Saudi regime by turncoat tribes he bought off. Abdulaziz and his descendants have thus tried to settle the bedouin, and chip away at tribal loyalty and organization. Cole says that although Abdulaziz was considered a desert king associated with bedouin, "he, perhaps more than anyone else, set in motion the destruction of the traditional basis of their tribal life and began their incorporation into the Islamic-based Saudi state.[10]

Abdulaziz tried to use Islamic bonds to weaken tribal ties, much as the Prophet Mohammed had done. He thus devised the "brotherhood" (Ikhwan) to harness them. The bedouin were indoctrinated in Islam, and prepared for waging war on enemies of the Al-Saud. This not only separated tribe members from their tribes, but forced them into contact with other tribes. Abdulaziz also tried to demolish the economic foundations of nomadism by encouraging agriculture. This failed, and the Ikhwan settlements survived through government assistance and war booty.

After the Ikhwan revolted and were defeated, the bedouin abandoned the villages. Some tribes still sing bitter songs of the time when Abdulaziz bombed them. Bligh says that in the 1979 Mecca insurrection, the two tribes hardest hit in suppression of the 1928-1930 Ikhwan rebellion were the most heavily represented.

The second attempt to settle the bedouin began in the Fifties. The Wadi Sirhan, Haradh, and Habrin settlement projects soon proved failures. The state found more success by controlling access to resources, starting in 1925, when Abdulaziz deprived the tribes of exclusive use and management of their own grazing regions. In 1968 a new law stated that bedouin can gain land after farming it for three years, and further eroded communal ownership. This favored tribal leaders who could exploit their ties with local princes, said Cole.[11]

Tribal sheikhs play an important, but declining role in the Kingdom by providing soldiers for the traditional levy, and helping distribute government largesse. Tribal passions still cause problems. Privates of noble camel-raising tribes sometimes refuse to take orders from sergeants of lesser tribes. The threat of Iraq, however, is helping to forge a greater feeling of national identity both among the bedouin, and the townsfolk people of differing regions.

REGIONAL GROUPS

It is natural that a country unified only 50 years ago, has problems with regionalism. The authorities tried to combat this by building an infrastructure linking the nation together. Fahad distributes as much money as he can to the rural areas because this consolidates the Kingdom and erodes the roots of the conservatives' natural constituency.

The heartland of the Kingdom is the Nejd, where the Al-Saud originated. It is one of the least populated and technologically advanced regions of the Kingdom, yeet it benefits disproportionately from government expenditure.

The Western Region, the Hejaz, which contains Mecca and Medina was, under the Sherif Hussein, an independent kingdom. Hejazis hav dealt with pilgrims and caravans for centuries. They consider themselves more cosmopolitan and advanced than the Nejdis. The Nejdis, for their part, contemptuously call Hejazis "the Mixed Breeds" because many have the blood of pilgrims from India, the Far East, and Africa settled after completing their Hajj.

When the Kingdom was first founded, Hejazis dominated government because they were the only educated Saudis. Today, everything has been moved to Riyadh, including SAMA, the Ministry of Foreign Affairs, and all foreign embassies. Under Fahad, the Hejazis have lost ground to Nejdis. Minister of Finance and National Economy, Mohammed Abalkhail is well-known for promoting those of his Qassim background. Like other ministers, he is referred to to as H.E. (His Excellency), but disgruntled SAMA employees say the H.E. stands for Hejazis Exit.[12]

The date- and oil-rich, Eastern Province, which has a large Shia minority, is another problem area. The Shia saw that most of the money earned from its oil went to build Riyadh and the Western provinces. Since the Qatif riots, the government has taken more interest in the region.

The Asir, the last region conquered by the Al-Saud, is, still, according to revanchist Northern Yemenis, part of Yemen. Certainly, the people have more in common with their neighbors than they do with their Nejdi overlords. The coastal Asiris who live in African style huts called Kraals still harken back to Africa. Despite cultural links, a vast majority prefer their life in the Kingdom compared to the lives their brothers lead in Yemen.

CONCLUSION

The Saudi state, founded by a radical Muslim movement, Wahhabism, is susceptible to militant Islamic fundamentalism. To stave off such a threat during a period of economic recession, the regime gave concessions to traditionalists for support. Strangely, the Iraqi threat stands to change the equation. If the crises gives the Kingdom a greater sense of nationhood, demands are likely to increase for participation in decision-making. The presence of foreign troops, however, will exacerbate anti-foreign sentiment, especially among the most destabilizing group, the underemployed youth. It is too early to say what will evolve, but if the youth prevail, it will not be as pro-Western as the present ambivalent government is.

3

FOREIGN POLICY

"Our ties with the world countries are ties of interest. There are no emotions...If we find our requirements with a friendly country and if she gives us what we want, she does so in return for our money. Nobody provides anything for free...We buy weapons but we do not buy ideologies," **King Fahad addressing military officers after Iran boycotted the 1988 Hajj.** [1]

When Iraq's armor units halted on the Kingdom's borders, having just smashed Kuwait, the Saudis witnessed the ultimate failure of checkbook diplomacy. For she, as well as Kuwait, bankrolled Iraq's war with Iraq, to the tune of $30 billion. Kuwait was repaid with explosive shells, rape, and plunder. The Kingdom was next in Saddam Hussein's sights. Fahad first appealed to the Arab League, but when its meeting was cancelled at the last moment, he turned to his last option: to wait and hope the United States would unilaterally save it.

The Kuwait invasion was but one of many Saudi foreign policy disasters in the past five years. Iran and Iraq are both enemies. Kuwait, a member of the Kingdom's Gulf Cooperation Council (GCC) is occupied by Iraq. The Yemens are uniting. The policy of putting distance between the Kingdom and its big brother, the United States was undone by the need for American military protection. In short, nearly every goal of Saudi foreign policy has been wrecked, mostly as a direct result of the oil downturn.

The Iraqi dictator presented the Kuwaitis with several ultimatums, most of which were oil-related. He ordered Kuwait to stop over-producing and driving oil prices down. He further demanded payment for petroleum extracted from a border oilfield. Although conquest was his primary goal, Hussein, like all oil producers, was suffering from low crude prices. He wanted cash to rebuild after his ruinous war with Iran.

The Saudis also suffered from low production and depressed prices. Though the oil glut should have emasculated the Kingdom's checkbook diplomacy, it forced it to become smarter and tougher. Though they had less to give, what aid they provided became more valuable since the other oil powers were suffering worse than the Kingdom was.

If Saudi foreign policy seemed a bit indecisive during the oil glut period, it was because Fahad uses a collegiate approach. The Minister of Foreign Affairs, Pr. Saud Al-Faisal is a career diplomat, but he is often circumvented by members of the Al-Fahad. Sultan was the resident Yemen expert. Abdullah was familiar with Syria. Sultan's son, the fighter pilot-turned ambassador to the United States, Pr. Bandar Bin Sultan, became the regime's version of Henry Kissinger. He helped organize one of Lebanon's many cease-fires, pushed arms sales through Congress, and was instrumental in the Chinese missile deal.

None of these capable men was prepared for Iraq's invasion. Kuwaiti Foreign Minister Sheikh Sabah Al-Ahmed Al-Sabah said Fahad and others warned the Kuwaitis not to mobilize for fear of antagonizing Hussein and assured him no attacks would take place.[2] That night, the Kuwaiti royal family fled for its lives. The Gulf Cooperation Council, based in Riyadh, and fashioned by the Saudis, proved powerless to stop Iraq.

According to its charter, the GCC states, Saudi Arabia, Kuwait, Oman, Bahrain, Qatar, and the United Arab Emirates, are pledged to go to war to protect each other. This has not been done.

Instead, the Kingdom, backbone of the group, was so paralyzed by the invasion, that its news media was forbidden to mention the invasion the day it took place. The Kingdom even closed the Saudi-Bahraini Causeway in nervous reaction.

The impotence of the GCC is a blow to the Kingdom, because it hoped it would become a small version of the European Community, contributing to greater stability and prosperity in the Gulf. The Saudis assumed they would dominate, but found GCC members were obstinately independent. Oman refused to break relations with Egypt after the Camp David Accords with Israel, and two members declined to break relations with Iran after the Mecca riots and the sacking of the Kingdom's Tehran embassy.

One of the ironies of the Saudis' effort to contain Iraqi expansion was that they were hegemonistic themselves earlier in the century. The British had to stop the Ikhwan from raiding Jordan and Iraq in the Twenties. Kuwait, after sheltering Abdulaziz and his father, found itself seeking British protection from his Ikhwan warriors. Qatar was threatened with annexation. Bahrain's ruler paid Abdulaziz secret protection money. Oman at one time had to fend off Saudi land claims. The Saudis have oscillated between threatening and buying off the Emirates. Abdulaziz tried claiming four fifths of Abu Dhabi's land. In 1974, Sheikh Zaid of Abu Dhabi surrendered slices of territory, including the Zarrara oil field, but the Buraimi Oasis remained part of Abu Dhabi.

The GCC rulers are not close, and take potshots at each other through the subsidized Arabic press in London. One particularly scurrilous rag is edited and published in London by a paid employee of the Saudi embassy. These publications find embarrassing information on leaders, threaten to print it, and then accept hush money. The Saudi publication frequently trashes the Nahyans of the UAE, and Qaboos of Oman, who offended Fahad by having his favorite son, Abdulaziz, removed from a state meeting. After one magazine was ordered not to publish more photographs of a daughter of UAE ruler, Zayid Al-Nahyan, its editor published a plea to King Fahad for financial compensation.

While the Saudis still hope to forge greater unity within the GCC (a distinct possibility since the riskiness of the neighborhood is more obvious than ever) they have had to break with their normal caution in dealing with other Arab countries. Those countries that backed Iraq have reaped scorn from the Kingdom's rulers. When the Tunisian head of the Arab League, Chadli Klibi, waffled over the invasion of Kuwait, the Saudis secured his resignation.

After Palestine Liberation Organization (PLO) chairman Yasir Arafat publicly supported Saddam Hussein, the Saudis announced that payments would dry up. "From now on, we support causes, not people," one a well-placed Saudi told the New York Times. "We are making the point that Yasir Arafat is finished here, but that other Palestinian leaders who appreciate all the financial help we have extended to the Palestinian movement over the years and who have not turned against us will be welcome."[3] After turning down a request by Arafat to visit the Kingdom, Fahad received Hani Al-Hassan, a senior PLO official sympathetic to Gulf monarchies. Officials later said his visit was pointless.

The Saudis' sense of betrayal by the PLO is palpable. Just a few years before, the PLO admitted that its only reliable finance came from the Kingdom. Riyadh Governor Prince Salman headed a group that raised additional private funds for the Palestinians. The Kingdom built a PLO embassy, but peculiarly erected it just outside of the Diplomatic Quarter. Despite one author's claim of risk, the worst a visitor can expect is to be inundated with political pamphlets.[4]

Perhaps the only country whose relationship will remain the same is Israel. While Israel is referred to in the media as the Israeli Enemy, or the Zionist Entity, Riyadh has no desire to confront Tel Aviv, a fact missed by opponents of arms sales. Sources say the Saudis have actually held talks with the Israelis, simply to keep out of each other's way.

IRAQ AND THE ACC

The Saudis had problems with Iraq from the earliest days, but the threat increased dramatically when the aggressive socialist Arabic Baath Party assumed control. In recognition of possible Iraqi aggression, the huge King Khaled Military City was built at Hafr Al-Batin along the probable invasion route.

During the 9-year Iran-Iraq War, the Saudis used the preoccupation of the two regional powers to fashion its GCC. The Saudis supported Iraq's attack on Iran, and even serviced some Iraqi aircraft at the airbase in Riyadh. Later, when it appeared that Iran might win, the Saudis scaled back their support and overt enthusiasm. In 1985, the Saudis sought to normalize relations with Iran, and restricted Iraqi oil exports through the East-West Petroline, blaming pumping problems. Iraqi agents detonated a bomb on Riyadh's Thalateen street as a warning not to get too pro-Iranian. A shoestore was blasted, a few passing Filipinos were killed, and the Saudis got the message. They played it cool with the visiting Iranian minister.

"When Saddam attacked Kuwait, he really calculated that we will back down," a cabinet minister told New York Times reporter Youssef Ibrahim. "Eventually they thought the PLO would dominated Kuwaiti using the 400,000 Palestinians living there to govern, and that Yemen would get a territorial adjustment in the South, taking some land from us there. Jordan and Iraq would reap substantial financial aid from a subdued Saudi Arabia and Kuwait."[5]

This assessment handily sums up Saudi apprehensions about Iraq's creation, in 1988, of the Arab Cooperation Council (ACC). This bound together the two Yemens, Egypt, Jordan, and Iraq. The ACC surrounds the nervous Saudis. Each of the member countries is poorer than the Kingdom, and most have a larger population. Fahad inked a non-aggression pact with Iraq as a result.

The Yemen Arab Republic (North Yemen) and the People's Democratic Republic of Yemen (South Yemen) have a combined population 1.5 times greater than that of the Kingdom, and make their neighbor nervous. Iraq, even before formation of the ACC, had close links with North Yemen, and was able to generate border incidents there to put pressure on Riyadh.

To counteract Iraqi influence and win the hearts of the Yemenis, the Saudis give generous foreign aid; free hospitals, subsidized food, and infrastructure. Despite this, they are still unpopular south of the border because of envy, and resentment over the treatment 1 million Yemeni guest workers receive in the Kingdom. Yemenis were the only nationality that needed no entry visa to work the Kingdom, and most filled lowest level manual labor jobs. After the Yemenis supported Iraq's invasion of Kuwait, the Riyadh revoked their favored status and now requries them to apply for visas like everyone else.

The Asir Province, conquered by Abdulaziz, still rankles Yemen, whose official maps still include it. Near the edge of the Rhub Al-Khali, among barren sand dunes as high as small mountains, Saudi border posts keep watch for Yemeni smugglers. South of the Saudi town of Shurura, in a place called Wadiah, the Saudis maintain a base inside internationally accepted, though never formally defined, North Yemen borders.

Smugglers crisscross the mountainous border of the Asir and the deserts farther East, Yemenis smuggle alcohol, drugs and firearms to the Kingdom, and sneak consumer goods and gasoline into Yemen. Both sides are armed and occasionally clash. A 1988 attempt to move border markers drew the Saudi and Yemeni military into small-scale clashes.

Saudi policy was always directed, despite Arab solidarity rhetoric, at keeping the two Yemens separated. Saudi money buys tribal loyalty and keeps the pot stirring. Some say the Saudis have underwritten select political assassinations. In spite of these efforts, against most predictions, the Yemens have united, and the bond seems to be sticking. North Yemen's new oil discoveries will help free the country from Saudi pursestrings. Production levels are already over 75,000 bpd.

THE SPECIAL RELATIONSHIP

"It will be forever imprinted in our minds and hearts the fact that you came so quickly to our assistance," an emotional Fahad told a delegation of 36 Senators and Congressmen.[6] Yet a few weeks before, he had to be persuaded by his brothers to let the Americans come in to ward off a possible Iraqi invasion. When the Americans arrived, Fahad's policy of holding the Americans at arms' distance collapsed.

While the Iraqis drew a ring of allies around the Kingdom and her Gulf brethren, the Saudis were busily distancing themselves from the Americans. The drift began after Washington rebuffed a request for additional F-15 jets, and the Saudis placed the biggest arms order ever for Anglo-German-Italian Tornado fighter- bombers. The "special relationship," so often referred to by the U.S. State Department, was not so special after all. In 1987 Riyadh announced a second British Tornado arms deal as a calculated insult to Washington. The purchase of Chinese missiles was another message. When Ambassador Hume Horan communicated Washington's displeasure, Fahad demanded his recall. When Iran began attacking shipping in the Gulf. They refused to openly ask for the U.S. fleet to enter the Gulf, but quietly provided AWACS cover for the ships after Kuwait reflagged its Tankers with the United States.

The Saudis didn't sever ties completely. They hoped to mollify the Americans by purchasing of over a billion dollars worth of M- 1 tanks and Bradley armored personnel carriers. Riyadh also helped finance the Contras and Afghan Mujahadeen in support of Washington's covert policy.

Although pro-Israeli critics hammer the Saudis for not backing American policy, they forget that there are limits to what the Saudis could do, even if they wanted to. Not only do they come up against resistance from stronger Arab governments, but they risk alienating their own people. America's all-out support for Israel has bedeviled the relationship since 1948, when Truman remarked that he had Jews, not Arabs, as constituents.

The Saudis for their part resent the beating they take from the American press and pro-Israeli Congressmen. "Why do we have to accept restrictions when we buy weapons for cash, and you just give them to Israel?" they ask.

American friendship has been a double-edged thing. On one level, the Saudis prefer Americans to other Westerners, possibly because the Americans never colonized an Arab country and are easier-going than most Europeans. Many of the Saudi elite have studied in America as well. On the other hand, the average Saudi finds it hard to countenance a non-Muslim non-Arab country fighting a brother nation, no matter how brutal it is. Certainly, the United States should expect little popular gratitude from any but the Kuwaitis after the crisis is finally settled.

This is why the American troops are being kept isolated from the population. If the people are constantly reminded of a foreign presence, and that female soldiers are helping defend the regime, it weakens the House of Saud. Demands by American feminists that the government "liberate" Saudi women would be even more damaging. It would make the House of Saud look like cringing servants of outsiders.

The announcement of a $23 Billion arms deal not only improves the status of the government, but is a way the Saudis can repay the Americans for their assistance. Further, by openly paying much of the costs for the American soldiers, the government places itself, in the peoples' eye, of hiring helpers, not begging for assistance.

EGYPT

The Saudis don't experience the same difficulties when accepting military help from Egypt. Historically, the regions were close. Egypt provided technical help and foreign aid early in the century. Relations grew hostile late in the reign of Farouk, and hit their nadir during the Presidency of Gamal Abdul Nasser. Nasser's Arab Socialism called for destruction of the anachronistic Gulf monarchies. He engineered a coup in North Yemen and sent in 100,000 troops. The Saudis, under Faisal, successfully held Egypt at bay by financing a civil war.

Faisal rebuilt bridges to Egypt's Anwar Sadat and wielded the oil weapon in support of the Yom Kippur October War. However, when Sadat signed the Camp David Accords with Israel, a deeply divided Royal Family finally opted to excoriate Egypt, and vote for its expulsion from the Arab League. Sultan, in Egypt to oversee a joint Arab munitions industry, was unceremoniously packed out of the country, and still harbors a grudge for his treatment. As time passed, the Saudis quietly re-established links with Cairo. When Iran looked on the verge of defeating Iraq, the Saudis were able to muster enough support to win them re-admittance to the League, even without repudiating the Camp David agreements.

This was just in time for some 5,000-10,000 Egyptian soldiers to provide security for the 1988 Hajj in response to threats of disruption by Iran. The Saudis untruthfully denied that they were assisted by the Egyptian military.[7]

Thus, Egyptian President Hosni Mubarak was welcome when he offered to send 5,000 of his troops to guard against an Iraqi invasion. The more Arab troops that attend, the easier it is for the Saudis to defend charges that they have become American stooges.

PAN-ISLAMIC POLICY

The other method for countering charges of selling out to the West is to mobilize Pan-Islamic support for American assistance against Iran. On the home front, Sheikh Bin Baz said Allah would reward the good deeds of the Christians and infidels who came to defend the Holy Places. When the Muslim Brotherhood issued its usual venomous condemnation of non-Muslim America's Satanic presence in the Holy Land, the Saudis intervened. The fanatical Muslim Brotherhood is only one of many Islamic revolutionary movements that live off of Saudi money. "The Saudis pulled the purse strings, and suddenly they were singing a different tune," said one official.[8] In the post-oil boom environment, the Saudis are one of the few nations to honor pledges to Islamic causes and groups.

Pan-Islamism and the Saudis are intertwined since the days the House of Saud rose to power on the fundamentalist Wahhabi Islamic movement. Faisal countered Nasser's Arab Populism by founding the Organization of Islamic Countries (OIC) in Jeddah. This organization consists of over 40 Muslim countries. The World Association of Muslim Youth (WAMY), the Islamic Development Bank, and other Pan-Islamic groups are based in the Kingdom as well. Saudi petro-dollars subsidize Islamic groups and help construct mosques all over the United States and Europe. Muslims from Cat Stevens to Idi Amin, take Saudi hand-outs. Big Daddy Amin lives in Jeddah as a guest of the government.

The Saudis fund Islamic extremists from Filipino Moros to Thai Muslim separationists. When the Eritrean guerilla groups were on the verge of signing a peace document in 1989, the

Saudi-funded splinter Muslim Eritrean groups protested loudly. Saudi money subsidized anti-Rushdie marches in Europe, only to be outbid for Islamic fervor by Iran, which called for the author's execution. The great irony of Saudi-funded Islamic fundamentalism is that it may one day turn against them. Most radical fundamentalists attack the monarchy as corrupt, and too friendly with the heathen West. These charges take on weight as the infidel troops of the Great Satan America take up positions to defend the monarchy.

Although former secularist Saddam Hussein now cloaks himself in Islam, the Kingdom's true religious rival is Iran. Relations were frosty, but bearable during the Shah's reign. Centuries of Arab- Persian animosity were aggravated by the Iranian ruler's goal of dominating the Gulf. The Shah was never as threatening as the Islamic Revolutionary Republic that destroyed him. The Ayatollah Khomeini and his heirs will destroy the monarchy by challenging it on its fundamental level of legitimacy; the stewardship of Mecca and Medina. Iran argues that Islam's holiest shrines should be administered by an international Muslim committee.

This was a reason why the Saudis encouraged Iraq to attack Iran. After authorities uncovered an Iranian-backed coup against Bahrain's Emir, the Saudis spent billions to construct the gigantic Saudi- Bahrain Causeway. In 1987, with characteristic humility, Fahad inaugurated the bridge, named after himself.

Iranian anger at Saudi support for Iraq festered. In 1986, Saudi customs found plastic explosives smuggled in by Iranian pilgrims, but tried to hush it up. After hundreds died when Saudi troops clashed with Iranian rioters in the 1987 Hajj, and Iranians looted the Saudi embassy in Tehran, the Kingdom broke relations. The next year, 4 Saudi Shia set off bombs in a petrochemical plant in Jubail, and set bombs elsewhere. They were caught and executed. Pro-Iranian agents vowed to kill an equal number of Saudi diplomats, and by January of 1989, 3 Saudi diplomats were gunned down.

The Saudis stuck to their position, and called in favors to secure pan-Islamic condemnation of Iran, both for the riots, and for later bombs set by Kuwaiti Shia in 1989. Sixteen Kuwaitis were executed for setting the bombs. They also mobilized support for quotas on pilgrims to Mecca, a move bitterly denounced by the Ayatollah. The Saudi Regime was branded unIslamic, but once again, it uncharacteristically stayed the course. When Iran threatened a boycott if its quota were not raised, the Saudis held fast. No official Iranian pilgrim groups have attended the Hajj since then, but the Saudi claim to be proper overseers of the city was weakened when over a thousand pilgrims were killed in a tunnel during the 1990 Hajj.

COMMUNIST NATIONS

If anything exemplifies the bolder post-oil boom foreign policy, it is the purchase of Inter-mediate Range ballistic Missiles from the Peoples Republic of China. The Saudis not only made a huge arms purchase without consulting their pals, the Americans; they signed the deal with an athiestic communist nation with whom they had no formal relations.

Ties with Communist China had already been building on a small scale, but were accelerated by the Ambassador to the United States, Prince Bandar bin Sultan. The Peoples Republic of China is the first communist nation to have official relations with the Kingdom since the the thirties.

China is not the only communist nation seeing more of the Saudis since the oil glut began. The Soviet Union and the Kingdom have established relations severed when Joseph Stalin refused to let Soviet pilgrims come to Mecca for the Hajj. To gain religious approval, Fahad had the Minister of Pilgrim Affairs, Abdul Wasie, participate in most of the talks. Soviet Embassies had already opened (with Saudi approval) in Kuwait, the Emirates and Oman. Lower level Saudi officials have long argued that once the Soviets removed the barrier of its Afghan involvement, the Kingdom could play the Soviet Union off against the Americans. Besides, the countries have several things in common: both are oil producers and both have large muslim populations.

CONCLUSION

While Saudi foreign policy has become more decisive due to the drop in oil revenues, it did not become reckless. There is a decided pragmatic streak in all except its bid for leadership in the Islamic community. Yet all of the Kingdom's patient work in building Arab consensus spectacularly failed with the invasion of Kuwait.

Some sources say that Abdullah will shift the Kingdom toward a more non-aligned status when he assumes the throne, but that is impossible while Iraq is ranged on the Kingdom's borders. This incredibly complicates the Kingdom's foreign and domestic policy, since the regime has always tried to keep some distance from the Americans. Once the crisis is over, and especially until the United States acts in a more pro-Arab fashion on the Palestinian-israeli question, the Kingdom will most likely revert to form, and try to establish some distance between itself and the United States.

4

MILITARY AND SECURITY

"It is not in the mind of the Kingdom to prepare for war...we never have any expansionist ambitions and all our arms are for the protection of the homeland and its holy sanctuaries," Prince Sultan, Minister of Defense and Aviation, on the Tornado aircraft sale.

Weapons are only as good as the warriors that wield them. When Iraqi tanks rolled through Kuwait, the Saudis trembled and called upon the United States to save them. The invasion made the Kingdom's billion dollar arms purchases seem pointless. The Saudis never let a deteriorating financial situation hamper weapons procurement, rather, deals seemed to increase the more oil revenue fell. The latest buy, a package worth some $23 billion, helps defense contractors in the United States, but doesn't cure the primary weakness of the Saudi military: a shortage of manpower.

The government has tried to make military careers attracive. Soldiers, spared general government salary cuts, get free housing and earn twice what civil servants do. Yet recruitment remained low until the invasion. Saudi males then volunteered for the new Reserve Force to receive basic training. They will be called up if needed. The tribal-based Saudi National Guard is ending enlistment quotas that prevented specific tribes from dominating the organization. Still, no draft has been imposed, because such a move would be bitterly resented by the male population.The government has considered conscription, but while the Minister of Defense, Prince Sultan, thinks it is a good idea, Crown Prince and National Guard Commander, Prince Abdullah, thinks it would introduce undesirable elements in the military forces.

The Kuwaiti invasion propelled the Kingdom into the embrace of the United States just two years after King Fahad distanced himself by purchasing 40-50 Chinese missiles and demanding the recall of the American ambassador who complained. The inability of checkbook diplomacy to influence Iran prompted the purchase of a deterrent weapon that risked no Saudi lives. The Intermediate Range Ballistic "Dong-Feng Oh" ballistic missiles also showed the Americans, said a Ministry of Foreign Affairs official, " we can buy arms wherever we want to."

The Chinese deal caught the U.S. flat-footed, despite the presence of CIA and other American intelligence operatives. It took an adventurous nurse exploring the desert to discover the missiles. "Satellites only see things where they are told to look," one defense attache mused. "Who would have guessed the Saudis would buy missiles?"

The regime doesn't really trust its armed forces, and compartmentalizes them to make it difficult to launch a broad-based coup. The Air Force and Army are drawn from cities. The police are weighted with Asiris. The National Guard is drawn from the bedouin. This keeps them divided and hurts military effectiveness, but the Al-Saud prefer safety to efficiency. The Saudis bank on the Americans to come to their rescue because their country is so strategically important. If an invasion should take place, commanders will trade territory for time and use the Army and National Guard to wear the enemy down while the air force hammers the invaders' supply lines.

The Saudis built strongpoints on each of the three most likely avenues of attack. If the Iraqis or Iranians invade, the Saudis will try to channel the assault along a narrow axis in the Northern edge of the Peninsula past King Khaled Military City (KKMC), at Hafr Al-Batin. Invasions from

Jordan, Egypt, or Israel would pass through the relatively empty North-West region past Tabouk, which contains an airbase, paratroopers, commandos, and half of the Kingdom's heavy armor. In the South, the Yemens, far from critical targets, can invade only along two easily defended land routes guarded by two mechanized brigades and armored units based at Khamis Mushayt. The Yemens could, however, seal off the straits at the mouth of the Red Sea.[1]

The big defense headaches are the desalination, oil and petrochemical facilities on or near the coasts. These facilities can be damaged by commando action, but the true worry is an air strike. This is why the Saudi Air Force is the most important branch of the armed forces. It is capital intensive, and requires less combat manpower per fighting unit than the army or navy, covers a wider area, and reacts more quickly.

ROYAL SAUDI AIR FORCE.

The Saudis have put together one of the world's most sophisticated air defense systems. Its eyes are five American- built Boeing EC-3A Airborne Warning and Control System (AWACS) jets. The planes are similar to American versions, but the Saudis insisted on equipping their aircraft with higher-rated SNECMA French-made engines, which give the aircraft a slightly higher operating ceiling, and therefore, slightly greater range. Thus, the software had to be modified for increased height. Further, the increased heat output of the engines reduces the effectiveness of the plane's heat-seeking missile countermeasures. Further, the Saudi versions of the aircraft contain radar and computers, but not electronic surveillance or countermeasure equipment. This is now considered a great gap in Saudi intelligence gathering capability, and they have begun looking at electronic snooping aircraft.

One of the many expatriate myths about the AWACS, and one that was repeated in Sandra Mackey's book, "The Saudis," is that the AWACS has helped Saudi officials track and capture smugglers driving truckloads of alcohol across the desert.[2] AWACS radars do not pick up objects going less than 90 miles per hour to avoid screen clutter from ground vehicles.

The AWACS jets are tied into the air defense system through the Peace Shield program. Peace Shield is a Command, Communications, Control, and Intelligence (C3I) system. This is the air defense the United States Air Force would love to buy, but cannot afford. The AWACS' 350-mile radar sweep gives the Saudis a critical 15 minutes warning before enemy aircraft can hit their coastal oil and water installations. The outermost layer of air defense is the F-15 Eagle. These jets shot down Iranian intruders in May, 1985,[3] by guiding a Saudi pilot to the target. It is presumed that the two Iranian crewmen were killed by his missile's direct hit. The F-15s are bolstered by 24 Air Defense variants of the Panavia Tornado fighters, which have a longer flight endurance than the F-15s, and nearly as much speed.

The next line of defense consists of the Northrop F-5E fighter. These supersonic aircraft have a combat radius of 1,056 km, or 656 miles. The Saudis' British-made Hawk trainers can carry armament in a pinch, fly at Mach .88 and have a combat radius similar to that of the F-5E. If an intruder evades the interceptors, he confronts the first line of missile defenses. These are improved Hawk missiles, that can hit aircraft at altitudes up to 16,000 meters at a range of 40 km. The next line of defense uses the Shahine, which is an improved version of the French Crotale missiles. The Shahines have a range of 15 km, and can hit aircraft at a height of up to 6,800 meters. The Shahines are mobile and can be shifted to areas in need of additional air defense. The final defense system consists of Swiss Oerlikon anti-aircraft guns, and French 30 mm twin anti-aircraft guns, with an approximate range of 3,500 meters. The Saudis also possess Stinger shoulder-fired anti-aircraft missiles for close-in defense. This layered defense is one of the most advanced in the world. The defenses use both the AWACS jets and ground-based GE radars for "eyes."

The system is not perfect. In 1982, a defecting Iranian F-4 Phantom jet capable of carrying 9.75 tons of bombs flew to Dhahran, and passed over Ras Tanura. It landed as the Kingdom's F-5s were taking off. That same year, a defecting Iran Air Boeing 707 crossed the Gulf, Saudi Arabia, and landed at Cairo, undetected by the AWACS aircraft.[4]

The proposed $23 billion arms package would provide the Kingdom with the Patriot Anti-Aircraft missile. This would not only extend the range of the missile shield, but would provide a badly-needed measure of defense against ballistic missiles. The deal would also add 24 F-15s, to give the Kingdom a total of 110 of the jets.

Saudi interest in air power began long before oil was discovered. King Abdulaziz, some authors say, was "obsessed" with having an air force after Britain's Royal Air Force (RAF) annihilated a raiding party of some 2,000 Ikhwan. The camel-borne raiders massacred a small village in Jordan. The RAF and armored car squadrons killed all but 8 of the King's religious warriors. He received the first planes of his fledgling air force from Britain in the Twenties and Thirties, and paid expatriates to fly them. By 1953, when Abdulaziz died, the Americans supplanted the British as suppliers. They provided transports and trainers to the Air Force.

Britain scored a big sale in 1965, during the Yemen Civil War, when the Kingdom paid $154 million for aircraft and missiles, $70 million for radars, and $1.6 million for training. This deal, for 40 Lightnings, demonstrated how Saudi arms deals got entangled in global politics.

The Saudis were looking for a long-range interceptor with ground attack capabilities the Lightning lacked. They wavered between two American fighters, Lockheed's Starfighter, and Northrop's F-5. Instead, as Anthony Sampson writes, the British and American governments struck a deal behind the Saudis' and the American companies' backs. In return for a British agreement to scrap their fighter-bomber project and buy American FB-111 aircraft, the Americans backed Britain's bid for the deal. Two months after the British celebrated their "biggest ever export deal," they announced their decision to buy F-111s. They later reneged, and the Saudis were stuck with unreliable, poorly supported short- range interceptors. "The Saudis in the end had been persuaded to buy British planes that they did not want, to allow Britain to pay for American planes that they could not afford."[5]

Eventually, the Saudis bought F-5 fighters, and now have 65 F- 5Es, 24 F-5Fs, and 16 F-5Bs. They also have Lockheed Hercules C-130 transports that refuel the F-5s in-flight. The next big purchase was the McDonnell Douglas F-15 Eagle. This pitted Saudi Arabia and its American corporate allies against the Israeli lobby in congressional combat. The Carter administration managed, against predictions of defeat, to push the sale through in 1978, by a vote of 54 to 44. The Saudis were restricted from basing their F-15s in Tabouk, near the Israeli border. The deal provided the Saudis with 62 F-15s, and an option of ordering another 50.

The F-15 is more than a match for any aircraft in the region, but has slightly less (as the average Saudi knows) capability than the Israeli versions. The drawback is that it places heavy demands on Saudi manpower. It takes 80 men to keep the F-15 flying compared to 40 per F-5.

After the fall of the Shah in 1979, the vulnerability of Saudi oil installations became apparent. Land-based radar could give no more than two to 4 minutes warning on low-flying jets, which is insufficient to enable interceptors to scramble to defend oil or desalination facilities. They saw their solution when President Carter flew several AWACS planes over during Iran's revolution in 1979. Carter sent the aircraft at the same time he made one of his most peculiar and irrelevant symbolic gestures, the dispatch of a flight of unarmed F-15s to Saudi Arabia. The embarrassing F-15s were quickly removed, but the AWACS mission stayed on. ELF-1 became the only U.S.

military mission on Saudi soil, until the anti-Iraq build- up. This group, which operated 4 E3-A AWACS jets and several tankers, started in October, 1980 and ended in 1989. Some 500 Air Force personnel were involved. Most of the "Elves," as they were called, lived in what was formerly one of the best hotels of Riyadh, the Al-Yamamah. It was fortified to resemble a prison compound. Across the street sat the old Ministry of Interior, and on at least one occasion, an airman was arrested for innocently taking pictures near it. The proximity of the Ministry of Interior did not spell security. After President Ronald Reagan began the Kuwaiti tanker reflagging exercise in 1987, a terrorist bomb left a small crater in the road outside of the hotel compound.[6]

Carter prepared an $8.5 billion package of 5 AWACS E-3A aircraft, and 8 KC-3 tankers, but left it to incoming President Ronald Reagan to push it through Congress. A group of Israeli lobbyists took out a full-page ad in the May 29, 1981 New York Times and other papers which was emblazoned with an imaginary headline: "Saudi Arabian Defectors Steal Secret U.S. Air Defense System For Russians," and then asked why should the United States sell the AWACS to an "oil arrogant" "Supposedly stable" country.[7] Exxon, Mobil, and other companies with business interests in the Kingdom weighed in on the side of the Saudis. Final approval of delivery was linked to Saudi support of peace initiatives with Israel.

The Saudis won, but their pride suffered from the public attacks from congressmen. They bitterly ask why Israel has carte blanche for free weapons, while the Kingdom, which pays cash, has to fight for permission to buy. The Kingdom avoided another Congressional battle, by turning to Britain for a $7.5 billion deal. They bought 48 ground attack versions of the Anglo-Italian-German Tornado fighter-bomber, 24 of the Interceptor-variants, 30 British Aerospace Hawk jet trainers, and 30 Swiss Pilatus propeller trainers.

The Tornado was tightly contested by France's Mirage 2000, until the Al-Ibrahim family erred by muscling in on the deal. Dassault compounded the problem by agreeing to deal secretly with them. This angered Sultan, who has an exclusive arrangement with SOFRESA (Societe Francaise D' Exportation Des Systems D'Armes), a French quasi-governmental arms agency. Then, Sultan's son, Bandar, the ambassador to Washington, lent the same talents that won the AWACS and F-15 sales, to the Tornado's cause.

British joy was compounded when the Saudis made a $15 billion second order for more Tornados and Hawks, plus approximately 90 Westland helicopters and some minesweepers. That was hardly indicative of a military feeling a budgetary squeeze from low oil revenue.

The Tornado adds potent ground attack capabilities to the Kingdom's air force, but vastly complicates supply, maintenance and training. Even though the F-5s and the F-15s are made by different companies, they still share a general American lay-out. The Swiss Pilatus, British Hawk, and Anglo-German-Italian Tornado all use different systems. The Tornados have also been devouring engines at a faster than expected rate.

If the Saudis had been permitted to acquire additional F-15s, the new planes would have been assimilated relatively painlessly. Instead, the new jets aggravate the manpower shortage faced by the Air Force. Saudis like to fly, and are perhaps the best pilots in the Gulf region, but there are only so many of them. The F-15 is a single-seater; the Tornado is a two-man bird.

The Air Force's second important role is to move troops and supplies quickly over the vast, thinly populated areas. The RSAF has 63 C-130 transports, plus 6 KC-130 air refueling transports. Several of the C-130s are configured as "Flying Hospitals" with operating theaters and life support systems. These fly around the country providing aid, and carry victims of disaster or disease to large hospitals. Other aircraft include two C-140 Jet Star transports, 12 Cessna 172 Light transports and "Mini-Hercs" made by CASA of Spain.

The RSAF has not neglected land facilities. The F-15s in Taif are housed in special bomb-resistant bunkers. Safran adds that "The Saudis have built military facilities and ordered or acquired military equipment with an eye not only to their use by their own, actual, or planned, armed forces, but also with a view to their possible use by friendly forces in case of need." This has proven useful during the Iraq invasion threat. Saudi officials have explained that some of the new F-15s will be available for American pilots in the event of future problems.

Most of the Air Force bases are located near the cities, probably to enable ground forces to respond quickly in the event of coups. Conversely, army bases are located far from most city centers.

THE SAUDI ARABIAN LAND FORCES (SALF) - The Army

The modern Saudi Army was not established until after unification of the country was essentially complete, and therefore does not have a tradition as some armies do, of helping create the state. It was formed out of Sherif Hussein's Hejaz army, consisting of several thousand Turkish-trained infantry armed with a few vehicles and light artillery pieces. Abdulaziz deactivated most of them, and then broke the army up into small detachments for border control and police duties.

After a British attempt to modernize the Army fizzled out due to official bungling, the regular army in 1951 stood at 7,500-8,000.[8] Today the Saudi army consists of somewhat over 50,000 men, similar in size to the Saudi National Guard. It possesses armor units, paratroop units, artillery detachments, and Air Defense Artillery (anti-aircraft) units. It is organized loosely along the American model.

The Kingdom has not invested billions in defense out of megalomania, says a deputy minister. "Sometimes, in Third world countries, it is easier to take a bunch of guys, put them in uniform for two or three years, educate and train them, and then release them to society. You can see that many of our successful businessmen are former military men."

Hameed gives Saudis high marks for training. Between 1971-78, when defense expenditures were highest, 50 percent went for construction, 30 percent went to training, and only 20 percent was spent on hardware.[9] The Army, like the other services, spends lavishly on housing for its soldiers. The SR18 billion ($4.8 billion) KKMC is an example. KKMC was built under U.S. Corps of Engineers supervision, in a wasteland. From the air, it appears as a large octagon in an uncluttered sandbox. But this octagon is an entire military city complete with water and power supplies, homes, mosques, maintenance facilities, and hospitals. It is designed to hold over 50,000 persons. The base was originally slated to hold some 3 brigades, but this number was halved due to manpower problems. Although the base is top-secret, the author found full blueprints to the entire base in the desert near Riyadh where one of the Korean contractors discarded them.

The Saudi army currently has 550 main battle tanks, of which 250 are U.S.-built M-60 A3 and 300 French AMX-30s. New American M-1 tanks are on the way. Some 200 Fox and Ferret armored cars are used in scout units. The Saudis like everything about the French tanks but their unreliable drivetrains. Saudi mechanized infantry units use 600 U.S.-built M-113 Armored Personnel Carriers (APCs) plus 250 French AMX-10P tracked APCs. They also have over 400 of the new Bradley Infantry Combat Vehicle.

All combat vehicles are tested in the Rhub Al-Khali, which may be the toughest proving ground in the world. The site, near the South Yemen border, has temperatures soaring over 115 degrees. The sand is almost as fine as talcum powder, and grinds gearboxes and treads down.

The Army is increasing mobility with U.S.-built Blackhawk helicopters, plus nearly 90 British Sikorski-licensed versions from Westland under the second Tornado deal. It has paratroop units that are trained and stationed at Tabouk. According to Hameed in "Arabia Imperilled," it takes the Saudi army a week to ten days to concentrate significant forces on a front. In 1979, during an outbreak of fighting between the PDRY and the YAR, the Kingdom had to request U.S. Air Force C-5As to redeploy tanks to the south.[11] Iraq's invasion found the Army rounding up absentee soldiers and hustling to get units in place. Saudi and other Arab units are forming the first echelon of defense against Iraqi attack. Behind them, like a backbone, are the American airborne and armored troops.

The Saudis have the weapons, but can they fight? Their army has had limited recent combat experience. Troops saw some action during the Sixties during the Yemen Civil War, and in 1979 on the Yemen border. A token brigade was stationed in Jordan during the 1967 Arab-Israeli war. During the 1979 seizure of the Grand Mosque of Mecca, National Guard, security and Army units fought bravely, but not well. The Saudis admit that its security forces suffered 578 casualties, of whom 127 were killed, during the two-week battle. The rebels lost 272 men captured or killed while fighting 3,000 Saudi troops.[11]

Some reports claimed French anti-terrorist specialists were called in toward the end of the battle. A high level source said the French offered the Saudis concussion grenades which could be used without destroying the mosque with shrapnel. French experts flew into the nearby town of Taif and rapidly trained Saudis in the use of the grenades. They never entered Mecca, he said.

THE NAVY

During 1987, a French-built Saudi frigate prepared to pass through the Straits of Hormuz. Her commander waited until nightfall, struck his colors, turned off the lights, and steamed through the straits. "What nationality is your ship?" the Iranians demanded over the radio.

"We are French, we are French," the Saudi vessel replied. One of the most powerful ships possessed by a Gulf nation cravenly slinked through the Gulf.

Although the Kingdom is a massive peninsula surrounded by water, its people, excluding some pearlers and fishermen, do not have a maritime tradition. Nonetheless, billions of dollars have been invested in the Saudi Navy. The reasons are strategic. The Kingdom's oil is shipped through two narrow bodies of water. The Gulf's Straits of Hormuz are easily sealed. The Red Sea has two chokepoints: the Suez Canal, and the narrow strait between Yemen and Ethiopia.

Most of the money went into American-designed bases in Jeddah and Jubail. Most of the Kingdom's ships, however, are French. France supplied four frigates more advanced than any in the French navy. The 2,600 ton frigates are armed with Otomat missiles, Crotale naval SAMs, plus automatic 100 mm cannon. The $3.45 Billion deal also supplied two "Durance" class oilers, 24 missile-armed Dauphin helicopters, and shore defense missile systems. After the Iraqi invasion of Kuwait, the French agreed to sell the Saudis a larger and more powerful frigate.

The frigates are the backbone of Saudi forces in the Red Sea and the Gulf. The Saudis also have 3 Jaguar fast attack patrol craft, 53 coastal patrolboats, 6 landing craft, and 4 small minesweepers. When an unknown country (most people suspect Libya) laid mines in the Red Sea in 1984, the Saudis realized they had inadequate minesweepers. The United States and other NATO nations helped out by scouring the area for more mines. The second Tornado Fighter deal included four British minesweepers. The 2,200-man Navy is looking at two more acquisitions: naval patrol aircraft and submarines.

The Saudis are oscillating between the American Lockheed Orion PC-3 naval patrol craft, and France's as-yet unbuilt Atlantique II. Such planes would add significant new capabilities to the Saudi Navy and would enable it to better patrol the Saudi coastlines.

If there is a case for naval patrol craft, the opposite is true for the Saudi proposal to build sub pens and purchase 8 submarines at a cost of several billion dollars. The Gulf has a maximum depth of 80 meters and is too shallow for submarine operations. At times, submerged subs in the Gulf can be seen by pilots flying overhead.

Britain, France, Germany, Holland, and Italy pushed their submarines. The Germans hurriedly pushed prior approval through the Bundestag. Britain worried that its slow progress on the Tornado Offset Investment program would scuttle its chances. Most countries lost interest when a decision was still not made by 1987, and pulled their teams out.

The Navy, dependent, as the other services are, on foreign maintenance, seems to be the least effective of the forces. Of the two frigates stationed in the Eastern Province, one almost never leaves the mouth of the base harbor, and the other usually patrols within eyesight of the coast. As long as it keeps its eye on the land, the Saudi Navy is unlikely to evolve into an effective force with a high esprit de corps.

THE SAUDI NATIONAL GUARD

Never, ever, riot near Saudi National Guardsmen. They shoot. When Shia demonstrators rioted in Hofuf during the 1979 seizure of the Mecca Mosque, Guardsmen shot them down. They opened fire again during the 1987 riots in Mecca.

The Harass Al-Watani "Guard of the Nation" is commanded by Crown Prince Abdullah. It follows his orders, and buys equipment he chooses. Its trucks are Austrian Steyrs, a company Abdullah represents. His officers started driving new Ford Crown Victorias in 1987, not just because Ford got off the Arab boycott, but because the new Ford agent happens to be Brigadier General Prince Miteb, Abdullah's favorite son. Miteb is commander of the Guard's King Abdulaziz Military Academy.

In another country, this sort of action would invite intense public scrutiny. But in Saudi Arabia, this has attracted little more than indignation in the business community. After all, the deal indirectly involves the Saudi National Guard, and the National Guard is Abdullah's. Miteb's entry into the car business is an example of increased competition between princes and commoners.

The Guard is the only Saudi military arm that has native roots; it evolved from the tribal levies of Abdulaziz, sometimes called the "White Army." It is not a reserve force in the mold of the U.S. National Guard. It is a full-time force, wholly independent of the Ministry of Defense. It has its own logistics, weaponry, and organization and does not train with the regular army. This is because the Guard's mission is not so much to deter foreign aggression as to provide internal security. Its troops protect sensitive domestic installations such as desalination plants, oil facilities, and power stations.

Abdullah so values the Guard, and the clout it gives him with the bedouin tribes, that he refused to surrender his portfolio upon being named Crown Prince. Fahad, who quit the Ministry of Interior when he was named Crown Prince, insisted Abdullah relinquish the Guard. Abdullah refused, because he had no full brother to pass it on to, and because his biggest rival for the throne is the Minister of Defense, Prince Sultan. Abdullah's adamancy caused a succession crisis which was only defused with the mediation of King Hassan II, of Morocco. The notion that Guard and the Army are counterweights annoys officials, who say the Guard is a vehicle for occupying the tribes, while supplying them income and training.

The regime does use the various services to counterbalance each other. The Royal Family wants a strong military, but fears it may turn on its masters. Since officers and men trained overseas are the least reliable, the Air Force, trained extensively in the United States and Britain, has proven most susceptible to the coup virus. In 1945, Abdullah Al-Mandeli, a pilot, tried to bomb King Abdulaziz's encampment on Mount Arafat, but missed. He was arrested and executed. In 1958, Some Air Force officers were arrested for conspiracy to kill King Saud after the July 14, 1958 Iraqi revolution. In 1962, Six Air Force officers were jailed for communicating with the Liberal Princes in Cairo. During 1969, an attempted coup was uncovered, and 100 military personnel arrested. Then, in 1977, some army officers were court-martialed for having roles in an attempted coup.[12]

The Royal Family protects itself by keeping princes in the armed services. Bandar, Ambassador to the United States, was one of many princely fighter pilots. Others hold various ranks in the National Guard and military, and keep an eye on the rank and file.

The Guardsmen are easily distinguished from their regular force counterparts by their uniforms. The regular, full-time SANG soldiers wear dark green fatigues, with the red-checkered "Ghutra" head-dress. Some of the modernized unit soldiers wear red berets. The Liwa units, consisting of men that can be mobilized by tribal leaders for service, wear a more traditional Arab thobe, with crossed bandoleers. Some observers dismiss the Guard, particularly the Liwa, as an anachronism. Jordan's King Hussein would not agree. During the bloody battles in 1969 and 1970 between Hussein and the PLO, untrained but armed Bedouin shifted the balance in Hussein's favor.

The SANG has an authorized strength of 35,000-45,000 though actual combat strength may be 18,000 to 25,000. Its irregular Liwa soldiers are paid a stipend for reporting to an occasional muster. Most Liwa are equipped by the Kingdom with old rifles, but many of them have personal AK-47s. These men have no established transport system, and are mustered when needed by their tribal sheikhs.

The "Firqa" non-modernized units are light infantry who have little organic fire support or heavy weapons, and use trucks for transportation. Firqa units are organized along tribal lines and guard installations and embassies. Their bedouin background supposedly makes the men less vulnerable than townsmen to subversion. Sometimes, Firqa soldiers are told to get out of uniform and hang out in troublesome areas such as Hofuf. They listen to street talk, and report what they hear.

The modernized brigades were established under a U.S.-Saudi agreement. As early as 1971, the U.S. was invited to assess the role of the National Guard. By 1973, an agreement was concluded to arm and train the National Guard. A private firm, Vinnell, was hired to oversee the training process. The New Brigades are light mechanized units. In many ways, their choice of military equipment is more intelligent than that of the regular army. Instead of buying complicated maintenance-intensive tracked vehicles, the Guard purchased wheeled armored cars. These are usually faster than tracked machines, and have good mobility since much of the Saudi desert consists of hard rocky plains.

The Two New brigades are armed with U.S.-built weapons. Their workhorse, the V-150 Cadillac Gage armored car, stops shrapnel, but is vulnerable to .50 caliber or similar weapons. It is used in several different configurations. Some units mount Vulcan anti-aircraft guns. Others carry TOW anti-tank missiles or 90 mm high velocity anti-tank guns. Each company has an anti-armor platoon, but the Second Brigade doubled the anti-tank weapons in its anti-armor units.

The 1st Brigade uses 105 mm howitzers, while the 2nd uses the 155mm howitzer. The ageing Cadillac Gages might be replaced by the Swiss-Austrian Mowag amphibious wheeled carrier chosen by the United States Marine Corps. Whatever vehicle is chosen, it will be picked for reliability. The Guard has purchased new weapons at a slower pace than the regular Army. Because of this, and because it has chosen its weapons with an eye to simplicity, it may prove more combat capable than the regular forces. But its limitations in armor would prove a heavy liability in a punch-up against a determined regular army equipped with tanks.

Trainers say the Guardsmen are relatively good soldiers, are responsive to their officers and have more esprit de corps than the regular army units. Tribalism influences operations in the Modern Brigades, but the new units are not organized along these lines. Interestingly, the trainers say the bedouin do not tend to be good shots, legends to the contrary.

"The Guard's biggest problem is education," said one trainer. "Over the years, the trainers have seen progressively better officers and better enlisted men, and more of them can read." Poor education levels mean "The National Guard is not yet capable of supporting itself in maintenance," trainers add.

Richard Johns and David Holden report that when the British showed a film of the Vigilant wire-guided antitank missile in the sixties, one Colonel asked where men could be found to attach the wires, and Crown Prince Abdullah asked if it could be fired from the back of a camel. "Only if the National Guard were prepared to expend a beast for each one fired, replied a B.A.C. man wryly. 'Of camels, we have plenty,' retorted Abdullah."[13]

The relative unsophistication of Guardsmen requires special videos to acquaint soldiers and their families to new government housing on bases. The films described how to operate toilets, washing machines, lights, and refrigerators. The films also discouraged cooking on the floor of the houses, and encourage the use of the stove. "Don't butcher your sheep in the yard," the video tells the new residents. "Take the animals to the neighborhood slaughterhouse."

REGIONAL MILITARY

Given the premise that the Saudi grand strategy is to trade space for time and seek foreign protection, it would seem natural for them to cooperate with local allies. On the Gulf level, the Saudis staged joint military maneuvers with the 5 other GCC countries. A nearly non-existent GCC Rapid Deployment Force (RDF) was established with a core of Saudi units. The Iraqi invasion dispelled any illusions that the GCC would have military clout.

On paper, the GCC forces seemed potent. The Kuwaitis, in particular, had 200 British-built tanks. Oman, with the only battle-tested army of the region, has only 33 tanks, reflecting its orientation against guerilla forces. Qatar has 24 tanks, the divided United Arab Emirates have 156. Unfortunately, most countries have not coordinated on arms purchases. The only similarities are that most use NATO standard ammunition.

While common military purchases would make a lot of sense from the standpoint of cost, spare parts, and training, few steps have been taken in this direction. So far, the closest coordination of purchases took place when Qatar bought Mirage F-1s because Kuwait had them. Several of the GCC countries also have U.S.-built Hawk SAMs. This is a waste of resources. Bahrain, Kuwait, Qatar and the UAE all face critical diseconomies of scale by separately spending large amounts of money on forces too small to be effective, says Hameed.

The air force is the key to regional defense. Hameed says that the RSAF is most important arm in the entire GCC, and its AWACS- based Command system should provide the GCC a means of coordinating their disparate armed forces.[14]

The GCC countries have overbought military hardware. Hameed states that no army can increase its holdings of military equipment at more than 10 to 15 percent per year without adverse effect. This includes advanced NATO forces. Most of the GCC exceeds this amount, but he says that the Saudis and Omanis are more reasonable in their buildup than other GCC countries.[15]

MERCENARIES

The idea of having others fight Saudi battles is not exactly new. Abdulaziz bought tribal soldiers and loyalty with gold. The Saudi Air Force used Britons and Pakistanis in the Yemen conflict.[16] In 1980, a Ministry of Information denial betrayed the presence of 20,000 to 30,000 Pakistani mercenaries. Approximately 10,000 to 15,000 were hired as combat troops, and served mainly in armored brigades. For several years the Pakistanis bolstered the Saudi military. Although the Pakistanis were supposed to avoid combat, the Saudis used a few on the Yemen border, where they either performed badly, or refused to perform at all. This, plus the fact that many were Shia Baluchis, who are susceptible to Iranian subversion, led to termination in 1987 of the mercenary agreement.

The Saudis had demurred on signing another 3-year contract for the Pakistani troops. Rather than agree to another contract extension, President Zia Al-Haq pulled the troops home. Pakistan lost money, but improved its security. The Saudi posting proved detrimental to Pakistan's military preparedness, because many officers earned enough to quit the service upon their return to Pakistan and set up businesses. Zia also had to placate the Iranians, who threatened to foment trouble in Baluchistan if he maintained the mercenary deal.

When the Pakistanis left, the Saudis said they would shoulder their own defense burdens. Sources say that on Jan. 9, 1988, Egyptian President Hosni Mubarak, now armed with official diplomatic recognition from most of the Arab countries, signed a $5 billion deal for 15,000 Egyptian mercenaries. Egyptians provided security for the Hajj in 1988, and participated in the multi-Arab force after the Iraqi invasion of Kuwait. Even if the Kingdom's combat units remain all-Saudi, foreigners will still be required in support and maintenance positions, say trainers. The Saudis can buy and operate sophisticated weapons, but are a long way from being able to service them.

MILITARY FACTORIES

Military security depends upon safe supplies of arms and ammunition, so the Saudis have taken steps to build a domestic and regional arms industry. Domestic arms production takes place near Riyadh in a town called Al-Kharj. These factories produce machineguns and other light arms, under license from Hoechler & Koch, of West Germany. The factories also produce various types of small-bore ammunition, and will make uniforms. Rhienmettal has built a plant to produce mortar shells. Rhienmettal and Thyssen are seeking a contract to produce 155mm howitzer projectiles as well. A Saudi, Abdullah Al-Farsi, built his own custom armored personnel carrier several years ago, and was lauded in the local press. Prince Sultan subsequently pledged to build at least 10 of them.[17] Sultan also announced that four new factories were authorized in 1987. Under the Offset Investment Program, discussed in a different chapter, an electronics plant has been established to produce military radios. The avionics, airframe, and turbine engine repair joint venture companies all give the Kingdom advanced warplane repair and modification facilities.

The Saudis also sought to broaden regional arms independence. In 1975, the Saudis formed the Arab Military Industries Organization (AMIO) with Egypt. AMIO began to produce spare parts and equipment needed to wean Egypt's forces from overdependence upon the Soviet Union. When the Camp David accords were signed the Kingdom pulled out of the organization.

NUCLEAR

Although the chances of the Saudis going nuclear are slim, they are negotiating the purchase of a small research nuclear reactor from the West Germans. The secrecy surrounding the negotiations demonstrate that Bonn and Riyadh are concerned about adverse international reaction.

MILITARY INFRASTRUCTURE

"Do they think they will win a war with headquarters?" one Saudi asked, contemplating the row of Military headquarters on Riyadh's Airport Street. At the cost of hundreds of millions of dollars, each service has built its own headquarters, equipped with special underground bunkers designed to withstand a nuclear war.

The same mentality that drives the Saudis to prepare for a nuclear war has also driven them to expend billions for other security related projects. The King Fahad Saudi-Bahrain Causeway, erected at a cost of $654 million. permits Saudi troops to drive to Bahrain in less than half an hour. Safran links the decision to build the causeway to a 1981 coup attempt.[19]

The latest investment in general security is the Strategic Reserve program, that will see Swedish firms Skanska AB and ABV building hardened underground oil and refined product storage in caverns. An extensive fortified cavern system interconnected by pipelines will be built over a period of 7 years, at a cost of perhaps $4 billion. Like the Tornado deal, this will be paid by oil barter.

ARMS DEALS

The Saudi appetite for expensive armaments is due mostly to greater insecurity, but also to commissions paid on the deals. This pattern was established from the start. An order for Lockheed Hercules C-130 transport aircraft set Adnan Khashoggi on the path toward wealth. He originally served as agent for Lockheed and picked up Northrop, Rolls Royce, and Marconi. His well-rewarded efforts were so spectacular that he earned himself his own chapter in Anthony Sampson's "The Arms Bazaar," a book about the international weapons trade. Khashoggi was also linked to the 1987 Iran arms for-hostages scandal.

Khashoggi, whose empire has begun crumbling in recent years, led Northrop and Lockheed executives through the maze of Saudi royal intrigue. Sampson writes that by the end of the Seventies, Khashoggi earned $106 million from Lockheed, and $54 million from Northrop.

During U.S. Congressional investigations into the Lockheed and Northrop influence-buying scandals, the senate was astounded to learn how generals, as well as princes, crowded at the "commission" trough. Those revelations prompted the Saudis to enact rules to prevent such embarrassing incidents from recurring. But quiet conversations with companies as small as air conditioner suppliers, reveal that today, majors, colonels, and generals are still demanding and receiving pay-offs.

Although these scams increase the cost of the military, and provide money for the small-fry, the real action is in big weapons. The Tornado deal yielded $400 million in commissions, according to the British press, a figure backed at least in part by other sources. This was denied by the British Ministry of Defense and the Saudis who claim the deal was done government-to government and involved no commissions. The Tornados were purchased on an oil barter deal that periodically ran into trouble because of falling oil prices.

MINISTRY OF INTERIOR

"Remember how powerful he is," a senior Prince warned a senior United Nations official of Prince Naif. "His writ goes far." This is true. Every governate in the Kingdom reports directly to him. He has more men under arms, than either the National Guard or the regular Army. His Ministry of Interior, by some estimates, makes up from one-third to one-half of the government. The Ministry was Fahad's stepping stone to Crown Prince. Naif, Fahad's full brother, has another full-brother, Ahmed, as his deputy. The separate sections of the Ministry are:

The Royal Guard: This semi-independent branch of the ministry is heavily armed and responsible for protection of the Royal family.

The Mubaheth: These secret policemen are silent thobe-wearing enforcers.

The Muruur: These traffic police drive green and white patrolcars.

Criminal police: They drive blue and white cruisers.

Prison Police: They drive sinister all-black or black and white vehicles. They are responsible for public executions.

Coast Guard: This military unit is armed with helicopters and 8 SRN-6 hovercraft.

Frontier Forces: This paramilitary organization patrols the borders, and handles customs inspections.

Civil Defense: These units include fire brigades and rescue teams.

Mujahidoun: Their name is the same as the Afghan guerrillas, and means "fighters." This shadowy adjunct of 40,000 armed men is a secret, plain-clothes reserve available at an instant. They are recruited from direct descendants of King Abdulaziz's men, and report once a month for their pay. They silently watch at night over sensitive locations in town, such as banks, or telephone exchanges.

The organization's headquarters is a broad three-story concrete building behind a 10-foot high iron fence. Its sign, contrary to the government's bilingual rules, is written only in Arabic: Mujahidoun. Ministry of the Interior." They report to the Minister of Interior, and are only vaguely known by the general public. The deputy President of the religious police, the Mutawwa, told the Author, "We are not the same thing at all," but would not elaborate.

THE ROLE OF THE MINISTRY

The Ministry of Interior's police state apparatus took its present form during the reign of King Faisal, who cracked down after several abortive coups. The Ministry exercises control over whether an applicant can get a new telephone line, and taps it when they do. The phone system built by Philips and Ericsson was designed to accommodate a centralized wire-tapping system. The Ministry enforces controls on expatriates. They need letters to travel between cities, do the Hajj, buy cars, or leave the country. When the Ministry works in concert with the Religious police (which it often does) then no personal habit is above investigation. For all its power, the Ministry of Interior is not a Gestapo. Saudis are wary of the Mubaheth Secret Police, but are not terrorized.

The Royal Family is relatively benign, and while some torture does take place, disappearances and brutality are relatively rare. The group most likely to suffer torture is the Shia community in the Eastern Province. Amnesty International reported that several Shia have died under torture, and that many are held without cause.

TECHNOLOGICAL INNOVATIONS

Naif has augmented old-fashioned Saudi suspiciousness with technology. The key improvement is the "Big Brother" computer Center, called the National Information Center (NIC). Computer Services Corp. (CSC) of the United States won the SR1 billion (over $300 million) contract to computerize the Kingdom's security system. Three Univacs were installed in a special building erected in Riyadh. A system was installed to permit communication with 8 regional offices. From there, a communication network of 1,100 computer terminals is maintained. Every Saudi and Foreigner in the Kingdom, whether on a Hajj visa or resident permit, is issued his or her special number that permits the computers to pull all records.

The computer maintains records divided into drivers license, Hajj pilgrims, vehicle registration, Iqama, visas, and both Citizen's Identification books, and passports. The computer also maintains criminal records, foreign worker registrations, applications by foreigners for visas, and their passports. The most interesting file is labeled Mumnuween (forbidden). When a person's name is entered into this category, life becomes hell. Any time he or she is checked on the computer, this mumnuween flag alerts the operator to the undesirable status of the person before him. Thus, interminable delays and investigations will be part of this person's life.

The computer is part big brother and part necessary modernization. Every expatriate repeats the hoary myth that so and so went to the police department to find out what happened to his request for a drivers license/car registration/ visa, only to find it was used in lieu of a missing leg to prop up a desk/chair/filing cabinet. Like most expatriate myths, the story has some truth to it. The old system was inefficient. Saudis themselves took advantage of this. On those rare occasions when a Saudi's driving was so spectacularly awful that his driving license was revoked, he simply traveled to another town to apply for a new license.

The Ministry of Interior computers are also modernizing the Majlis system. Saudis can present petitions directly to any government official, up to and including the King himself. If an applicant is turned down by one prince, he goes to diferent Majlis sessions until one prince, somewhere, grants his petition. That puts the Ministry in the difficult position of trying to enforce two separate royal decisions. The computer system tracks Majlis petitions, and the action taken on them to prevent contradictory rulings. Univac meets Ibn Saud.

The NIC is a centralized computer system. The mainframes are connected to specialized terminals. Passport control terminal operators, for instance, cannot search for traffic offense records. The system uses tape backup archives, flat stacking disk drives, and a technology called revolving drum storage. This last technology gives fast access, but has become outdated since the computer system was designed.

In addition to Big Brother, the Ministry is investing in a Japanese fingerprint storage computer and French command centers linked to helicopters equipped with television cameras and audio systems. These will film riots and other disturbances and transmit the information to the command center. The first such center was built for Eastern Province Governor, Mohammed Bin Fahad. Naif installed one as well. Prince Salman of Riyadh now wants one.

High technology is knocking on the door of customs searches as well. The Ministry is interested in cargo container X-ray machines capable of scanning an entire truck trailer, or shipborne cargo container full of goods without opening the container. A small hole would be drilled in the container to permit an electronic "sniffer" to sample the the air inside to detect alcohol, explosives, and drugs.

Saudi Customs wanted to install them at all of the major road, sea, and air entrances into the Kingdom. The deal could run up to several billion, a hefty sum that attracted Lockheed and British Aerospace, both of whom make the aircraft engine X-ray machines that are the heart of the machines. British Aerospace acquired two potent sponsors: Prince Saud Bin Naif, son of the Minister of Interior, and Mohammed Bin Fahad, but revenue shortages appear to have delayed the acquisition.

The ultimate symbol of the Ministry of Interior's power is its new headquarters building, erected by Hyundai at a cost of $193 million. The bizarre building resembles an inverted pyramid with a dome on top. Yet all of these expensive facilities cannot conceal one fact; the average Saudi policeman is usually illiterate. Journalist and author Peter Theroux, a fluent Arabist who worked in Saudi Arabia for 5 years, amused himself whenever policemen demanded his papers. He presented his papers upside down. Invariably the guard would examine the papers thoughtfully, frown, and then hand them back, still upside down. Many guards only recognize the signatures of their immediate superiors, which means that even if your documents had been signed by King Fahad himself, the guard would not accept them until they were cleared by his Sergeant or Lieutenant.

Expatriates are generally frightened of dealing with Saudi police. Third worlders are treated much more roughly than the fair-skinned Europeans and North Americans. The Saudi legal system has a penchant for locking people up while a case or accident is being sorted out, and this raises expatriate anxiety levels. Prisons are not notoriously brutal, but they are hot, crowded, and boring. Inmates must pay for their own food, supply their own blankets, and have little to do to pass the time.

Every once in a while, after a spectacular crime, such as a bank robbery or hit and run accident, the police set up checkpoints throughout the city, where they demand all the identification papers of those passing by. So many offenders are caught during the annual GCC Traffic Week, that buses are used to haul off those with improper identification papers. The police also assemble unhappy convoys by impressing some arrested drivers into using their cars as paddy wagons. To enforce sane driving, the police have taken to public canings of what they call "hot-rodders." To enlist peer pressure against hot-rodding, the Qadis, or judges, have ruled that those who are riding with the Hot-Rodding driver are also liable to public caning. Saudi law is not always sophisticated, but sometimes it makes good sense.

CONCLUSION

"The Saudi Armed Forces are Operetta. They do not exist," said one observer. The observer is not wholly correct, but one thing about operettas is that they are expensive productions. Armed forces such as those of the Saudis, are expensive to stage as well. The worrisome question for the Royal family is whether its armed forces can perform if the curtain goes up. The confrontation with Iraq shows how much confidence they have in their huge military investment.

5

RELIGION

"The Arabs of the Desert are the worst in unbelief and hypocrisy." Sura Tauba 9:97 the Koran.

It was pre-dawn in the Al-Rawdah suburb of Riyadh when Rafeeq, a Pakistani Muslim, and his co-workers returned to their company housing. The crew spent the night printing Saudi Research and Marketing's morning newspapers. They headed home around 5 a.m. to 6 a.m., and Rafeeq fell asleep while electronically- amplified dawn prayer calls echoed across the town.

"Alahu Akbar," called the Muezzin. "Ashaduwan, la Illaha Allah, Mohammed Rasul Allah. ("God is Great, There is no God but God, Mohammed is his Prophet.") This morning, the men heard heavy knocks on the door. The bewildered workers sleepily opened the door and confronted the angry visage of the "Umdah" or Old Man of the Neighborhood, an official charged with keeping an eye on his precinct.

"Why are you not at the mosque?" the man demanded. Clad in the short thobe of the pious, with a long grey beard, the official glared fiercely. He planted his sandal-clad feet in the doorway. The workers stammered that they worked a nightshift and needed to sleep, but the grizzled official cut them short.

"Prayer is a duty to God that must be fulfilled," he lectured. The fact the workers prayed at work was not good enough. They were all forced to report the local police station the next day. There they were informed that they had missed too many prayers at the mosque, and that if this continued, they faced beatings.

Saudi Arabia's ever-vigilant religious authorities pry, peek, push and shove in their zeal to enforce Islam and its five pillars: A profession of faith in one god, Allah, and his prophet, Mohammed; prayer in the direction of Mecca five times a day; fasting during the month of Ramadan, payment of alms, called zakat; and a pilgrimage to Mecca called the Hajj, by those who can afford it. Islam's holiest building is the Kaaba, a black cube, in the center of Mecca's Grand Mosque. Islam tolerates Jews and Christians provided they pay a special tax as a subject people; Pagans have it worse.

Islam and tradition are central to the Saudis' concept of who and what they are. Islam existed before oil, and will exist long after it is gone. Saudis are proud, not of oil, but of Mecca and Medina. Islamic Sharia law, based on the Koran, and the sayings and doings of the Prophet Mohammed and his companions, is the law of the land. The Kingdom is one of the few remaining countries that boldly bans religious freedom.

When oil wealth poured in during the reigns of the Faisal and Khaled, the people took it as a divine reward; when things turned sour, they assumed it was a punishment for drifting from Islam. The resulting renewed religious fervor plays into the hands of the Muslim conservatives who distrust the King. Saudi Kings have always relied on Islam to legitimize their rule. The family conquered the peninsula in alliance with the religious reformer, Muhammad Ibn Wahhab. Wahhab preached a return to the pure Islam of the days of Mohammed. In return for state support, the strict, puritanical preacher helped mobilize the bedouin to conquer the peninsula. Wahhab's descendants, known as the Al-Sheikh, continue to support and intermarry with the House of Saud.

THE RELIGIOUS AUTHORITIES

Oil money has helped smooth the relationship between the monarchs and their religious sheikhs during bouts of modernization. The late Kings Abdulaziz, Faisal, and Khaled also used their popularity and Islamic credentials to forced the conservatives to give grudging way to education of women and television. Fahad, however, is handicapped by widespread knowledge of his history of gambling, drinking, and extravagant consumption, and has had to give way before the religious authorities.

It isn't that they attack him from the pulpit. They can't, since their sermons must be approved in advance by the Ministry of Hajj and Endowments. Despite this, the religious conservatives can make their feelings known. Even more worrying to Fahad, fundamentalist youth have appeared at scattered mosques to distribute leaflets attacking the King for being too pro-Western.

Since the King has less money for buying off the religious watchdogs, he tosses them bones in the form of new religious restrictions on foreigners and women. The new regulations are laid upon an already substantial foundation of Koranic prohibitions. Alcohol, pork, and pornography are forbidden, though pornographic films are rife, and Koreans sometimes sell pork as "special meat." Any hint of foreign religion is forbidden. Cinemas, bars, and even video games are outlawed. Live music, considered a distraction from religion, is forbidden in hotels. The Ministry of Education recently expunged music instruction from school curricula. Each government building's religious official is authorized to punish any bureaucrat who fails to regularly attend prayers.

Today, the government implements even the silliest rulings of the Ulema, a board of religious scholars. In 1986, the government forbade the casual disposal of newspapers, because most contain phrases asking the blessings of Allah. One does not wrap fish in paper printed with the name of God. Because of this, several government ministries and at least one municipality installed separate trash bins for publications. Singer Michael Jackson's phenomenal popularity of 1985, during the release of his "Thriller" album, caused his music to be banned. Saudi youth imitated his hairstyle, bought his posters, and moonwalked about. In short, they idolized him, and Islam forbids idolatry.

Islam's prohibition against idolatry explains the dislike of the human image. The FAL Shopping Center in Riyadh was forced to tear down two-thirds of a SR250,000 neon sign because it featured human figures ice-skating and bowling. Other ads, whether featuring children or camels, have been modified or defaced by the religious police. Ironically, photos of the King and his brothers are everywhere.

The national airline, Saudia, spent millions repainting aircraft and reprinting tickets and posters because the white space between the S and the A inadvertently formed a cross. Saudi television cuts out scenes involving male-female contact, and silences any mention of Christianity on even the most inane of American situation comedies. The unintended result is beneficial; banal Hollywood offerings are shortened. Sadly, the censors, through unfamiliarity with English, sometimes allow the usual lame double entendres to slip through.

The English language papers purge their comics of crosses. Whenever Porky Pig appeared in the *Saudi Gazette* comics page, artists added silly ears and a black nose to make him "Porky Dog." *Arab News* finds it necessary to separate Dagwood and Blondie Bumstead whenever they exchange farewell kisses at the door. Hagar the Horrible's mugs of beer are erased, and every female character's cleavage is covered, and her skirt lengthened.

Religious censorship includes shopping malls. Expatriates buy artificial Christmas trees under-the counter as "Party Decorations." Frantic notices demanded action during the 1984

"Cruel Shoes" incident. A Chinese firm decided to put the name of "Allah" on the bottom of rubber sandals to boost sales, obviously forgetting how Muslims consider the feet unclean. The Taiwanese embassy immediately issued a statement that shoes so offensive to Muslim sensibilities could only have come from the athiestic Communist Chinese.

The Kingdom's hospitals obtained a Fatwa, or ruling, from the Ulema about the Islamic propriety of performing transplants. The Ulema replied that is permissible to take an organ from a Muslim or non-Muslim and put it into a Muslim, but pointedly omitted the permissibility of putting a Muslim's organ in a non-Muslim.[1] So far, the Ulema has not ruled on the practice of using Pig heart valves in the frequent Saudi heart operations. "We just don't tell the patients what they are made of," said a Saudi heart surgeon. "Why cause problems?"

ISLAM IN DAILY LIFE

Every day, near noon, early evening, and nightfall, a strange anxiety besets expatriates. Prayer call will soon start, and if they haven't finished their shopping, they will have to drop everything for a period averaging a half hour to an hour. The minute the Muezzin calls from the minarets, loudspeaker-equipped red and white Chevy Suburban trucks manned by Mutawas cruise the city streets, calling out, in Arabic, "Pray, Pray, Remember God," to loiterers and shopkeepers.

Shopkeepers hurriedly close the metal shutters on their stores. Restaurants clog up with clientele who cannot leave until prayers are finished. Sometimes that is not good enough. Waiters in Riyadh's Mexican Connection restaurant were arrested for serving people locked inside during prayer call. The religious police confiscated the store's music speakers for good measure.

Supermarkets use a compromise worked out by the Chambers of Commerce. Those inside the store must wait for the end of prayer call. Shoppers can continue filling their carts, but their purchases will not be rung up at the cash registers. Lights are dimmed, and a prayer room is provided. This compromise fails to satisfy fanatics, who have forced some stores to throw customers out anway. Again, this practice has increased due to official indulgence.

"It's a preposterous solution," Dr. Muhammed Masari, an American-educated Saudi biochemist told former *Saudi Gazette* reporter, Peter Theroux. Masri, who is a devout Muslim (his father was imam of King Abdulaziz's mosque in the town of Al-Kharj, outside of Riyadh), has scant respect for the Government's method of living with the religious establishment. "You end up with people wasting their precious time standing on the sidewalk, or wandering aimlessly inside. Whether, or when, you pray, or for how long, is between you and God. It has nothing to do with the machismo of the Mutawa. "It's only a competition; they don't trust each other. When you play a game called, 'which of us is the better Moslem?' That is very un-Islamic."

Many Westernized Saudis think the Al-Saud keep the religious zealots occupied with minutiae, such as checking to see taxis don't ferry unmarried women, or finding improper Arabic lettering on foodstuffs. Distracted by petty religious concessions, the Ulema never deals with weightier issues such as the Islamic legality of hereditary Kingship, immorality of rulers, construction of billion dollar palaces, and monopolization of power.

Religious oppression goes in cycles, usually getting stricter after upheavals, such as the 1987 Iranian riots in Mecca. The pattern of loosened and then tightened restrictions began long ago. The Wahhabis cracked down after Abdulaziz conquered the Hejaz in 1929. A few months later, on the anniversary of Abdulaziz's accession to the throne of the Hejaz, celebrations "Were organized on an unprecedented scale for Arabia and were obviously intended to impress both foreigners and Arabs alike...They may said to mark a definite departure from the rigid precepts which the Ikhwan had succeeded temporarily in imposing. Photographs were taken freely: an official photographer had in fact come from Egypt and photographed the Emir (Faisal) on every possible occasion. Smoking was indulged in openly, or with only a pretence at concealment."

Then, three months later, "The regulations issued by these committees nineteen months ago had been allowed practically to become a dead letter, and the local citizens, who had been congratulating themselves on the gradual evanescence of these tiresome restrictions, were greatly annoyed to find them resuscitated by lictors or special police imported from Nejd who carry out their duties with deplorable efficiency...small boys playing mouth organs have been the first to receive attention. These diminutive miscreants are given a spate of the cane and the offending instruments collected in baskets."[2]

Enforcement of Islamic rules include imprisonment of foreigners who dare eat food publicly while Muslims fast during daylight in the month of Ramadan. Christians hold underground worship services, some with priests smuggled in by embassies or large organizations. Many Christians say their spiritual life is more fulfilling in the Kingdom than back at home. People worship in the Kingdom because they want to, not because of social pressure.

On Feb. 26, 1987, a group of Eritrean Christians praying in the home of their lay leader were arrested by religious police. The following is the account of one of the women:

"On this Thursday, 26th February, there were 38 in the house including 8 children, and Abraham (the Pentecostal minister) was preaching. There was a knock at the door and I went to open it. Many police burst in, over 20. They punched me and pushed past. Some were in uniform with guns and others were in Saudi dress, and they had a video camera. They pointed their guns and told everyone to be quiet and started videoing everyone. We started singing (psalms). They took all our Bibles - in English, Arabic, and Amharic ... while we continued to sing and pray. They became very angry and told us to stop and threatened us with their guns - pointing one at a girl's head. They were very confused at our behavior, and said, "What are they doing, these messihi? (Messianists, or Christians)" The group was taken to prison, where they were were asked why they weren't Muslims. Some were treated roughly. "To our leader Yohanis, they offered him money, a house, and a job if he became a Muslim."[3]

The only protection for non-Muslims is that Saudi authorities are loathe to invade homes. This goes for either religious services or parties. But raids have been made, and are encouraged by the ever-watchful mutawa who try to infiltrate Christian worship services with Muslim Filipinos or Pakistanis. Religious persecution is not restricted to non-muslims. Other Muslim sects, such as the Shia, suffer under the Kingdom's strict Wahhabis.

The Saudis finance mosques throughout the world, and their press crowed about construction of a Mosque near the Vatican in Rome. Yet no churches are allowed in the Kingdom. After the Riyadh Diplomatic Quarter was established, the Western ambassadors made a request. Could they build a Westerners-only church without any exterior symbols of Christianity? The Ministry of Foreign Affairs rudely dismissed their request. It is no wonder that American chaplains are asked to remove their religious symbols when not directly with the troops.

When Minister of Hajj, Abdul Wasie imperiously asked the Swiss when they would grant permission to build a mosque in Geneva, the Swiss replied that permission would be granted as soon as they could build a church in Riyadh. The Saudis argue that the kingdom is all-Islamic, and that Christianity violates its peoples' traditions. Other Gulf countries, from Bahrain to Oman, have allowed construction of modest churches. Perhaps the government's biggest fear is that Saudis will convert, and that would force implementation of Sharia death penalty for apostasy.

In 1985, the European Parliament told its trade negotiators to bring up freedom of religion while holding talks with the Gulf Cooperation Council. The French head of one delegation shrugged and said in 1988, that freedom of religion will not stand in the way of making a deal.

The man on the street shares his government's dislike of Christianity. A local art dealer sold frames to a Saudi who had purchased two Monet paintings at a London auction for approximately 50,000 pounds each. He hung them in his bedroom, but something bothered him; it was a church steeple in one of the paintings. "He paid someone to paint over the cross," the dealer gasped while drinking a glass of homemade wine. Swedish flags flew in Riyadh for a state visit, and prompted angry letters to the local newspapers complaining about the display of the cross on the flags. Swissair's first office in Riyadh was physically attacked because the airline's logo contains the Swiss cross. King Khaled Eye Hospital's mainly expatriate staff was banned from giving a Christmas party for staff children because a "devout" Saudi resident complained.

Unsurprisingly, converts to Islam are highly valued, and some receive money. The local Imam records his or her attendance at prayers, and files a report at the end of the probationary period; the money is then awarded.

Life is not easy even for the majority Sunnites. Islam governs a Moslem's life to a degree that it is difficult to keep all the rules straight. The local newspapers and the television stations feature Islamic scholars who answer endless questions on marriage, divorce, inheritance, and the problem of paying interest to banks. Is it permissible to urinate while standing? Although most Muslims urinate squatting, one of the prophet's companions amazingly saw fit to record that he once saw Mohammed urinate while standing. What if you fart while praying? Start all over. God doesn't like farting. What if your wife converts from Islam to another religion? Well, in a Muslim country, she should be executed. If not, you still must divorce her. One man said his ritual ablutions were spoiled because of a urinary problem that caused him to dribble. The solution? Tie a plastic bag filled with absorbent material around the "appropriate part of the body." Then pray as usual. The scholar finished by saying that Islam makes things simple. One wonders how Muslims fared in the pre-polyethylene days. Every week or so, single males are told cryptically what the Imam thinks about masturbation. He writes, "The practice you mention, while not forbidden, is not encouraged."

One old man learned that his wife of 21 years, the mother of nine children, was his "sister." It so happened that his mother's milk dried up during a drought, and he was breastfed by an aunt. The aunt's husband had a second wife, the daughter of whom he eventually married. Islam forbids adoption, but says children become brothers and sisters if they suckle from the same woman. Two decades later, relatives planted doubt in his mind. "In my head, I kept asking myself, 'Is my marriage right or wrong in the light of Islamic Sharia?'" the distraught man told the Jeddah daily, Okaz. "...I went to Sheikh Abdulaziz Bin Baz, and he said, 'Divorce.'"

"I went home, not knowing how to explain all this to my wife. I finally told her. She had a shock from which she never recovered. She became insane."[4]

In early 1988, King Fahad announced that those prisoners who fully memorize the Koran (about a 2-year exercise for most people) will have half their sentences commuted. Nobody seems to know whether a thief could thus commute his sentence from a hand to his index finger.

RELIGIOUS SPENDING

Although revenues are down, the government still lavishes money on Mecca and Medina, Islam's two holiest cities. Even after the oil crunch, Fahad approved an additional SR5 billion for expansion projects. The expenditures, past and present, have been to accommodate the yearly Hajj. In Jeddah, a huge, but surprisingly airy terminal was constructed solely for Hajj flights. Solar-lighted tunnels and elevated walkways that are used just once a year, were built to help speed the pilgrims on their way. The total cost of these road projects topped SR10 billion.

Both the Grand Mosque of Mecca and the Prophet's Mosque in Medina are being expanded. The Prophet's Mosque will hold more than 650,000 worshippers, almost twice the year-round population of Medina itself. For comparison, the Houston Astrodome seats only 50,000. The expansion is being paid through oil barter. The Mosque in Mecca is being enlarged in a similar, billion dollar fashion. The Grand Mosque has specially-cooled floor tiles to prevent barefooted Muslims from burning their feet as they circumambulate the sacred Kaaba in its center.

Another demonstration of Islamic zeal is the support of Islamic guerilla groups and construction of mosques abroad. This is not simple cynicism. The Saudis feel a sense of Islamic solidarity with any number of Islamic revolutionary groups, ranging from the Moros of the Philippines, to the Afghan Mujahadeen. Idi Amin Dada, the former Ugandan dictator, lives comfortably in Jeddah on a government stipend because he says he is a Muslim. The Eritrean separatists cloak themselves in Islam for support, as do certain Burmese and Thai splinter groups. Most of the affected countries are too poor to protest this interference in their affairs.

THE RELIGIOUS RELATIONSHIP AND ITS USES

Most Saudis, regardless of their level of observance, believe in Islam. Saudis may discuss how, but never "if" Islam should be implemented. The Royal family thus gains legitimacy by wearing the Islamic cloak. This explains why attacks of a religious nature cause volcanic reactions. When American AWACS jets arrived in the Kingdom after the fall of the Shah, Libyan Leader Muammer Qaddafi claimed the Kingdom's leaders were committing a grave offense against Islam. Non-Muslim Americans could peek out of the jets at the forbidden Holy cities of Mecca and Medina. The next Friday, thousands of imams delivered thundering sermons condemning Qaddafi as a heretic, a madman, and one who consorted not only with strange women but Athiestic Russian communists. Qaddafi backed down and arrived in the Kingdom later to perform Umrah.

The presence of American troops makes the Authorities similarly nervous. As soon as Iraq can be forced to vacate Kuwait, it is likely that the Kingdom will ask the Americans to depart, or scale back their numbers.

THE RIOT

The quiet growl of a thousand murmured prayers emanated from the Grand Mosque in Mecca on the morning of July 31, 1987. Hundreds of thousands of pilgrims circumambulated the Kaaba clad in the simple two-piece white Ihram garment of the Hajj pilgrimage.

But as the day wore on, Mecca grew tenser. By 4:30 p.m., Saudi traffic police fidgeted nervously outside of the mosque. A phalanx of loudspeaker-carrying Iranians led 150,000 of their countrymen on a demonstration down the main street toward the Holy Mosque. Many of the pilgrims were Revolutionary Guards, led on this demonstration by A. Mortezavi, chief propagandist of the Tehran Friday prayers. Closely-linked with Hashemi Rafsanjani, speaker of the Iranian Parliament, he was joined by various officials, including the mastermind of the American embassy seizure. "Martyr Plan" was underway.

Saudi Radios crackled as the men reported to their superiors. The Iranians were massing. Forming up on side streets under color- coded posters of Khomeini, carrying banners "Down with Israel," "Down with America," they were led by by men chanting through loudspeakers suspended on poles. The mob marched behind a vanguard of women, including the Ayatollah's wife.

A few policemen nervously checked the switches on their electric shock riot batons. The Iranians came forward, implacable, irresistible, energized by Khomeini's exhortation to "turn the

Hajj into a battleground," and were armed with concealed knives, scissors, and other sharp implements bought in the local souks. Their goal was entrance into the holiest of Moslem Holies, the Grand Mosque. Prince Naif's instructions to his men were clear: do not let them in. In 1979, Muslim fanatics seize the Mosque, and it took over two weeks and heavy casualties to root them out.

Police formed a thin wall in front of the advancing protestors. The demonstration clogged the path of the faithful of other nations, many of whom urgently tried to squeeze past. Arguments started, pushing escalated into fighting, and several foreigners were stabbed.

"The Iranian women threw bottles (of gasoline) in the faces of pilgrims who refused to join the demonstration," one Egyptian pilgrim told press agencies upon his return to Egypt. One Nablus doctor saw two Jordanians stabbed because their Khaffiyeh headdresses were mistaken for Saudi garb.[5]

The enraged Iranian mob swept the truncheon-armed Saudi police before them. Officers were stabbed, motorcycles were burned, and rocks were thrown. Ministry of Interior forces were mobilized, as was the National Guard, a unit of which was stationed near the Mosque. The great doors of the Mosque were pushed closed and barred against the Iranians.

Saudis gathered on rooftops to hurl bottles and stones on the demonstrators. A Ministry of Interior helicopter began firing teargas canisters at the Iranians. The crowd of both Iranians and foreign pilgrims began to stampede but were restricted by Saudi police. After one Saudi policeman was killed, a lieutenant in the National Guard, opened fire on the Iranians with an automatic weapon. By 8 p.m., the streets were quiet, and the crowds dispersed, leaving bloody bodies on the streets outside of the Mosque. The casualties were 402 dead, and 649 wounded. Many of these were women trampled to death during the frightened stampede. One Saudi source said 25 were killed by Saudi gunfire.

The Saudi and Iranian propaganda machines went into action. For once, the Iranians underestimated a deathtoll, and said 200 were killed. The Saudi Minister of Information, Ali Al-Shaer, told an indefensible lie that he repeated through the next several weeks. He said no Saudi guns were fired. This propaganda blunder was dutifully parroted by the Saudi media. Al-Yamamah Magazine drew cartoons of Khomeini removing his turban to show horns, and printed an exclusive scoop: in Paris, Khomeini wore a fake beard which he took off when he went to bed.

Saudi television broadcast the first admission that during the previous Hajj, Iranian pilgrims were arrested while smuggling in up to 55 kilos of plastic explosives. The Iranian government gave its pilgrims identical pieces of luggage containing explosives in concealed compartments. The Saudi broadcast was meant to show the Kingdom's forbearance in publicizing Iranian perfidy.

The Iranians had touched a raw nerve, for they were also demanding that Mecca and Medina be internationalized as pan-Islamic cities. The Saudis purchased support for its handling of the riots from almost every Islamic organization in the world. Most nations thought the Iranians deserved being shot for rioting in Mecca anyway. Iran persisted. During the 1989 Hajj, two bombs blew up in Mecca; one killed a man and wounded 23 others. The other injured nobody. This was Iran's way of saying, "You can't have a truly safe Hajj without cooperating with us." The Saudi reply was to execute 16 Kuwaitis arrested in connection with the explosions. Ironically, the next year, around 1,000 pilgrims died in a tunnel stampede when cooling systems failed, and Iranians were not involved.

The Saudis orchestrated outrage against the publication of "Satanic Verses" by Indian-born British Author Salman Rushdie. Rushdie, a former Muslim, was accused of slandering Islam, Mohammed and Mohammed's wives. The Saudis financed the first series of anti-Rushdie demonstrations in Britain, but were upstaged when Iran put a $4 million price on the author's head. Riyadh hosted the 1988 OIC summit, which condemned Rushdie and demanded that he be tried for apostasy in an Islamic country. The government may have waffled for Western consumption, but other Saudis, from Western-educated businessmen to bedouin, said Rushdie should die.

Interestingly, official reaction to "Satanic Verses" was less severe than it was to the film, "Death of a Princess." This shows either that the Kingdom learned the limits of coercing the Western media, or that it takes blasphemy against its royals more seriously than blasphemy against Islam.

RELIGION TODAY

The Kingdom's religious elite sit on the Ulema, a board of 15 scholars who approve the succession to the throne and issue fatwas, or rulings, on government actions. When militant Muslim fundamentalists seized the great Mosque in Mecca during the Hajj of 1979, a Fatwa was procured permitting troops to fight within the hallowed sanctuary.

Chief of the Ulema is Sheikh Abdulaziz bin Baz, an ancient blind scholar. He sits in his office, attended by two younger men, frail, but stern, with opaque white eyes that glitter in the office twilight like marble chips. His skin is grey, and parchment-like, and he speaks in Nejdi-accented perfect classical Arabic. Bin Baz attracted worldwide notoriety when he published a tract claiming that the world is flat because it says so in the Koran. He also argued that the universe revolves around the Earth. King Faisal forced him to withdraw his claim about a flat Earth, but he maintains the pre-Copernican concept of an Earth-centered cosmos, in accordance with the infallible Koran.

His mental energy is undiminished, he answers questions with a battery of quotations from the Koran, or the 26 volumes of the Hadith. Bin Baz may be a fanatic but he is no fool. Every day, a line of petitioners wait before him to hear his rulings on their questions. He told one source that he knows the government supports Western-style banking which depends upon payment of interest. The Koran bans either the giving or taking of any interest whatsoever.

"It is the moral obligation of the government to promote Islamic banking," he said, adding that cosmetic cover-ups, such as calling interest "commissions" does not fool him. Bin Baz single-handedly forced the government to delay the 1988 issue of bonds. "How can an Islamic government issue interest-paying bonds?" he demanded.

In 1987, sources said, a Pakistani armed with a knife attacked him during a car trip. They add that the attack was staged by the Ministry of Interior to provide an excuse for posting guards nearby. This lets the Ministry control access to the influential Bin Baz. He is a curious guardian, this wizened old man, stern, unforgiving, ever vigilant, despite being locked in the darkness of the blind.

The House of Saud, says Niblock, has chipped slowly and persistently at the Ulema's power. Unlike the Shia clergy of Iran, the Saudi religious scholars have no hierarchy, and no income-generating lands of their own. Wahhabi imams are also more dependent upon the state for a living than other Sunni clergy, such as those of the conquered Hejaz, who lived off of gifts, or Waqf endowments. Wahhabis believe endowments should pay for mosques, charity, and works of God, not support clergy.

This dependence upon secular rulers for income inhibits the Saudi Ulema's independence and allows the Al-Saud to ignore some of its demands. "This talk of us being consulted during the Majlis is just 'sweetness' (window dressing)," one sheikh told a Canadian diplomat.

When the pro-Western Fahad succeeded Khaled to the throne, many Saudis expressed hope that he would liberalize the country. Instead, he has moved backwards. What little credibility he has with the religious conservatives is squandered on the construction of more palaces, and securing more jobs and commissions for his sons and the sons of his full brothers.

In 1987, Iranian propaganda goaded him into dropping his many pompous titles for "The Custodian of the Two Holy Harams" That meant Caretaker of the two forbidden (to non-Muslims) cities of Mecca and Medina. Newspapers were obliged to refer to Fahad in the first reference as the "Custodian, etc., etc." Crown Prince Abdullah, not to be outdone, began referring to himself as the Deputy Custodian of the Two Holy Harams, shortened by some, to, the "DC."

Before the oil prices collapsed. the regime felt strong enough to ignore the Ulema. When, in 1925, they called on Abdulaziz to stop the Shia of Al-Hasa from performing Shia rites, Abdulaziz refused. It has also cut down on the Ulema's participation in government. When Saud was Crown Prince, he used the Ulema as judges, imams of mosques, financial administrators and police officers.[6]

This changed after Mecca was conquered. Only two Ulema were selected for the domestic governing council of the region. A strategy was adopted, said Al-Yassini, to bureaucratize areas formerly under Ulema control, such as education and the judiciary, to loosen their grip.

"The extent of the Ulema's participation in the newly founded structures was influenced by the needs and orientation of the political sphere -- the Ulema were given prominence when religious legitimation was needed, and they assumed a secondary position when their stance contradicted that of the ruler or when other sources of legitimacy were invoked....; they became paid civil servants whose status, income, and general activities were governed by state regulations and objectives."[7]

Al-Yassini argues that the Ulama were channeled through several different organizations supported by the government. The Kingdom has two overtly religious ministries: the Ministry of Hajj and Endowments, and the Ministry of Justice.

THE MINISTRY OF HAJJ AND ENDOWMENTS

The Ministry of Hajj and Endowments helps with the tremendous burden of the yearly Hajj. Actual control of the Hajj rests with the Ministry of Interior. The Ministry of Hajj is concerned purely with the logistics of caring for the pilgrims.

This is a gargantuan feat. Each year, almost 2 million pilgrims converge on Mecca. Food, water, transportation and medical care must be supplied to people speaking dozens of different languages. Hundreds of Medical clinics are established to care for the pilgrims. In the old days, pilgrims tended to die off from whatever diseases existed in their groups long before they made it to Mecca. Today, they get off the planes hot with whatever exotic contagion they left home with. Saudi medical authorities desperately try to screen these people out but they are not always successful. Viral spinal meningitis broke out during the 1987 Hajj. After the Hajj is finished, Jeddah and the Western province becomes awash with influenzas and other diseases brought in by the pilgrims.

A fleet of over 1,200 buses sits idle until Hajj takes place. Small passenger cars were banned from Mecca during Hajj starting in 1984, because of traffic and the fact that cars have been used to smuggle in weapons and explosives.

Because part of the hajj rites entail animal sacrifice, more than 500,000 sheep are slaughtered during each pilgrimage. In the old days, the pilgrims would give the extra meat to the poor of

Mecca. By the Seventies, the waste was scandalous, so a program was started to fast-freeze the meat and fly it to other Islamic countries.

Mecca is a tremendous security headache. The Hajj is difficult enough without being forced to admit Iranians, Lebanese, and Libyans. In 1985, a load of Libyans arrived armed with machineguns. The Saudis refused permission to disembark with the weapons and eventually, the Libyans returned whence they came.

The Iranians proved more troublesome. Fear of Iranian anger at first led the Saudis to permit the Iranians to boost their pilgrims to 150,000, a number greater than those sent by more populous Islamic countries, such as Egypt or Indonesia. After the 1987 riots, the Saudis decided to cut the number of Iranian pilgrims entering the Kingdom without appearing to single Iran out. In the March meeting of the OIC, the Saudis asked for the right to limit pilgrims according to population. The ongoing construction projects in the two holy cities was the justification. Iran's delegate stormed out of the meeting. The Saudis secured near-unanimous approval.

In fairness to the Saudis, efforts had already been made to cut back the number of pilgrims flooding into Mecca. In the early Eighties, they said Muslim guest workers can perform the Hajj only once every five years. Before this, many guest workers made the pilgrimage each year. The decree cut the numbers going to Hajj by up to 400,000. A less crowded Hajj is part of the Saudis' determination to do all it can for the "guests of God."

ENDOWMENTS

Under Islam, the wealthy could make endowments, called Waqf, to support charities such as Mosques, hospitals, or schools. The Ministry also oversees these charitable trusts and foundations. Charity is one of Islam's strongest features, and the Saudis respond well.

MINISTRY OF JUSTICE

Perhaps the best example of bureaucratization of the Ulema is the Ministry of Justice. In the beginning of the Saudi state, the leaders ruled on general matters; the Ulema restricted themselves to religion and crime. With institution of Islamic Sharia law by Abdulaziz, the religious men became Qadis, or judges. Further discussion of this ministry is in the Chapter on Physical and Human Infrastructure.

DIRECTORATE OF RELIGIOUS RESEARCH IFTAA', DAWA, AND GUIDANCE.

This is the primary channel for the Ulema's activities. Its chief has the rank of a Minister-at-Large and reports directly to the King. The Directorate sponsors seminars, research, and propagation of Islam.

Its scholars also write books that the Directorate publishes. Several of these tomes are:

Sheikh Sulayman Ibn Muhammad Al-Hamidi's *"Al-Turuq Al- Shari'ya li hal al-Mashakel al-Zawijji"* (Legal ways of solving marital problems).

Abd al-Rahman ibn Muhammad Ibn Qassim al-Asmi al-Hanbali's, *"Tahrim Halq al-Lihi"* (The Religious Prohibition of shaving off beards).

Sheikh Hamad Ibn Nasser Ibn Uthman Ibn Mu'amar's, *"Ishad al- Muslimin fi al-Rad ala al-Quburiyin"* (The Guidance of Muslims in Answering those who Advocate Visitation of Graves).[8]

Membership of the directorate is 15 men appointed by the King. Today, only one is an Al-Sheikh. This does not mean the Al-Sheikh have lost power. They head the Ministries of Agriculture and Water, Justice, and Education.

The Ministry of Education, Ministry of Higher Education, and General Presidency of Girls Education, the General Presidency of Youth Welfare and the Ministry of Information all propagate Islamic values. The Ministry of Finance has a special division for collecting the Islamic Zakat tax from companies. The Ministry of Interior cooperates closely with the religious authorities, and provides backup for the Mutawas. Non-ministerial organizations are also powerful.

RELIGIOUS POLICE

The best known is "Al-Amr Bil Am'Arouf Wal Nehi 'an Al- Munkar" - "Committee for Propagation (commanding) of Virtue and Forbidding of Evil." A Committee member is known as a "volunteer" or "Mutawa." Expatriates call them Mutawas as well.

Expatriate dinner parties are rife with entertaining, blood-curdling, and often inaccurate stories of the Mutawa. Mutawas are not all wrinkled old men clutching staffs, wearing short thobes, and Ghutra headdresses without the black Iggal band. Actually, approximately 25 percent of the 20,000 or so Mutawa actually wear police uniforms. Many of them are quite young, the products of the Kingdom's religious universities as well as some foreign schools. Most eschew gold or silk (forbidden by the Prophet because they are adornment for women) and wear long beards and short thobes as marks of piety.

The Committee functions as an independent and powerful government agency. Their Acting President Abdulrahman Bin Ahmed Al Al-Sheikh sits in an office, located in an old white-washed villa guarded by several uniformed police. Abdulrahman is a young man, in his thirties, whose English is fair, and whose demeanor seemed pleasant but severe. It was a shock to see him wearing a gold watch and gold cufflinks, but an Islamic column said gold-plating is permissible, though pure gold is not.

"To begin with, we must point out that the existence of such a body (the Committee) in this Islamic State is a realization of what was set forth in the Holy Koran: "Let there arise out of you a band of people inviting to all that is good, enjoining what is right and forbidding what is wrong: They are the ones to attain felicity," he said. "This country, thanks to God, is an Islamic country that came into being on the basis of Islam, and will remain so, if God wills. I will sum up the objectives of the Committee in one phrase, i.e., 'To guide people to Truth.' This is one of the legal definitions of the propagation of virtue and suppression of vice...as a whole, the Committee tries to prevent evil so as to facilitate the spread of good," he replied.

The Mutawa can probably trace their ancestry to a group of "Zealators" founded in 1855 by Imam Faisal. These 22 men carried canes for punishing those who wore gold or silk, or who smoked, sang, played musical instruments, or were lax in religious observances.[9]

Sheikh Abdulaziz Ibn Abdulatif Al-Sheikh founded the first "modern" committees in 1903 to patrol Riyadh. The mutawas were empowered to arrest, bring to trial, imprison or punish those who commit offenses. It was dangerous to smoke in Riyadh 40 years ago, because the smell of tobacco would bring a Mutawa to your door. The committees were extended to the Hejaz in the late 1920s, and were promoted through a fatwa by Meccan theologians. When King Abdulaziz found that the Mutawa were opposing some of his policies in 1930, he had them incorporated into the Directorate General of the police. They were restricted to reporting crimes to police and were stripped of arrest powers.

In 1960, civil service regulations were extended to the Committees. The sybaritic King Saud bolstered them in a bid to refurbish his Islamic credentials. The head of the committees was assigned Ministerial status in 1396AH (1975).

Al-Yassini contends that by incorporating them into the bureaucracy, they have been stripped of power. This is not true. After the oil bust, Fahad has granted them more leeway to take arbitrary action against individuals. One businessman recounted a dining experience in a Chinese restaurant. The Mutawas thought the Filipino staff was too slow in closing up for prayer call. The waiters and kitchen staff were taken outside and beaten on the spot. A foreigner arrested for drugs in the Hotel Al-Khozama was expelled from the Kingdom, with a proviso that if he returned, he would be taken to the lobby of the hotel for a public flogging.

Mutawas take the names of persons they decide are indecently dressed. The offenders are not only women with bare arms; men in running shorts are liable to be rebuked with a swat of a cane. The Mutawa are arbitrary: One day, a woman will be get accosted for failing to wear an Ubayya (common in Riyadh, less so in Jeddah or Al-Khobar) and the next she won't.

Offenders are taken to a local mosque for a grilling, and may be detained for hours, days or even weeks. The Mutawas answer to none but their leaders and certain high-level authorities. Detainees are usually released only after signing confessions and pledges not to indulge in vice again.

While recruits were formerly selected solely on the basis of moral qualifications, administrators now take the competitive Civil Service examinations. There are no female mutawa. "All the members of the Committee are government employees and not volunteers and they get their salaries from the government like the other government employees," Abdulrahman said.

ISLAMIC ORGANIZATIONS

The World Association of Muslim Youth (WAMY), founded by the Saudis in 1972 to propagate Islam abroad. Al-Yassini says WAMY is designed to assert Saudi leadership of Muslim youth. WAMY issues warnings on a regular basis about the insidious activities of Christian missionaries. In 1987, it accused the ultra-ecumenical World Council of Churches of sponsoring the destruction of Sudanese mosques by rebel guerrillas.

The Jeddah-based Organization of Islamic Countries (OIC) is not exactly a Saudi organization, but was founded at Saudi instigation when Nasser threatened the Kingdom with pan-Arabism. It contains 46 Islamic countries, from Palestine to Turkey, and is the most important forum for Islam in the world.

The OIC almost always supports the Saudis on such touchy issues as its handling of the Iranian rioters in 1987. The Kingdom, in turn, is one of the few countries that meets its financial obligations to the organization. Deadbeat members and lack of funds forced the OIC to fold its Islamic International News Agency. The best way for a reporter to get to know members of these groups is to attend cocktail parties. Officials of the Islamic Development Bank, OIC, and MWL, are frequently located near the bar.

RELIGIOUS OPPOSITION

In a country without political parties, religion functions as the premier consensus builder. Those that do not agree fall into opposition. Religious Saudis were always concerned about the corrosive effects of oil wealth, but lower revenue seems to have aggravated their discontent, and given weight to their arguments.

Some religious opposition comes from schismatic sects, such as the Bani Yam tribe of Wadi Najran and 250,000 Shia in the Eastern Province. The Shia are second-class citizens, mainly because the Wahhabis regard their sect of Islam as heretical. They are banned from performing the self-flagellation and processions that commemorate the martyrdom of Hussein during Ashura. There are only three Shia deputy ministers. When well to-do Shia offered to pay for repairs to their mosques in the Eastern Province themselves, permission to perform comprehensive repairs was denied. Community leaders are getting better results from the new Eastern Province Governor, King Fahad's son, Mohammed. In the meantime, they tread softly out of fear of radicalizing the Shia community.

"The Shia will not risk anything until they are sure of the outcome," said one diplomat. "Some of them must sympathize with Iran, but they are waiting to see what happens." Their cautious attitude is influenced by the government's historical willingness to shoot and kill Shia demonstrators.

Some radical Shia have joined the Iranian-sponsored Organization of the Islamic revolution, which may have supplied volunteers to plant bombs in petrochemical plants and refineries in 1987, but most religious opposition comes from Sunni zealots dissatisfied with what they perceive as a corrupt and pro-Western government. Nothing is more dangerous than a true believer, and the Kingdom's Islamic universities are producing herds of these.

Umm Al-Qura in Mecca, and the Islamic University in Medina have professors such as Dr. Ali Mushref Al-Amri, who claims a 80 - 100 percent cure rate for the "Evil Eye" and evil spirits using Koranic verses. The largest of the Islamic institutions is Al Imam Muhammed Al Saud Islamic University of Riyadh. Its new billion dollar campus stands near the King Khaled International Airport. The country needs engineers and doctors, yet the Islamic schools grind out religion and Arabic language graduates.

The government and religious conservatives have clashed in the past. The most famous incident was the seizure of the Grand Mosque in Mecca in November, 1979. A group of almost 400 zealots seized the Mosque on November 20, 1979, During the two-week battle, Shia were killed in an unauthorized Ashura procession in the Eastern province.

After the fundamentalists in the Kaaba surrendered, they were interrogated, and then dispatched to the corners of the Kingdom for execution. The Al-Saud were particularly shaken, because the revolt came not from the Shia or Hejazis, but supposedly stalwart Nejdis in their early 30s. Many of the fighters had served in Crown Prince Abdullah's National Guard, which heretofore had been regarded as the most politically-reliable of the armed forces.

After they seized the mosque, the radicals issued statements attacking corruption and "innovations" in the Kingdom. The targets were familiar. Technology, relations with foreign powers, and un-Islamic attitudes held by the Royal family. The leader and chief theologian of these Muslim revolutionaries, a young man named Juhaiman, was once examined and cleared by Bin Baz. After the revolt was crushed, King Khaled summoned Bin Baz. One court observer said the normally placid King Khaled thundered at the blind religious scholar, "You are like an empty can. You make a great noise when beaten with a stick, but you have nothing inside."

THE RELIGIOUS-POLITICAL SYSTEM OF ISLAM

"You know what the difference is?" one Muslim woman told a friend. "Christians 'love' God. In Islam, love doesn't enter it. We 'obey' him." When Mohammed revealed his new religion to the Arabs, he called his new religion "Islam" or "Submission" to the will of God. It is the final perfect revelation, built on the foundation of Judaism and Christianity. Followers of these religions are given special consideration by Muslim rulers, because they, like the Muslims, received divine revelations, which makes all three "People of the Book." The difference is that they perverted their revelations. This allows Muslim men to marry Jewish or Christian girls (though not vice versa). Though non-Muslims were distinctly second-class citizens under Islamic regimes, Jews usually fared better under Muslims than under Christians in the Middle Ages.

Although Mohammed is revered as the perfect model of a man, he is not worshipped. He is said to be the last of a line of prophets including the Jewish prophets and Jesus Christ. Muslims accept the virgin birth and second coming of Jesus, but deny he is the son of God. They likewise reject the crucifixion. Islam accepts angels. Gabriel (Jibreel in Arabic) transmitted the Koran to Mohammed. Other spirits, called Jinn, exist. During the Ramadan of 1987, religious authorities made an announcement. A "Jinn" or spirit, with a tiger's head appeared to the Grand Mufti of Mecca. It claimed it was Buddhist, but after the Grand Mufti explained Islam to it, it converted, and then disappeared.

The central miracle of Islam is the Koran. The earthly version is said to be a copy of an original that existed before the dawn of creation. Only the most fundamentalist of Christians attribute to the Bible the kind of authority the Koran claims for itself. Very little of the Bible consists of quotes from God. The entire Koran is dictation taken from God and given to Mohammed.

Islam rejects the idea of fallen man, but instead hedges men with restrictions to force them to do good. Every human is accountable to a merciful God and therefore is never quite sure (unless it is for a period of time after making the Hajj pilgrimage), that all his or her sins are forgiven.

A Muslim is absolutely certain of forgiveness only if he commits a sin either through ignorance, or by compulsion, in other words, though no fault of his own. This leads, in the author's opinion, to a tendency to avoid personal responsibility. Because of their religion, Christians perform a mea culpa and then feel forgiven. Performing a Mea Culpa in Islam does not gain forgiveness, it simply means that you have saddled yourself with responsibility for a sin.

Regulations cover every aspect of a Muslim's life. Animals must be slaughtered "Halal" though Kosher will do in a pinch. Taxes, inheritance, divorce, how hard one may beat one's wife, and what types of punishment should be meted out for crimes, are covered by laws deduced from the Koran and the sayings, or doings of the Prophet, collected as the "Hadith" or "Sunna."

Religious duties are so complicated, that Saudi schools give primary and secondary students two hours or more a day of Koran memorization, and on how to perform the religious duties of Islam. For instance, a Muslim must walk around the Kaaba in a specific direction seven times. His daily prayer follows a specific pattern of bowing, standing, hand-clasping, and kneeling. The niceties of performing proper ceremonial cleansing "ablution" are complicated as well. The prayers follow established verbal formulas and a specific choreography. Muslims also gain credit for good works.

One Arab Muslim confided that his Hajj turned him into an atheist. A recent convert to Islam attended the annual Hajj and said that far from being edifying, the rites were grueling. He was surrounded by a million pious Muslims terrified that by forgetting some minute element of ritual, their Hajj would be invalid, and they would be consigned to hellfire. When he started drinking a Coke, he was admonished, "The Prophet never drank a Coke with his left hand."

One Christian woman, smuggled into Mecca by a rich Saudi, said that non-Hajj Mecca had an aura of peaceful, religious purpose that was beautiful. Most Muslims agree.

Religious and social law grew so complex that four major schools of jurisprudence sprang up to interpret the Sunna and Koran. These were the relatively liberal Hanafis, the Malikis, the Shafis, and the most conservative of all, the Hanbalis. The Hejazis emphasized Maliki

EXECUTIONS

The following is the author's eyewitness account of an execution:

The unannounced executions, called "Chops," are held in the parking lots near the main mosque in most towns. They attract thousands of spectators. I have not seen, nor spoken to anyone who has seen the victim poked by a sharp stick to make him stiffen before the blade falls, nor nor have I seen or heard of the police dispersing the crowd with whips. That is not to say such things occurred in the past.

To see a "chop" in Riyadh, you must go downtown on Friday morning to the clocktower outside of the central Mosque. When the parking lot in front of the clock tower contains cars, no execution will take place. If parked cars have been cleared away, then the execution occurs after noon prayers. A large crowd gathers early. I arrived early to one execution and was able to stand about 10 meters (30 feet) from the place where it took place. The crowd, of Saudis, Pakistanis, Egyptians, and others, was packed 12 deep. People stood on cars, climbed the few date palms. and clambered for views. It was hot, and we were packed elbow to armpit, with convulsive heaves as people tried to elbow their way to the front. The myth of Westerners being pushed to the front to watch was laughable. It took considerable muscle just to maintain one's place.

The heat was intense as the guards began to deploy. Armed police watched from the nearby rooftops. A ring of young recruits with automatic rifles formed an circle and watched the front row of the crowd. A second ring of older soldiers, armed with submachine guns, looked out over the crowd. Plainclothesmen circulated in the crowd to ensure no aggrieved relative tried a rescue.

The site was in front of the old Emirate (or governate) office of Prince Salman. Parked by its steps were two small black windowless mini-buses. Each contained a condemned man.. Several men lounged beside the vans. One, with an ammunition bandolier, carried a shining sword. His thobe was immaculate, and his headgear was a standard red-checked ghutra. He was a medium-sized older man, black, and wore glasses. He chatted nonchalantly with a doctor dressed in a lab smock.

The prayers of the mosque echoed across the square from the loudspeakers. I was thirsty, hot, and suffering from the smell of a thousand tightly packed unwashed bodies, when the last prayer ended. The wall of bodies heaved from the impact of thousands pouring out of the mosque to get a look. I noticed some small boys brought by their father to watch.

When the final prayer ended, a police officer announced in Arabic the names of the criminals, and their crimes. He ended, as always, with the statement that the Kingdom is keen to preserve social peace through application of Islamic Sharia. As his words ceased, two men were led from the parked buses. Ahmad Sheikh Al-Din a large Somali, and Oman Salem Muhammed, a small Yemeni, had broken into a Kaki Money Exchanger and cracked the safe to steal dollars and gold.

The men were blindfolded with cotton taped over their eyes. Their hands were bound behind their backs, and their feet were manacled. Muhammed stumbled, and his face appeared as if he had been weeping. Both appeared drugged. They were led to the center of the square, and stopped. A guard then grabbed their thobes, and ripped them, pulling them down about their shoulders. The feeling of heat left me, and I felt a chill. This was it. This was for real. I wondered what I would be thinking about in their place. The men were then turned to face Mecca, and forced onto their knees, about ten feet apart. (one friend who witnessed some Filipinos being executed remembered one man rising slightly from his knees as they were burnt by the hot tar).

The executioner silently stalked to the small man., and unsheathed a normal sword, not a heavy scimitar. He raised the blade halfway in the air, and brought it down on the Muhammad's neck. He crumpled without a sound, his head still partly attached to his neck. I expected some sort of quirky-jerking reaction to death, but he lay still. Blood began to pool on the pavement. Without stopping, the executioner walked on to Al-Din, raised the blade, and brought it on the neck of the big Somalian. The blade bit into the vertebrae with a "tchuck!" and the African pitched forward with a groan onto his forehead.

The crowd rippled with polite applause.

But the Somalian was not dead. The executioner repositioned the Somalian's head, and daintily chopped the partially-severed neck. He then wiped the blade on the dying man's thobe and stepped back. The Egyptian doctor walked forward to check the two men. The Yemeni was dead; the big Somalian still clung to life. The executioner walked forward again, moved the head around by its hair, and made another dainty chop or two before cleaning the blade on the man's clothes and stepping back.

The whole procedure took perhaps 90 seconds from the police announcement to the death. Afterwards, Firemen hosed the blood down drains, and the square became a parking lot once more.

jurisprudence, while the Nejdis subscribed to Ibn Wahhab's even more rigid modifications of Hanbali doctrine.

THE STATE

Islam is inherently undemocratic, because while it may be "just" to subject peoples, it does not grant them a say in their affairs. Islam exhorts its people to assume control of any community they live in, if possible, and then impose the rules of the Islamic "Ummah" or community. This aspect of Islam is why many countries with sizable Muslim minorities experience separatist and communal troubles.

The Saudis still hate Turkey's Kemal Ataturk because he abolished the Caliphate, dropped the Arabic alphabet, and made Turkey a secular state. The Turkish Minister for Religious affairs was astonished by Abdul Wasie at a Pan-Islamic meeting. Wasie read a statement which spent nearly three pages damning the Turks and their secular government to Hell. The offending sections were removed only after a strong diplomatic protest.

When it comes to hammering out separation of church and state, or dealing with modern life, Christians have more room to maneuver than Muslims because the New Testament contains little social legislation compared to the Koran. The Koran is full of detailed instructions, and it is hard to fudge these laws without calling into question the veracity of the book itself.

Sharia law can be considered harsh. It requires public execution for murder, rape, armed robbery, adultery and apostasy. Thieves may suffer amputations. Yet the rules of evidence are strict. Adultery must be proven by several eye-witnesses, for instance. Amputations take place only after multiple convictions. The victim of a crime, not the state, has the right to extend clemency. The survivors of the victim can opt to take blood money compensation instead of asking for the criminal's head. Every once in a while, the first male survivor of a murdered man is an infant. In that event, the courts wait until the boy reaches the age of majority. At that point, he can decide to take blood money or go ahead with the execution. A laconic official execution announcement then states that the criminal had to wait 15 years or so for the male heir to mature. Some executions seem deliberately, cruelly, botched and slow, while others are quick.. One friend saw a young executioner lop a head off with an underhanded swipe. The body remained kneeling, spurting jets of blood from the neck, before slowly sinking to the ground. The crowd applauded loudly. The crowd spit in the blood of a different man convicted of murdering a little girl. In 1989, after a spate of partricularly gruesome highway rapes, murders and robberies near Riyadh, the culprits were executed, and their bodies suspended from engine hoists in the center of town for six hours.

Scott Pendleton, a former *Arab News* reporter, witnessed a stoning. "They throw small stones, and they don't throw them very hard. The guy looked like he just fell asleep." Expatriate mythology maintains that the Saudis have modernized stoning. A large dump truck full of stones backs up to the victim, a lever is pulled, and voila! we have an instant stoning. It sounds too good to be true, and it isn't.

Those facing amputation are taken to the town square in a single black windowless van, just like those facing stoning or beheading. After the sentence is read out, a group clusters around the convicted felon. Although the man is drugged, sometimes a cry can be heard. A brief flurry of movement takes place while the executioner amputates the hand neatly at the wrist. The bleeding is staunched, and a police officer holds the hand up on a string to show to the crowd. Polite applause is heard.

Amputations are very rare, and stonings even less common. These punishments can take place in any town square in the Kingdom. There is none of the drama or trappings of a Western beheading or hanging. There is no special equipment, and no ceremony. To a good Moslem, it is much like garbage disposal, and could be as quickly achieved in a supermarket lot as the town square.

Executions send the country a message. Before the 1987 Hajj, the Saudis departed from usual practice, and executed criminals on weekdays as well as weekends. The Iranian rioters failed to heed the warning. The Somalian and Yemeni execution was one of a series following several bank robberies. When some Filipinos had been arrested for raping their mistress and killing her husband (he had supposedly cheated them out of their pay) they were killed in an almost deliberately inept (and therefore painful) fashion, and their sentence was read in English for the benefit of Filipinos in the crowd.

The most famous execution was that of young Princess Mishaal bint Fahad bin Muhammed. She and her lover were executed on the orders of her grandfather, the hot-tempered Muhammed. Her crime was adultery, and her story was chronicled in the movie "Death of a Princess."

Executioner Saeed Al-Sayyaf, is one of Kingdom's professional executioners. He has executed more than 600 people in more than 35 years on the job. He has had 24 wives, 25 sons, and many daughters, living off of the commission of SR500 per head. He says he uses a sword for men, and a pistol for women. A sharp- edged knife is used for cutting wrists (sixty hands have been removed by him).

"I have a feeling of delight and satisfaction," he told Al-Medina newspaper. "Thank God who gave me the power to put an end to what is against the law of God....the job involves a lot of fun sometimes, and when I set with relatives or friends, I hear from them jokes. Once I joked with the Crown Prince, His Royal Highness Prince Abdullah bin Abdulaziz and said to him, 'Your Royal Highness, the market suffers a lot these days suffers a lot of recession! No heads to chop! No wrists to cut!'"[10]

Although some expatriates say the executions are barbaric, most concede the Kingdom is safe as a result. Some argue that the Kingdom's low crime rate is due to tight family structure and wealth, but forget that crime was rampant in that same society before implementation of Sharia law.

When the executioner's blade falls, it is an affirmation of Saudi Arabia's religious system in action. Religion made the law, religion set the legal procedures, and religion established the punishment. Once again, the expatriates and Saudis see clearly that the banner of Islam waves high in the Kingdom.

CONCLUSION

The biggest challenge to the present regime is how to manage the disappointed expectations of young Saudis, and how to ride the tiger of Islamic fundamentalism. The royals have bought off the traditionalists with religious concessions. But now that the Islamic universities are cranking out greater numbers of young fanatics, the problem is growing worse.

Fanaticism might lead to outbursts, and perhaps an assassination, but it will probably not result in any overthrow unless economic conditions completely alienate the middle class. Again, the longer the Americans remain, the more it will chafe the fundamentalists. The liberal elite hopes the presence of foreigners, and the immense world goodwill shown to the Kingdom will loosen hold of fundamentalist moslem leaders, writes Youssef Ibrahim, of the New York Times.[11] Whether it will, is another thing altogether.

6

SOCIAL

"Ye shall certainly be tried and tested in your possessions and in your selves and you shall certainly have much that will grieve you. but if you persevere patiently and guard against evil, then that shall be a determining factor in all affairs." Surah Nissah (Women) V. 186

Saudi Arabia's isolated tribal-oriented Islamic society survived rapid modernization during the oil boom without too much damage, but the downturn is creating new stress. Lower oil revenues finds increasing numbers of coddled, demanding youth who feel cheated by a drop in affluence. The past struggle between conservatives and modernizers took place within the context of family, religion, and tradition, and it is likely that adjustments to a downturn will be made within this context as well.

The West, while seductive, has not changed Saudi society as much as expected. Its influence is held at bay by the strong conservative tendencies of a culture which was never traumatized by the experience of colonization. Another trait that mitigated the stress of rapid change is the Saudi tradition of consensus-building. The Saudis, like the Japanese, try to reach agreement and avoid open disagreement. Consensus is hammered out in the Majlis, a sort of get-together that purveys information and gossip up and down the hierarchy. Saudi homes have a Majlis instead of a living room, where the men, or women, get together, drink tea, and talk. There are two types of Majlis, and each serves a different function. A Majlis between equals, say, of the senior princes, is used to develop consensus. A Majlis attended by subordinates, such as King Fahad's Tuesday Majlis, allows the common man to vent complaints and get assistance from his ruler. This does not mean consensus methods are always used. Families and businesses are usually run autocratically by the head male.

Civility is another trait the Saudis share with the Japanese. Good manners keep things running with minimum friction in a society which, until recently, had a propensity for taking insult easily and carrying on blood feuds. When two Muslim men meet, whether they are Saudi or not, a series of formulaic greetings are exchanged. "Salam Allaykoum (Peace of God with you)" says the first. "Allay koum Salam" (And peace of God to you) the other replies. Then comes several different ways of asking about one's health, to which the reply is affirmative, with the phrase "Ill hamdu' lillah" (Thanks be to God.)" Then various blessings and good wishes are exchanged, until finally, the men begin a conversation.

Well-mannered foreigners do not point the bottoms of their feet at Saudis, or eat with their left hands. The bottom of the foot is considered unclean. In pre-toilet paper days, the left hand was used for wiping one's posterior. This stricture is not hard to understand, given that Saudi meals are traditionally served on a communal basis without forks, spoons, or other utinsels. This has spawned the nickname "lamb-grab" for the feasts.

Saudis and Japanese share an insular outlook, which means they have an exclusive idea of who is in their group. Islam is anti-racist, but many Arab-looking Saudis look askance at countrymen who appear Negroid. A man's name is a brief introduction to his genealogy. If he is Hassan bin Walid Bin Sultan Al-Dhossary, you have learned that he is Hassan, the son of Walid, who was son of Sultan, of the Al-Dhossary tribe. Saudis are often aware of each other's family trees.

Concern for bloodlines and the example of the Prophet Mohammed promote first cousin marriages. This keeps wealth within the tribe, but results in a plethora of birth defects. The emphasis on kinship makes for a small society. The Kingdom has a total population half the size of New York, and only a small part of it deals with foreigners. People, particularly within a certain social strata, seem to know everyone else, either personally, or through in-laws. Businessmen are advised to watch their words. An off-hand insult about a Saudi across the country has a disconcerting ability to travel on the gossip hotline.

FAMILY AND ISLAM

Saudi society rests on religion and the family. Islam provides a social system that leaves little room for doubts, and provides believers rules for their personal, public, and religious lives. It encourages life in a greater religious community built on the foundation of strong families.

The family, and by extension, the tribe, provides the individual an emotional and financial safety net. If a man is out of work, his father, brothers, or cousins will support him. This cushions the effect of the downturn. Large families are the rule, and the Western practice of sending aged parents to nursing homes is considered disgraceful. Unfortunately, Saudis are embarrassed to send their mentally and physically handicapped relatives out into public, and keep them home, out of institutes that could provide help. Since the family is so important, Saudi employees think nothing of taking time off to take care of various domestic problems.

The extended family has been weakened, not so much by economics, as by the government. When a Saudi is sent to one of the industrial cities to work, or a soldier is assigned to some remote part of the Kingdom, he is torn from the bosom of his extended family.

The oil glut has caused a decline in rents which permits young families to build their own homes or simply rent apartments. This movement has been accelerated because the advantages conferred by extended families are being whittled away. At one time, it helped to have several wives who cooperated on housework, child-rearing, and labor-intensive meals. Inexpensive maids and technology have changed this. "The big family is no longer necessary," said one Saudi housewife. "For instance, using a modern kitchen, one woman can cook for many."

PRIVACY

Reputation is important to the Saudi male, and he takes pains to keep his family and affairs private. Walls, like veils, are designed to prevent other men from looking at a man's wife, daughters, or sisters. Robert Frost may have written that "Something there is that does not love a wall," but he never visited the Kingdom. Fahad's palaces are surrounded by walls over 10 meters high while most residential streets are corridors between bland tan-colored cement or cinder-block walls. Saudis do not like prying eyes, and sometimes top the 8-foot high walls with additional screens. Jeddah homes, reflecting their owners' more open personalities, have lower walls than those of Riyadh. Jeddah, a port, and Mecca, with its yearly influx of pilgrims, have always been less puritanical than Riyadh.

Riyadh authorities assume foreigners share their obsession with privacy. When the Al-Riyadh Development Authority approved construction plans of embassies in the Diplomatic Quarter, they regulated windows to prevent diplomats from peeking at women of other nations. The British had to secure written permission from the Swiss before they were permitted to add windows on the Swiss side of their embassy. The New Zealanders had to change the design of rooftop ventilation panels, because it was feared that, if they did not, someone might be able to stand on their tiptoes to peer through the slots at women in an adjacent embassy compound. "This tells us a lot about the way they think," one disgruntled ambassador from an Islamic country confided.

The persons most likely to stare at another man's women are bachelors, which explains why single males are segregated. An article entitled "Bachelor-phobia" in Al-Bilad said many apartment owners only rent on a "family" basis and will evict single Saudi men. The article lamented that more leeway is granted to foreign bachelors who are considered less likely to cause problems than Saudi males.[1]

Saudi attitudes toward foreigners are explored in "Cities of Salt," a fictionalized account of the arrival of the first American oil workers. Saudi novelist Abdelrahman Munif chronicles the reaction of villagers to the Americans. The government desires the money that will come from the oil. The villagers dislike the Americans because they are different, and call the American wives sluts, because they wear no veils. They resent the arrival of the Twentieth Century. The xenophobic reaction of the villagers still exists today as Saudis wrestle with the changes wrought by technological advance.

It seems hard to reconcile the Arab tradition of hospitality with this dislike of outsiders. Custom says a host must show at least three days of hospitality to everyone, even enemies, who come to his tent. This tradition arose because no man knew when he, too, might become lost in the merciless desert, and require help. Hospitality is an obligation, not an act of friendship. It is no wonder then, that as the years wore on, citydwellers wearied of foreigners, while countryfolk still like meeting them. Even in long-term relationships, foreigners are rarely invited to a Saudi's home, and will almost never see a man's sister. This is not discrimination, since few Saudi males ever see their best friend's sister, either.

Saudi generosity is also famous. In the old days, if a guest expressed admiration of his host's possessions, the host would give those things to him. Stinginess is a terrible reputation. Some Westerners abuse this trait by asking for gifts that a polite Saudi finds difficult to refuse. Then, when the Westerner refuses to reciprocate, he adds to the general Western reputation of greed and ingratitude.

Some young Saudis befriend Westerners in the Kingdom in expectation of tapping into a supply of alcohol, pornography, or females. Former Saudi Gazette journalist, Peter Theroux was badgered by Saudi co-workers to introduce them to nurses. After months of importuning, he revealed he found interested women. His delighted coworkers pressed him with questions. Did they like sex? Were they pretty? Did they drink? He replied in the affirmative. Impatiently, they demanded what nationality these wonderful, loose women were. He replied "Saudis." "Impossible," his scowling coworkers said. "A Saudi girl would never be so shameful," and never pestered him again.

Arms dealer Adnan Khashoggi was a master of pragmatic "generosity." He dealt in high-priced prostitutes and wild parties, according to one of his women, a former Miss India, Pamella Bordes. She was one of Khashoggi's "gifts" to foreigners and members of the Saudi Royal family.

Saudis also inform newcomers that "an Arab's Word is his Bond," but cultural differences cause problems. Saudis think telling someone "no," is rude, and prefer to be indirect. An evasion which would be an overwhelming "nay" to a Saudi sounds like a "maybe," or even a "yes," to a foreigner. Even when a Saudi is determined to redeem a pledge, you never have any guarantee as to when it will be done and insistence upon immediate fulfillment of the pledge is resented.

SOCIAL ADJUSTMENT

Absorption of new technology was not always easy; resistance to television led to a shoot-out at the broadcast station in Riyadh. Few had qualms about the automobile, but it has probably been more damaging to family insularity than television. Cars allow youth to leave the family for recreation. Many bored teenagers cruise down boulevards for entertainment. Kids spin their cars and pickup trucks in circles, called "Doughnuts" by American teenagers, and "fives" by Saudis, since the Arabic symbol for five looks like a Zero. Some engage in aggressive road races that frequently end fatally. For a while, traffic fatalities undid the diligent procreation practiced by good Saudi mothers. The police gradually imposed a limited amount of order on Saudi streets. To curb hotrodding the police finally began to cane offenders. However, police infrequently pull people over (partly out of fear of stopping a prince) unless the driving plumbs the depths of psycophathic insanity.

Cars encouraged urban sprawl, and disrupted old neighborhoods. Before the advent of autos, women could do all their shopping in the nearby souk. Now they need transport. The cure was hiring a driver. Soon almost all middle and upper middle class families hired Filipino, Pakistani, or Indonesian drivers. This created an unwanted intrusion by foreign males in a household. A maid is one thing, because if a husband has sex with her, it is understandable. For a wife to sleep with her driver, which happens with greater frequency than Saudis care to admit, is absolutely unacceptable. The Saudi Gazette killed a story about the large number of babies found, dead, in trash recepticles in Jeddah. Most were Saudi-Asian.

The growing dependence of families upon foreign domestic help was another oil-related phenomenon. Domestics are just another version of slave labor, which existed in a literal fashion up until 1962, and figuratively up till now. Saudis found servants useful, and socially prestigious.

"These maids are now seen in almost every flat and villa...in markets and shops...they are moved by a Western mentality and lifestyle and will destroy our children and family," an unnamed Saudi lamented to the Islamic newspaper, Al-Muslimoon.[2]

Huda, another Saudi, related the following horrifying incident. "I saw them (her children) sitting around a fire along with the governess performing certain religious rites. I could not control myself any longer and asked her to get out of the house immediately." One Filipina who knew karate practiced her moves in the privacy of her own room. Her eavesdropping employer felt threatened and had the woman arrested by police. The downturn has not halted the use of domestics, it simply means that abuse of, and refusal to pay domestics has increased.[3]

ATTITUDES

It is difficult to get a true feel for Saudi sentiment, because there are few avenues for Saudis to get together en masse. There are no labor unions. The few literary clubs are so effete and elitist that their effect is negligible. Charitable foundations provide citizens a chance to work together, but most have princes or princesses on their boards, and therefore lend themselves to pro-regime activities. Religion is the main non-family mass event. Yet, all sermons must be approved in advance by government officials. Thus, the imams may dish out anti-Israeli, anti-Christian, and anti-Western sermons, but never anything anti-government.

Soccer games and sports competitions are the only other mass activity allowed. Sports Clubs, sustained by government subsidies, are often maintained out of political motives. One team, Al-Nasser, was always heavily backed by the sons of the late King Saud, mainly to rehabilitate his name. Hilal (Crescent), in Riyadh, is called the Government's Team. Ittihad, in Jeddah is the darling of would-be liberals and Hejazis who dislike the Nejdis.

Further, during and after games, the reactions of the youth reveal their attitudes. After victories, young Saudi males weave through the streets, honking horns and trailing the colors of their favorite teams. After the Kingdom beat Iran in the semi- finals of the 1989 Asia Cup, the youth went wild. On Thalateen Street, a Westerner was pulled from his car and beaten. Windshields were smashed. When police tried to intervene, they were severely beaten. The worsening economy seemed to foster the violent anti-foreign outbreak. Taken aback by the eruption, the government posted contingents of police at intersections, blocking off favorite cruising boulevards, and designated specific "celebration" sites at the various soccer clubs.

TEENAGERS

Violent soccer fans are symptomatic of the "teenager" problem. Bored, undisciplined youth have long harassed Third World workers, hurling eggs at Asians, and driving aggressively. Many randomly dial telephones, in the hopes of hearing a woman answer the phone. Some women also do this.

"It is the boredom in my leisure time that forces me to take a drive after midnight," Nabeeh Ribh told Okaz "I feel like running away from home after remaining inside for so long. I stop my car by the side of a telephone booth and begin to dial indiscriminately in search of someone who will answer."[4]

"What am I to do after sending a whole day studying?" asked Sami Abdullah, another youth. "I have no friend but the telephone. I am tired of loneliness and want to break the monotony of reading books and studying my lessons." Another youth said, "As the eyes of my family are all-pervading, I resort to this when my friends are away. I don't practice any hobby or play sport, and I am bored of my studies."[5]

Saudi youths, like other teenagers, are often sexually frustrated. Many bother Asian and Western women in shopping malls. When the Religious Police catch offenders, they are not any kinder than they are with foreigners. In Riyadh, 254 "Romeos" were arrested and jailed seven days each for disturbing women.[6]

The result is that upper class youth go on trips abroad. The most popular spot is Bangkok, where sex is inexpensive and readily available. A Thai journalist once confided to some colleagues that Saudis are a Thai prostitute's least favorite customer.

Others stick to home, where Eritreans and Ethiopians dominate the lower end of the prostitution market. They cross the Red Sea as refugees, and most eventually settle in Jeddah. There they take jobs as housemaids, but often supplement their meager incomes through a little "moon-lighting." Lebanese and Egyptians dominate the higher end of the market. There are stories in Riyadh of bored Saudi college students participating in higher-class bordellos both to make extra money and to have something to do. Those that do, face death at the hands of their fathers or brothers if they are caught. For a long time, the air hostesses of Saudia Airlines in Jeddah had a reputation as "hostitutes," because of the activities of some stewardesses. Some nurses are also lured by the easy money as well. Prostitutes makes life hard for other women who are then treated as if they, too, are for sale.

Homosexuality, and frequent use of prostitutes means that Saudis are vulnerable to AIDS. The government restricts information about Saudis suffering from AIDS, and claims that the only Saudis to suffer have been victims of tainted blood transfusions. The other cases are blamed on foreigners, who have to be tested for AIDS to get a visa. Saudis traveling abroad, though, get pamphlets warning about the disease.

DRUGS AND ALCOHOL

Despite being outlawed, brand name liquor is available in most upper class Saudi homes. A fifth of Johnny Walker Black Label costs $100. Most is smuggled from Yemen and the United Arab Emirates, although containers are smuggled by ship. Embassies are allowed to bring in booze, and this privilege is sometimes abused. Western diplomats who sell liquor are sent home, but Filipino and African diplomats have been jailed.

Eritreans, Filipinos, and Somalians dominate in production and sale of Saudi moonshine, called "Siddiqi" which means "Friend" in Arabic. If genuine alcohol is rare, beer and wine are even scarcer because they carry less "kick per liter." The difficulty and expense of obtaining "real" alcohol leads many expatriates to brew their own. This will be discussed further in the end of this chapter, when we look at expatriate lifestyles and society.

Many young men turn to drugs. Saudis pick up drug habits in India, Thailand, or the West.It is not impossible find run across hashish being smoked at certain parties. One heroin-addicted Princess, who called herself "Jo" for "Johara" passed out in California after an overdose, and awoke in the drug treatment ward of Riyadh's King Faisal Specialist Hospital.

The Ulema issued a 1987 Fatwa authorizing death for drug dealing. Effective anti-narcotics officers get cash rewards. One officer in Jeddah had won SR750,000 ($200,000) by mid-1989. By June, of 1989, police said the anti-drug campaigns and death penalty threat combined to cut the number of addicts by 60 percent, said Maj. General Ibrahim Al-Maiman, head of the Drug Combating Department of the Ministry of Interior. Drug use fell 26 percent at the same time.[7] Since the penalty was announced in 1987, more than 111 pushers were arrested, and several had been executed. One, a Chadian, was said to be a diplomat.

The battle against drugs continues, with urgency and determination. The biggest weakness is that some princes abuse their privilege to smuggle drugs. As long as they can bring drugs into the country, anti-drug efforts are undermined. Officials are combating addiction with three "Amal" or "Hope" hospitals for drug and alcohol abusers.

BEDOUIN

"Arabian culture embodies two contradictory currents of thought," says Cole. "One, stemming from the sedentary Arabs, is based on literacy; it includes an erudite knowledge of Islam and classical Arabic literature. The other stems from the nomadic desert Arabs, who in their simple tribal life embody the ideals of austerity, endurance, justice, and hospitality. In the past, many urban families sent their children to live among the bedouin to absorb the positive values of living in a simple society in the purity of the desert with the camels."[8]

To cartoonists, the Saudi is a ghutra-clad fellow riding a camel past an oil well. Yet most Saudis are not bedouin, and few have ever ridden a camel. Bedouin constitute only 20 percent or so of the Kingdom's population, and many of these live in towns.[9] Their past influence over the townsfolk was disproportionate because the tribes possessed superior mobility. On the other hand, the sedentary arabs were not exactly at the mercy of the bedouin. When Abdulaziz crushed his bedouin Ikhwan warriors, he used townspeople to do so.

Like most peoples, the Saudis have a weakness for an idealized pastoral past. The bedouin's mercurial, excitable and warlike qualities are admired and praised, yet their unsophistication, and slyness are the subject of jokes. An in-depth discussion of tribal organization is not terribly interesting, or particularly useful. In brief, the tribes have organized themselves according to kinship. The tribe is the largest unit, and claims descent from a mythical founder. The tribe breaks down into into various branches, all of which are reckoned by descent. Eventually, the bedouin fragment to the basic building block, the family unit. At certain watering holes, during times of war, or times of plentiful rain, the tribes agglomerate and form large groups. This ability to break down into small groups, or to concentrate when needed, gives the bedouin organizational flexibility.

Each tribe is run by a Sheikh, literally the "old man." His job is often hereditary, but not necessarily so. A tribe cannot stake its survival in the harsh desert on the niceties of succession. The ruler is someone who has built a reputation for wisdom in amicably solving disputes, by bravery in battle, and by having a more than average amount of luck.

Sheikhs seldom rule autocratically. Decisions are best reached by consensus and enforced by peer pressure. In a culture where reputation is so important, few bedouin are unlikely to risk censure by the tribe. Today, the importance of the sheikhs is declining. The government defers to them in matters involving tribal matters. If a crime is committed, the local Amir will summon the sheikh and tell him to deliver the offender. This preserves tribal pride. If a member of a tribe requires government aid, he might address his request through his sheikhs.

Nonetheless, the Sheikhs' role in securing government gifts or favors has declined, mainly due to the increase of bureaucracy. A sheikh doesn't hand out a Real Estate Development Loan, a civil servant does. Nonetheless, the sheikhs are treated with respect. Their fellow Bedouin ignore the periodic government plea for citizens to turn in their weapons. Most Saudis, rural or urban, have a firearm. The leather craftsmen in the old Riyadh souk make gaily colored scabbards for the bedouin favorite: the AK-47. Lebanon is a source of weapons, but most are smuggled from Yemen. The Saudi weapons souk is said to be located near Khamis Mushayt, in the South.

The tribes are not only well-armed; they are trained. Bedouin are the backbone of the Saudi Arabian National guard (SANG) described in the military chapter. This is a system for handing out grants to the Bedouin, keeping them busy, and building them into a usable, and reliable force.

The bedouin and rural peasants constitute most of the Kingdom's poor. The number of poor is increasing, and they receive fewer benefits than they did during the heyday of the oil boom. A destitute Saudi depends on generous Majlis sessions, numerous philanthropic societies and the strong Islamic tradition of alms- giving. Further, free medical care and educations are provided for the most humble. To an extent, Saudis choose how poor they will be, for most young men have many government-provided opportunities.

INTELLECTUAL LIFE

"What's the difference between Saudi Arabia and Yoghurt?" goes one joke. "Yoghurt has a living culture," is the reply. Compared to Egypt or Syria, the Kingdom is a cultural as well as physical desert. The Kingdom's most famous novelist, Munif, lives in exile. Literary societies and newspapers are all subsidized and controlled by the government. The Ministry of Information approves the chief editors of the local papers, and directly operates television and radio. Foreign publications are rigorously censored, not only for poitical items about the Kingdom, Islam, or Israel, but also for advertisements showing too much cleavage or legs. Armies of censors clip out or use black markers to color over offending elements in every foreign publication that enters Saudi Arabia. Domestic Arabic and English publications are subject to after-the-fact censorship, and therefore censor themselves. Most of the journalists, who are non-Saudi Arabs, Indians and

---

MY FINAL EXIT

I, too, was fired on government orders. My freelancing finally caught up with me. I started out selling articles under various nom de plumes: Finn Barre, for *The Financial Times*, Finbar James for *The Sunday Times*, James Rabnif for *The Christian Science Monitor,* and even Sylvester Cheeseworth, for *Middle East Agribusiness.* Later, I began using my real name. An article about the Bradley Armored vehicle sale, which ran in *Businessweek's* international edition, may have been the last straw. Prince Turki Al-Faisal's General Directorate of Intelligence ordered my publisher to fire me. *Arab News* delayed, but finally agreed. I was given ample time to prepare my things and depart with all my wages. The Saudis were very decent about it all. The Syrians and Iraqis, for instance, kill journalists they don't like.

Pakistanis, value their jobs more than they value controversy. When a transgression is made, the government sometimes fires the editor. This happened when *Al-Jazira* printed a derogatory poem by the then-Health Minister Al-Gosaibi. At other times, the government orders the paper to fire the offending person. The most popular cartoonist in the Kingdom, Khanafir of the *Al-Riyadh* and the *Riyadh Daily*, was forced to stop in 1989 because he drew a cartoon showing a Saudi contractor asking a Ministry for payment before the oil bust and afterwards. In the first, he is getting paid. In the second panel, the contractor is in chains. To a government stiffing its creditors, it was not funny.

The Polish-American managing editor of the Saudi Gazette was expelled from the Kingdom after an Indian co-worker coveting his job sent the Ministry of Interior a letter claiming the man's parents were Jewish WW II concentration camp survivors. Jews are not allowed in the Kingdom.

The press attacks Israel, Jews, the West and non-Muslims. Each issue of the *Arab News* contains a section of short items that seem designed to show the West is decadent and bizarre. Priests seducing children, husbands turning their wives into Doberman Pinscher smorgasbords, and disasters all make it into the paper.

The Saudi press comes into its own when it publishes "exposes." The *Saudi Gazette* published the virulent anti-Semitic tract, "The International Jew," by Henry Ford, claiming that the "important work" was removed from library shelves by Zionist "sneakthieves." To add extra kick to the various chapters, such as "The Jew and Jazz," the Gazette weighed in with excerpts from the old Czarist forgery, "The Protocols of Zion." The *Riyadh Daily* published the amazing Medieval fable of Jewish cabals kidnapping non-Jewish babies for sacrifices.

Of course, journalistic standards vary immensely inthe Third World than they do in the United States. Several Indian colleagues were renowned for demanding gifts or money for writing stories about hotels. An American did much the same thing. Gazette reporters were ordred to stop loafing. "I want three stories and three letters to the editor each week," their editor ordered.

Letters to the Editor were perhaps the most popular part of the Arab News, and a section the Gazette wanted to emulate. A handful of inveterate letter writers would declaim on anything from Western perfidy, to one Francis Andrew's constant call for re-imposition of the British Empire. Often the letters would be the most vigorous part of the paper because it gave most people their only chance to speak out on a myriad of issues. The most famous letter was written in jest. It began by congratulating Saudi TV on its educational programs, including Sesame Street and the medical shows. It then suggested that Dr. Linda Lovelace's show on Oral Exercise be broadcast. The writer signed off as Mrs. I. Suckett.

The next day, sales of the paper reached historic levels, and the management was running for cover. One of the many offended Saudis who called in exclaimed, "Everyone knows who Linda Lovelace is." (Linda Lovelace starred in a pornographic movie about oral sex entitled "Deep

Throat") The poor Pakistani in charge of editing letters to the editor did not. In the ensuing weeks, the paper was shelled with letters written by Harry Butt, Red N. Sore, and others.

One of the biggest obstacles to journalism in the Kingdom lays in the fact that any Saudi can complain to the Ministry and kill a story. The government is less concerned with the content of the English language press than with the Arabic press, because the average Saudi, if he can read, reads only Arabic. Consequently, many senior Saudis augment their morning doses of the BBC's news with a glance at the English dailies.

The Kingdom produces an absurdly high number of papers and magazines because of subsidies. Nine Arabic dailies, seven Arabic weeklies, and 3 English language dailies are published. A vast number of periodicals are also printed. Many papers have princely investors. A large chunk of the media giant, Saudi Research and Marketing, publisher of *Asharq Al-Awsat, Al-Majalla,* and *Arab News*, is owned by Prince Salman.

ELECTRONIC MEDIA

Saudi radio is so bad, it is not worth discussing, so we shall skip to television. Up until 1984, the Ministry of Information had only its Arabic Channel 1, which broadcast some English language programs for its expatriates. It broadcast the news in English as well as Arabic. Its seminal contribution to television awfulness was "The News In French." News presenters with bad French accents dished out endless reels of King Fahad meeting people.

Channel 2 was a humane contribution to expatriate life, providing entertainment for bored foreigners. It was an expensive proposition that provided little benefit for native Saudis, so despite its shortcomings, its creation has to be viewed as a generous act. Up until then, a few English language programs were carried on Saudi television. The only English speakers who were treated to decent television were those in the Eastern Province, who saw the superior output of Aramco's Channel 3, and Bahraini TV. Jeddah-dwelling Saudis and Arabs orient their antennae to Egypt and live off of that nation's steady output of films and soap operas. Saudi television's most popular imported show is professional wrestling, which is translated into Arabic. Every once in a while, Hindi movies are shown with Arabic subtitles.

Lower oil revenues forced the Ministry of Information to generate more income, so in 1986, the first television commercials were aired, and proved as big a draw on the stations as the shows themselves. Officials forbade advertisers to use religion, sex, ridicule or even direct comparisons to other products. Nonetheless, television revenues proved a boon, and newspapers saw advertising decline for several years. By 1989, both newspapers and television were doing well, as advertisers learned that print media exposure was still necessary to sell products.

Even more hours are spent using Video Cassette Recorders (VCRs). Japanese exporters say the Kingdom has more Video Cassette Recorders (VCRs) per capita than any other nation. Approved government Video sales shops do a brisk business in approved videos. These are edited to remove excessive skin, but are not as rigorously censored as the broadcasts. A film costs approximately $6 because all the films, even the latest releases, are pirate copies. The Kingdom recently signed a copyright protection agreement, but this has had little effect either on tapes, or the booming business in pirate computer programs and equipment.

Pirate pornographic tapes also flourish. When travelers arrive, their videos are all taken by airport personnel and screened for pornography. Yet somehow or other, blue movies of all descriptions flood in. These are watched separately by men and women. Perhaps the most unfortunate side-effect of the wide circulation of pornographic films in the Kingdom is that it gives Saudis distorted ideas of Western society in general and Western women in particular.

ENTERTAINMENT

The government has spent millions to provide recreation for families. Parks exist in almost all cities. These are rigidly segregated by sex. More spectacular are the Corniches. Jeddah's Corniche is a spectacular seaside drive, replete with modernistic sculptures that can be both fanciful and bizarre. A similar Corniche is being constructed in the Eastern Province. These driveways provide families a pleasant place to picnic in the evenings. Youths bring their instruments and play music together. Others watch television. Inland Saudis camp beside desert roads to share meals.

Riyadh has the biggest zoo. Another is operated in Taif. Many individuals own exotic animals, ranging from chimpanzees to tigers. Several National Parks have been built in the Asir mountains.

The National Guard sponsors the annual Heritage Festival and giant camel race near RIyadh. The General Presidency of Youth Welfare, run by King Fahad's oldest son, Faisal, also funds traditional dance troupes as well as soccer clubs. Faisal is building the Kingdom's first Opera House, though what it will eventually be used for is not clear. He justified it to conservatives as a performance venue for traditional dance.

The private sector weighs in with numerous amusement parks and a few beachfront resorts. All of these have separate sections or days for families and men.

EXPAT LIFESTYLE

The existence of English language papers is testimony to the size of the expatriate community. "Expatriate Society" differs, depending upon the foreigner's background. It is generally divided between the European or American "Khuwajjas" and the Third Country Nationals, called TCNs.

Khuwajjas are better-paid, and better-treated by the Saudis. Each nationality tends to stick to itself, but the Americans and Australians seem less clannish than the British and French. Among TCNs, the Indians, Pakistanis, Bangladeshis, and Sri Lankans group together. Filipinos, Koreans, Thais, and other Far East Asians are different. Among these Far East Asians, language barriers prevent much mixing on the blue collar level.

All these different nationalities need to communicate, and English is the Lingua Franca. This makes it difficult to learn Arabic in the Kingdom. Unless the student works in a hospital, most of those Saudis he or she meets during the day speak English. The general lack of contact with Saudis, plus the dearth of information, leads to dependence upon rumors. The government won't allow even such mundane reportage as murders or auto accidents. Riyadh Governor Prince Salman has an absurd fear of bad news in his city. Stories on fires, car wrecks, or building collapses were consistently spiked on his orders.

Rumors take on the cloak of reality in the absence of hard information. Supposedly knowledgeable people regurgitate bits and pieces of expatriate mythology. Even embassies cast for rumors in the swirling dust storms of the country. Is GOSI paying? Are the Saudis expelling all the Lebanese? Did you hear of the 12 Filipino nurses whose bodies were discovered in the abandoned Rush Housing Project? When power is so tightly concentrated, it is difficult for anyone, even a high government official, to know what will happen, or why something has taken place. These shifting rumors are just another reason why expatriates never feel truly secure in the Kingdom. This feeling is enhanced because expatriate society doesn't mix much with Saudis. Saudis seldom socialize with Third Worlders and Westerners always deal with the same upperclass Westernized Saudis. Embassy functions put out a little booze, and are attended by the same Saudis all the time, a phenomenon known as "Rent-A-Thobe."

Most expatriates are single males: married status is granted only to professional level workers. Nurses and airline hostesses are the only available women. Western nurses have more freedom than their Asian co-workers. All women, even doctors, who are accorded a slightly higher status, are forced to meet curfews and are forbidden from consorting with men. They are segregated in compounds and guarded, not only from going out, but from having people come in. They are viewed with a jaundiced eye, since no decent woman would leave her family to work among men.

Dating is a cloak and dagger affair. Since it is illegal for men and women who are either unmarried or closely related to be in the same car, it is risky to drive around. Police normally do not stop cars without cause. Yet chance accidents and spot checks occur. During routine police roadblocks, a white skin is helpful. Often, a European wearing a tie is not ever stopped. Conversely, American blacks or orientals suffer until they prove they are not TCNs.

The longer an expatriate lives in the Kingdom, the more likely he or she will suffer personality regression. Their lives are externally controlled. They are generally well-taken care of, and have few responsibilities. Since they cannot build any future for themselves in the Kingdom, many become short-term-oriented. A surprising number of expatriates leave the kingdom with very little saved. They spend years in the kingdom complaining about the Saudis, yet every year, they renew their contracts. It is a "Honey Trap," similar to pitcher plants. Flies are lured into the plant by sweet nectar, cannot escape, and are eventually digested.

For the Muslim TCNs, working in the Kingdom is fulfillment of a dream. They not only earn high incomes, but are near the two holy cities. They try to perform the Hajj the first year, and then invite their relatives to come and make the Hajj themselves. During the weekends, many foreigners living in Jeddah go to Mecca, but with the tremendous construction now taking place, the city has lost a great deal of its former charm.

The Kingdom's guest workers are unlikely to pose a serious threat to the government. First of all, the populace distrusts them. Second, the different groups of expatriates generally dislike each other. The Saudi talent for compartmentalization works as well in labor recruitment as it does in other aspects of government.

TRADITIONAL LIFE

Fifty years ago, the day started early. The break of dawn was greeted in every village and town by the thin melodic cry of the Muezzin, who called the faithful to prayer.

"Eshadu'an, Allahu Akbar. Allah Akbar..."

"Listen, God is Great, God is great..." he called, urging the faithful to come to the Mosque for prayer. Prayer five times each day is only one aspect of religion's influence in Saudi behavior. Islamic fatalism and belief in a hereafter allows acceptance of harsh conditions: both evil and good come from God, and must be accepted as his will.

Until the coming of the Wahhabi religious police, attendance at prayer, particularly at morning prayers, was not always high. But the day began with prayer call nonetheless. The people stirred. Wives started fires. Children yawned and stretched, and merchants set out to open up shops.

Caravan traders sleepily put out their fires, reloaded their camels, and prepared to resume their drifting across the desert.

Farmers trudged out to work their fields and raise precious water from wells, while the bedouin set out to watch their herds of camels, and flocks of sheep and goats.

In towns, people normally dealt with the "Old Man of the Neighborhood," who still functions like a communist block chairman, by providing recommendations as to the moral qualities of the people in his neighborhood. This is necessary for certain travel permits and government jobs.

People personally presented petitions to the town "amirs," who was backed by a slave-dominated palace guards. Abdulaziz provided some order by implementing Sharia law, and stamping out brigandage.

Children, mostly boys, learned a few verses of the Koran from the local Imam. Some dreamed of the day they could leave with a Caravan to travel, perhaps as far as fabled Cairo or Damascus, and make their fortune. Many Saudis migrated abroad to find work.

Girls married young, bore many children and worked hard. Women often played a more important social role than Westerners realize. Saudi rural and urban women maintained social links even when their menfolk broke into their interminable quarreling. When tribes went to war, a virgin on a camel would accompany the men. Some would bare their torsos to spur the men on to victory.

People took siestas after afternoon prayers to escape the brutal heat. In winter, men wore fleece-lined cloaks, and women bundled up. After the siesta, work resumed until evening prayers and dinner.

Life revolved around the family, both in the narrow sense of the extended family, and in the larger one of the tribe. A Saudi's existence was hard. Infant mortality, even as late as the Eighties, was appallingly high. Medicine consisted of Koranic verses, herbs, camel urine, and heated branding irons. Cauterizing with hot branding irons still occurs in the countryside, where it is believed to cure anything from bad backs to headaches.

Traditional medicine still exists side-by-side with ultra-modern hospitals and maintains its appeal to magic. A 13-year-old girl's parents begged Riyadh Zoo director Dr. Lawrence Curtis to let her see the wolf. The pleasant, veiled young girl conversed with her family in normal Arabic. The sight of the caged wolves sent her into convulsions. She howled, and jabbered in a masculine, deep-throated voice, demanding (in Arabic) escape. Her brothers restrained her with great difficulty. After a violent wrenching, she collapsed, and then spoke in a normal voice. Her overjoyed father begged to purchase the wolf to keep it near her, explaining the demons feared wolves. Zoo officials demurred. "Still," Curtis said, "It was the damnedest thing I ever did see."

Barring intrusions of the supernatural, and the vagaries of nature, the Saudi world was predictable, particularly after the coming of Abdulaziz. He put a stop to rampant banditry and murders. Wars stopped. Camel raiding, a favorite bedouin past time, was halted.

The crackdown on crime by implementation of Islamic Sharia law, was universally welcomed. When a crime did occur, the members of the Murrah Tribe of the Rhub Al-Khali, served as government trackers. These men can distinguish not only between male and female footprints, but of pregnant and non-pregnant females. One famous tracker, Rashoud Murshid Al-Sifri said, "It sounds a bit of hyperbole, but believe me, I can even differentiate the footprints of relatives and determine their degree of kinship."

Every Saudi, rich and poor, savored coffee. Hosts served guests coffee roasted over a fire, ground in a mortar, and cooked in a coffeepot, called the "Dallah." Those who could afford it would flavor the coffee with Cardamom; the more cardamom used, the more prestige for the host.Even today, coffee is the emblem of hospitality. It, and tea, are the beverages of choice for the Saudis. Businessmen drink countless glasses of sugary mint-flavored tea as they wait in offices.

Wealthy men still greet visitors with incense. The most valuable type is Oudh, which costs up to SR40,000 ($12,500) per kilo (approximately $6,000 per pound). When the King attends a function, attendants carry the distinctive Saudi incense burner to him, where he scoops the scent into his face, and onto his clothes. His guests do likewise.

The guest would be fed, if possible, with a freshly-slaughtered sheep or camel. Like other Arabs, a Saudi host was expected to have more than enough food for his guests. Leftovers were given to the servants and the poor people of the district. Muslim cities seldom had separate slums for the poor, a fact that enabled the impoverished to share in the joy and liberality of feast days. Before or after dinner, the guests might splash themselves with perfume; the preferred scent being the essence of rose petals taken from Taif or Damascus.

Talk took place before and during dinner. For lucky groups, a poet would stand and declaim his verses. On the more cosmopolitan coasts, a man might sing, possibly to the accompaniment of the Arabic Lute, and drums. Once the eating was done, the guests left quickly. Then, after the last evening prayers, men might sit around the campfire and talk, but most would soon turn in for the night. The next day everyone would arise to the sound of the call to prayer and the cycle would begin again.

The Saudis' holidays were all based on Islam. In the older days, the Prophet Mohammed's birthday was celebrated as it is in other countries, but this was stopped because it smacks, say the religious conservatives, of worshipping Mohammed, Thus the two big holidays remaining are Eid Al-Adha, the week of the Hajj, and Eid Al-Fitr, the last week of the month of Fasting, Ramadan. Eid Al-Adha is a week of celebrations and sacrifice of a sheep. Eid Al-Fitr is similar to Christmas, in that gifts are exchanged, and many dinners are held. Those who can afford it buy new clothes and distribute alms.

Other sources of festivities were weddings and circumcision. Drum beaters would precede the groom as he headed to the wife's house, depending, of course, upon the status and wealth of the bride and bridegroom. If at all possible, a wedding feast would be held. It was usually sexually segregated. That night, the groom would learn whether his wife was a virgin or not. If she weren't she would face humiliation at the least, and probable death at the hands of her brothers.

The ostentation of a circumcision celebration depended upon the finances of the family in question. The boy was expected to endure the cutting with Arab stoicism. This reflected well upon him and his family. Other smaller events marked life, but for the most part, life was monotonous work, in a yearly cycle unaltered since the distant past.

CONCLUSION

Oil altered this by introducing the tools of the Twentieth Century. Each had a corrosive effect. Cars and trucks carried sons to distant villages. Radios brought in news and music not only from distant Arab countries, but from non-Muslim lands as well. Radio, and later, Television, actually made families turn further inward, by making the old sources of news and entertainment, the coffeehouses, redundant.

Electricity and airconditioning modified the hours people kept, generally to the detriment of prayer call. Those who stayed up late under incandescent bulbs were disinclined to arise at daybreak to attend prayers. Better medical care, publications, education, and greater contact with foreigners all had their toll on Saudi society.

Now, the oil downturn is encouraging a re-examination of the value of all that has been achieved. The Saudis have not reached conclusions yet, but the verdict is likely to veer toward slower development, more disenchantment with the Royal monopoly on power, and greater conservatism.

7

WOMEN

"Before five years ago, a woman would go out to work out of leisure. Today a woman goes out to work out of economic necessity...Unemployment among women is high." - A Saudi feminist speaking confidentially.

It took the threat of Iraq to force King Fahad to call for more female participation in the Saudi economy. He ordered ministries "to accept those women volunteers who present themselves to carry on duties in the areas of human services and medical services within the context of fully preserving Islamic and social values."[1]

He said nothing new, really. Officials have often said women can work, provided they do so in an Islamic context. Yet, the fact that the King himself said it, is significant. Saudi Arabia spends billions on female education, and more billions on foreign workers, yet it won't let its women replace the expatriates. The petrodollar crunch increased economic pressure for greater female participation, but increased the relative strength of the religious conservatives who desire greater restrictions on women. The Kuwait invasion may have tilted the balance between a need for manpower and a need to placate traditionalists.

WOMEN AT WORK

The oil crunch has strengthened arguments for increased employment of Saudi women. They account for only 4 percent of the entire workforce even though many have good educations and can replace hundreds of thousands of foreign office workers and bureaucrats. Most women work as teachers, and have filled the available jobs in the cities. Aspiring teachers must commute to outlying villages. The problem is: they are banned from driving. "You have to pay room and salary (for a driver) and if you cannot afford that, you still must hire a limousine...more than half your salary goes to a driver," complained a professional Saudi woman.

The private sector is not much better for would-be women workers, mainly because the religious authorities say women can be employed only if they are completely segregated from men. This has discouraged most businesses from hiring women. Those that do, often establish women-only operations. This is ironic, for those Western feminists who argue for women-only businesses have reached a conclusion shared by the Kingdom's religious conservatives.

Aramco hired women as secretaries and geologists, but has been forced by religious pressure to scale back the hiring of Saudi women. Saudi Cable Company (SCC) is planning a women-only electronics plant. The idea is not as far-fetched as it sounds. Many Asian electronics plants depend upon nimble female fingers for assembly.

Many banks established women's branches during the closing days of the oil boom. The branches were expected to attract business-owning women. This has not worked, says a female banker, because lady customers think women employees would gossip about their deposits. Female banking scored better with employees than customers. When Al-Rajhi Company for Currency Exchange and Commerce opened women-only branches in Jeddah, regional manager Suleiman Al-Owayel expressed doubts. "When we opened the ladies branch, I thought we could never find enough Saudi girls to work. Even a year later, we were still getting job applications." Arab National Bank (ANB) deputy general manager Mohammed Abdulkader says bank work is popular with Saudi women. "It is a movement among Saudi women college graduates to work in banking because they see it as very prestigious."

ANB had to meet strict standards when it hired 45 women. "They are brought to work by husbands (some of whom work at the bank) or by brothers," said Abdulkader. "They are completely isolated according to all Islamic customs. Even the messenger is an older, religious person. He takes documents and delivers them to and from the women to the men. A phone is used when we need to talk. "They come to office 15 minutes later than the men, and leave 15 minutes later, so they can't mix during opening or closing. They even have a special elevator."

Women-only shopping centers have opened in Riyadh and Jeddah, providing employment for Saudi and expatriate women. Though the opening of the shopping centers was lauded by religious authorities, it appears the last thing female shoppers want is to see more women. In an article entitled "Women's Souks no Big Draw," one shopkeeper said, "Unfortunately, women think they need their husbands' opinions when buying things. Therefore they go to souks where their husbands can also go."[2]

Women are increasingly seeking employment. Cecile Rouchdy, general manager of the first Saudi girls' school, Dar Al-Hanaan in Jeddah, wrote in 1989 that many Saudi women need jobs because they got married early, divorced early, and cannot support themselves. Her school is offering practical skills courses to women.

"We think they are part of the society and that we should hire Saudis and work with Saudi women because, number one, they are capable, and secondly, they have no place else to go. We have all the university graduates who come out of the universities -- thousands of them every year. They used to go into teaching, in which the government is now almost self-sufficient," said Abdulkader. "So many of them are supporting their families. Many support their old father or mother. So this family actually depends upon this girl. Therefore we feel it is our duty to hire Saudi women to work."

A vast majority of employers say Saudi women are much more conscientious workers than their countrymen. Rouchdy, however, chided her graduates. "Most of the women working today, with the exception of a very small minority, don't take their jobs seriously. They consider it a hobby or just a way to fill their free time. Check her attendance sheet at the end of the year. 50 percent of the time, she is absent." [3]

The big impediment to female employment is the ban on women driving. "Women not driving causes a social problem. Having more than 50,000 foreign drivers in the Kingdom causes economic and family problems. The bedouin woman simply picks up her Toyota truck and drives in the country," a townswoman said with a touch of envy. "The government is introducing driving women in the village today."

The gradual introduction of driving women in the rural parts of the Kingdom is one method of effecting change using one of the more conservative elements of society. A bedouin, who cannot be accused of "Westernism," is not likely to complain about his wife driving, since her driving helps him do his work. Nobody sees the woman driving unless she makes an infrequent trip into a small town. This is a gradual approach to breaking down male resistance. Traditionalists say a woman has to remove her veil to drive, and will be prey to male drivers. One senior minister confidentially said, "We are worried that young men will deliberately cause accidents with women so they can meet them." When the Saudi-Bahrain Causeway allowed Saudis to drive into Bahrain, some deliberately ran into women drivers and bore out his prediction.

The *Arab News* is subtly encouraging this by printing photographs of female American soldiers driving trucks, and working alongside other soldiers. "As for women driving, some people talk about it," a woman with a doctoral degree told author Marianne Alireza. "Accident factor aside, it would be worse, because men unaccustomed to seeing women drive would follow and bother. It would be great sport!"[4]

Despite the ban on driving, Saudi women have made gains on working. "This is a matter of necessity," one Saudi feminist said. "If women have government support, then there is no problem in entering the workforce. Until now the University of Medicine is still open (where women train as doctors). Some serve as social workers in hospitals, so we can see that a man and a woman can work together in the field of medicine."

The erstwhile liberal Prince Nawwaf bin Abdulaziz, fought back in an editorial. "Therefore the university graduate girl who works outside her home and family and takes more interest in her work than her home is unworthy..."[5] His view is shared by many who think women should stick to their traditional role in society, yet better education and more severe demands on manpower make this attitude harder to defend.

EDUCATION

A little education is a dangerous thing for fundamentalist Wahhabis, especially when the recipients are women. The opening of the first girls' school in Riyadh was an occasion for riots. Religious sensitivity explains why girls as well as boys get so much religious instruction in school. They are taught the Koran, religious tradition, and methods of performing various rites. They are not permitted, by the way, to read the Koran while they are menstruating. By the time the girls leave High School, most are close to memorizing the Koran. Only university students get anything approximating comparative religion.

Girls attend school for the same number of years as the boys, and consistently outperform them on tests. Part of this is because boys can cruise the streets, while the girls are stuck at home with little else to do but study. Saudi educators churn out explanations why the mentally "superior" boys do not perform as well as their sisters.

Women in university are taught by expatriate women. Those few classes requiring a male teacher are taught using video cameras. Except for the medical schools, the female universities are in separate compounds surrounded by walls. The facilities are shabbier than the men's. When King Saud University moved to its $3.5 billion new campus, the women occupied the old campus and retained their old Olaysha campus -- an abandoned palace compound. The oil crunch hit female university students harder than their male colleagues. In 1988, the KSU Woman's University closed its women's book store. Teachers were reduced to photocopying textbooks, and had to pay for their own copy paper. The Ministry of Higher Education said it had no money to maintain the book subsidy.

The girls do not complain about their facilities, said one former teacher. "They don't perceive any advantage to being with the men, and are not aware of the fact that they have lesser facilities. They don't care about the discrepancy; the walled campus on Olaysha is large. It is like a garden, with many walkways under lots of trees. Most of the girls are so happy to come to place where they can walk, like in a park. Most just want to be with their friends, out of the house, strolling around, talking, laughing, and lying on the grass. It gives them something to do. They get a smaller (government-supplied university) allowance than the men, but it is still a nice part time job."

A lot of girls go to college just because they can't stand staying at home," one girl told said. "Many drop out of college just because they don't feel like it any more." Dropouts are not surprising, said one woman. "The goal of the Presidency of Girls Education is to produce a religious housewife," says one educated Saudi woman. "If you do that 12 years, do you expect she will come out with lots of ambition?"

The most pernicious effect of female education, according to religious scholars, has been to give them the idea that there is more to life than being a wife. They are concerned because a growing number of Saudi girls are post-poning marriage to earn higher degrees in universities.

MARRIAGE

Dr. Ahmad Jamal, a Saudi professor of Islamic Culture, wrote a book, "Our Girls and the Right Path," in which he condemns Saudi women who turn down marriage to pursue studies, saying, "For any female, marriage represents her first need and her fundamental obligation."[6] Many Saudi men are intimidated by educated women, and refuse to marry them, said female journalist Ebtisam Al-Manae, who holds a master's decree in education of the handicapped, "I have great respect for Saudi youth, but a point against them is their unwillingness to take educated Saudi girls as their wives."[7]

Arranged marriages were the rule in the old days, and are still preferred. Since most marriages were between first cousins, the two might have met as children, but not since puberty. Girls could refuse their husband, but few had the nerve to do so. Modern couples try to meet ahead of time, at least to talk. It is no longer adequate to simply glimpse a future groom in the flesh, or through a photograph. Even this limited contact is anathema to religious conservatives and families who would be dishonored if others knew their daughter met an unmarried man.

"It is not easy for Saudi girls," says one married Saudi woman. "Courtship is not accepted in our society, yet they see courtship on Egyptian TV which talks about love. The School says that love is forbidden; you should see your future husband only once and then marry. But, she wonders what to think. She goes to her girlfriend's house and hears her talk to a "boyfriend" on the telephone. Or she hears a popular Saudi performer singing a song written by Pr. Khaled Al-Faisal about love."

Some girls stay home home, drink tea, and watch videos -- the last ditch defense against boredom. A surprising amount of the videos are hard core pornography, a staple of male viewing as well. Often, the girls put on music, talk, or dance together.

Determined girls meet boys, but not in the fashion of the movie, "Death of A Princess." Princesses don't cruise to the desert to choose males. Exceptionally aggressive females, on rare occasions, approach men in fancy stores and pass their numbers on. Stores and malls are the only areas where a woman might meet a man. Cassette tape music shops were such common meeting places that the religious police banned men and women from shopping in those stores at the same time. They learned that teenagers would leave their phone numbers hidden in cassette cases.

For the shy, there is the telephone. Unconsummated phone love affairs are common. Both men and boys, women and girls, heterosexuals, and homosexuals, call randomly on the telephones, hoping for a friendly voice on the other end. Saudi males try for Western women, but many expatriate men have been disturbed by female obscene phone calls as well.

School officials seek to guard girls while they are out of their family's care. Female students are not allowed on the school bus (driven by a venerable old man) unless they are totally covered. Saudi teenage boys race beside the schoolbuses in their cars, flashing their phone numbers printed on large cards. Some girls write the numbers down, but have to do so discreetly. Each bus has at least one paid spy to tell officials if her sisters are "misbehaving."

Bolder girls skip classes at school, usually to shop, but occasionally for trysts. For a while, girls would tell their parents they weren't finishing school until 2 p.m., but would leave earlier. The school started requiring girls to carry cards saying when they were supposed to be finished.

Some women let the veil work in their favor. A brother lets her off at gate. She passes the watchman, who notes her. After she enters, she pulls a new set of her shoes out of her purse, changes them in the building, and half an hour later, walks out past the guard. All he knows is that a formless black-clad woman with green shoes walked in, and a formless black-clad woman wearing red shoes walked out.

Some women engage in affairs. One *Saudi Business* co-worker loaned his apartment to a Saudi friend for a tryst. The episode was over quickly because of a Saudi male's approach to sex. A woman, a former masseuse for a princess, said Saudi women climax quickly, because they are not so much oriented toward the act of intercourse itself, as the general idea of "romance" or pursuit. She added that, for the man, sexual enjoyment is purely a male affair. His objective, she says, is to have as many orgasms as possible; he is not concerned with the woman's enjoyment. "You should have seen this poor 13-year-old wife we saw," a nurse from the Riyadh Security Forces Hospital said. "She delivered a child, and we sewed her up, telling her husband no sex until she healed."

"The next day she came in, bleeding. All the stitches were ripped out, because he couldn't wait. We sewed her up again, and told the husband, 'No sex until she gets better.' She came in the next day, ripped up again, and we decided, 'Right, we'll fix that bastard.' So we sewed her up with stainless steel wire, and told the husband he had to stop this."

"The next day, he came in, all ripped up," the Australian said, smiling. "Served him right."

The girl consented because Islam forbids a woman to refuse sex to her husband. The Saudi Gazette's Islamic columnist, wrote that since a woman is a man's tilth, or field, and farmers "work " their fields, oral stimulation in sex is permissible. The Prophet, he added, said Allah will not look at those who practice anal sex, a prohibition that goes against common practice. The columnist got into severe trouble for his frank discussion.

Any discussion of Saudi sexual practice has to be made with the understanding that the most appalling untruths can be uttered without fear of contradiction, because nobody need fear contradiction by a Saudi version of the Hite Report.

Sex (for women) is restricted to a husband, who is often selected in an arranged marriage. Westerners shudder at the practice, but it has its defenders. One Pakistani hotelier said, "I suppose my wife and I never got to go through that phase of being totally head over heels in love. But if your parents do a good job in arranging a marriage, it gives your marriage a chance for success. They check to make sure both are from similar families, that your interests are similar, and that your educational backgrounds are close. The parents check to make sure the other partner has got a good reputation, is hard-working, and has a good temperament. These are the boring details that can wreck a marriage which many people in love overlook. I also think that over time, we have grown to love each other, as well."

MARRIAGE AND DOWRY

Unlike the Hindus, who require the bride to come up with the cash, the Arabs demand the groom pay a dowry to the bride. The dowry is a sort of divorce insurance for the wife because she keeps it in the event her husband divorces her. She uses the dowry to buy gold for herself, and furnishings for the couple's new home. Oil wealth caused dowry inflation. The higher the dowry, the more prestige one's daughter received. Soon, upper middleclass girls claimed dowries of

SR100,000. Meanwhile, lavish weddings and rented hotel ballrooms drove up the cost of nuptials. Entrepreneurs responded in the post-boom period by building "Festival Palaces" which cost less than hotels, but high prices still discouraged young men from marrying.

They avoided the financial squeeze by marrying foreigners. Their favorite hunting grounds were Egypt and Syria, whose women are Muslim, Arab, beautiful, and inexpensive. India provides the least expensive brides. Most of the few relatively few Western brides married Saudis studying abroad. Foreign marriages increased during the oil downturn to the point that they were banned. The Ministry of Interior approves foreign wives only if the Applicant is very old, and wants a woman to look after him. Violators are punished. A shepherd and his smuggled Yemeni bride were each fined SR1,000 and sentenced to six months in prison.[8]

The government is trying to drive down the cost of marriage. Sheikhs from many tribes encourage marriage without dowries and the press praises prominent men who give their daughters for token amounts. The government-owned Saudi Credit Bank (SCB) began loaning money for dowries, and by 1989, provided over SR1.01 Billion for 96,740 marriages.[9]

MARRIAGE AND POLYGAMY

High dowries have depressed the already declining practice of polygamy. Still, polygamy has many defenders and adherents. Mohammed, who had from 9 to 14 wives, said God limited all other Muslims to a maximum of 4 wives. The husband, he said, must treat them all equally, especially in the matter of sex.

Though this, most Saudis admit, is hard to do, the big question is whether the man can afford the dowry. The next is whether his present wife will object. "Today, the younger generation appreciates its privacy. We (young wives) remember the women and children fighting," said a young Saudi wife. The children of the different wives would form separate blocks in the family. These would often feud. "We don't want that any more. What woman really wants to share her husband with others?"

Dr. Faisal Zahir, professor of anatomy at King Abdulaziz University, argues that it would be "absolute egotism" for women to deny men polygamy. "Women raise the slogan of one wife simply because they are influenced by alien currents," writes Ismat Hamid on "How women react to Husband's Second Marriage" "Women contradict themselves by closing their eyes to what the husband does outside marital life as long as he doesn't bring another woman to the house. By so doing, they ignore the Koranic verse, "Then marry such as please you, of (other) women by twos and threes and fours." It is a biological fact that a man cannot settle for one wife because this would not fully satisfy his desires."[10]

Interestingly, a poll of King Abdulaziz University women revealed that 36 percent of the women would accept their husband taking a second wife, while only 32 percent said they would not.[11] This is lucky for the surplus Saudi women created by foreign marriages. Jeddah mothers founded a society that visits married Saudi women to request them to allow their husbands to marry another woman. This practice generated comment and complaints in the local press. The visits were generally unwelcome by wives, who call a husband's second marriage "Marrying Against them."

"This was really just part of the oil boom," one Saudi woman said. "People of my father's generation married more than one woman because he could afford it. People in our generation are already back to one wife."

MARRIAGE AND DIVORCE

A wife has few options if her husband marries another woman. More women are divorcing their husbands, but it is difficult and still fairly rare. A husband, however, only has to say: "I divorce thee" three times in front of a witness.

Columnist Maudha Al-Zahrani, in *Al-Riyadh*, writes about rich husbands who throw their first wives and children out under the influence of a new, young wife. "In case the women is divorced and demands monthly entitlements to provide for the needs of the children, the husband threatens to withdraw the children from her care," she complained.[11]

In earlier days, a divorce diminished a woman's dowry value, but was not a terrible social stain. A study of the Al Murrah bedouin showed that 45 percent of the old men of the Al Kurbi lineage had divorced at least once. Thirty-three percent of the old men had divorced three times. This implies that women re-married after divorce.[12]

Today, a divorced woman finds life tougher. Many divorcees depend upon a privately-funded philanthropic system of hospices called "ribat." To enter, the woman presents a certificate from the Umdah (old man of the Neighborhood). She gets extra money for the month of fasting, Ramadan. Many get free health care, electricity, and water. Some get food as well. Some of the Ribat admit non-Saudi Muslim women, too.

MOTHERHOOD

Although the role of women as peacemakers, communicators and homemakers is important, their ultimate purpose is to produce offspring, especially men. Male children were important because they would grow up to be warriors. A woman whose oldest boy is named Walid, will be called "Um Walid," "Mother of Walid," and the father is known as "Abu Walid" or "Father of Walid." Nobody is called the Mother or Father of a girl.

Muslim scholars say birth control on a personal basis is permitted, but that government population control programs are forbidden; God created women to have babies. Thus, infertility is a justifiable cause for divorce. Childlessness is almost shameful, and the the husband usually blames it on the wife. As soon as in-vitro fertilization made the news, the Saudis introduced the medical technology.

This drive to bear children, when coupled with first cousin marriages and Islamic fatalism, has tragic results. Some couples have child after child with horrible genetic deformities. The defects are never attributed to in-breeding (which is defended in the newspapers) but to the will of God. It does not help that at least one American geneticist prostituted himself by telling a Saudi medical seminar that first cousin marriages cause no birth defects.

Since breeding is important, a woman cannot use birth control without her husband's assent. Officials grew concerned that too many Saudi women were getting tubal ligations, and said hospitals are not permitted to perform tubal ligations unless they are approved on the grounds of medical necessity by a board of three doctors containing at least one Muslim.

Although the woman bears the child, she has no child custody rights in the event of divorce. She is allowed to raise them while they are very young. After that, they go to the father, a situation that tends to keep many Western women trapped in bad marriages in the Kingdom. If a Saudi husband kidnaps his child in the United States and brings it to the Kingdom, the woman will never regain custody. Conversely, some women try to spirit their children out of the Kingdom. The results are often tragic. At a dinner party, a female guest complained about the tyrannical control exercised by Saudi husbands over their Western wives.

The British hostess of the dinner, who had been fixing home-brewed drinks while most of the conversation took place, ventured, "Well, I say they are silly bitches for marrying them in the first place. All they do is marry them for their money."

Her husband nervously cleared his throat and said, "Dear, may I introduce you to Mrs. Ahmed Al-Shubaili?"

"I say, I guess I should go prepare the salad," she replied.

GENERAL RESTRICTIONS

Western wives are often overwhelmed when they first confront Saudi restrictions on their dress and behavior. These rules are embodied in the veil, a Turkish invention adopted by the Arabs. The Saudi veil is not the gauzy covering of Hollywood; it is part of the armor that shields a woman from male eyes. The face taboo is so culturally-ingrained that some woman patients will undress their bodies, yet refuse to uncover their faces. Many Westernized Saudi women resent the veil, but find it lends a comfortable anonymity similar to that of dark sunglasses. A Saudi woman may start out with skin-tight designer jeans or dress, but she adds a black outergarment made of sheer nylon or silk called the Ubbayya. She then covers her entire head with the veil, a sheer black cloth that allows her to see out, without strangers seeing in. If she is fastidious, she'll wear a medieval-looking black mask under the veil and don black gloves. The result is bottle-shaped black ghost. Interestingly, the veil is not mandated by Islam. The Prophet Mohammed only said women should cover their hair,

Girls adopt the veil when they reach puberty and are eligible for marriage. An Islamic advice column once told readers that a man could force his 9-year-old daughter to marry a 20-year-old man, but advised against it. He added that the husband should wait until the girl reaches puberty before consummating the marriage. But, it is permissible. After all, the Prophet married a girl so young, she carried her toys to his home. Child brides may be rare now, but pre-teen girls are still separated from all men except their father and brothers. Their frilly overdone party dresses are covered with black when they venture in public.

The veil is reflected in house design; the room where male guests are received is completely segregated from the rest of the home. This is done because women embody the honor of the family. Some husbands are so touchy about men viewing their women, that they refuse to present embassies with passport photos of their wives. The author of a *Saudi Gazette* article, "Photo Shop Menace," recounted the rage he felt when he spotted his wife's photograph. leafed through a friend's photo album of women. He forced the friend to reveal that the photos were purchased from Filipino employees of a film developing shop. "What kind of social degenerates do this sort of thing?" the author complained. "Some might keep the photos in their wardrobes, or underneath their pillows." It's no wonder that Polaroid's instant photographs are so popular in the Kingdom; only the photographer and his family ever see the prints.

This fear of having other men glance, even via photographs, at one's women, stems from a Saudi male's conviction that other men will bother them. Western and Asian women in the souk shopping areas are sometimes harassed, usually by stares and suggestive noises, but at times by groping hands or exposed genitals. Saudi men argue that these restrictions shield the woman, who is unable to resist her "animal" desires. This sexual apartheid "protects" women and grants them equal rights. The Koran forbids men from depriving women of their "rights," such as owning and operating businesses. It also says women get half shares of an inheritance compared their brothers, and that their testimony is worth only half of a man's. It orders men to cherish and protect them. Yet, while women are supposed to be more prone to sexual misconduct than men, it is they who must cover themselves up. They wear black, while men wear long, tight-fitting, thin, dress-like garments called Thobes.

The regular police and Mutawwas enforce sexual apartheid. The Mutawas swat immodestly-dressed women with canes. Zealots occasionally post notices in restaurants and shopping centers urging women to dress decently and behave in a "bashful" manner. Proper dress in Riyadh is stricter than it is in the more cosmopolitan Jeddah; women in Riyadh cannot even show an elbow. When the sports director at the Riyadh Intercontinental Hotel allowed mixed doubles matches at a tournament, he was jailed for two weeks. Pools, including the pool in Riyadh's Diplomatic Quarter, are segregated completely. A husband cannot swim with his wife. The Riyadh Zoo's family days were cancelled because the Religious Police assumed assignations were taking place amidst the animal cages. "We had already segregated the reptile house," mused Zoo Director, Dr. Curtis. "I guess that wasn't enough."

The Mutawas delight in harassing foreign women. This is partly cultural, since any single female bold enough to travel unaccompanied by her brothers is a harlot. Unaccompanied Saudia Airline hostesses, for instance, are forbidden to wear makeup in public, and must ride in veiled buses. Women must get a male's permission to travel, even if from city to city in the Kingdom. If she checks into a hotel, her name is registered with the local police station. Most hotels simply refuse female guests. For a while, Limousines were forbidden from carrying unaccompanied women, but the authorities relented after the hospitals complained that their nurses had no other transportation.

Mutawas diligently root out unmarried couples. In 1989, religious enforcers took advantage of the absence of Riyadh Governor Prince Salman, to increase raids on restaurants for unmarried couples in the segregated family sections. They set up a roadblock outside of King Faisal Specialist Hospital to catch nurses being dropped off by boyfriends. Fourteen nurses were forced to submit to pelvic examinations in the filthy environs of the decrepit downtown Shemaisy hospital. Some Western nurses revert to adolescent behavior under these restrictions. After all, working in the Kingdom is a bit like being in high school; their housing and food are provided; they must meet curfews; and are forbidden to drink alcohol.

Lest anyone think there is diplomatic immunity from the laws of God, the Mutawa also hound diplomats. An American diplomat who touched his fiance in public was arrested by them. The wife of the Tunisian ambassador was accosted while she shopped in Riyadh's popular Al-Akariyyah shopping mall.

"Are you a Muslim?" he demanded.

"Yes," she replied frostily and kept walking. She was several months pregnant.

"Why is your hair uncovered?" he demanded, taking hold of her arm. She replied that she was the wife of a diplomat, that it was none of his business, and shook his hand off her arm. He shoved her, she fell, and miscarried. The offending Mutawa was banned to a distant corner of the Kingdom.

Saudi women had expected less control when Fahad ascended the throne, but he has beaten a slow retreat on the matter of women's rights. "During the past 6 years, things have gotten worse," said a Saudi woman working in a hospital. "It is harder for women to travel abroad. Even most princesses have to apply in advance for permission from their husbands, fathers, or brothers. One Princess told me, 'They are harder on us than they are on you. I am watched all the time.'"

Whenever Western journalists, particularly female ones, visit the Kingdom, they feel obliged to write a "behind the veil" story on Saudi women. Most "Women in the Kingdom" articles paint a picture of Saudi women chafing under the restrictions, as if they were a herd of black-shrouded feminists desperate for American-style liberation. The visiting journalists always talk to the same batch of Westernized women, and unsurprisingly arrive at the same conclusions each time. This is wrong. Most Saudi women aren't feminists. For a long time, many did not know an alternative existed to their present system, and most still believe the present system is God-ordained. Nowadays, more are reading the Koran, and raising questions about male interpretations that restrict them. Nonetheless, most share their menfolk's conservative opinions on the separation of sexes. Women in rural areas are too busy working on the farm or herding their animals to think much about "liberation." Even students spend little time grousing about male oppression. "I don't recall them ever complaining about it," said one American educator at King Saud University's women's college.

Most Saudi women work in their homes by caring for large families. Domestic servants provide many middle class wives with leisure that is spent in endless tea parties and gossip. Few women are interested in sports, and would have difficulty finding facilities if they were. This sedentary life leads to obesity in women who are naturally graceful when young. Luckily for them, many Arab men prefer plump women.

Well-to-do women frequently throw parties where they try to outdo each other in clothes and jewelry. Upperclass women wear the latest Paris fashions, and are draped in gold. Few deign to wear platinum or white gold, simply because those metals would be mistaken for silver. The dresses tend to be boldly colored. At times, they are what a Westerner would consider tacky; the colors are too bright, the skirts too tight, and the overall design overdone. Prince Naif's wife, for example, has been seen wearing a dress with her husband's face sewn in glittering sequins on the front. This woman is renowned for espousing reformist ideas. It's always a matter of trying to show how rich you are," said an Arab American. "Often it is not so so much taste, but how many precious stones and how much gold you can wear." Women often dance together at these gatherings, or comb each others' hair.

An Egyptian-American student recounted her days at the Women's college of Riyadh's King Saud University. "You see, we are not allowed to smoke, so the girls all go on the roofs to light up. Eventually, they hired some Filipino women to sit on the roofs to try and catch those of us who smoked, but we still knew where to go. Once, a friend and I went up to the roof so she could smoke, when I stopped. There were two of our friends in a clinch." She added that lesbianism is a phase that usually ends at marriage.

CONCLUSION

Poor and lower middle class traditional women are often slaving away simply to take care of a husband and manage a large brood of children. Some women put their hopes in the crowning of Crown Prince Abdullah, whose bedouin background is said to make him more aware of the economic importance of working women.

"If under Abdullah, the Kingdom would improve the situation of the women, it would not be because of his personal opinion," said a feminist. "It would be because of the pressure and necessity of the women. None of the Royal Family has views as conservative on women as the Ulema, but they don't want to face them over it," she continued. "But change will come because of economic necessity."

"I would never have stayed in the United States," said a Saudi woman educated in California. "We are a family people, and most of us women decided that we would accept these things and make the sacrifice to join our families. But as things get worse, some of us are reconsidering." If they do, then the Kingdom will have inflicted a grave defeat on itself. The refusal to admit women into the workforce is now an unaffordable luxury.

8

THE MERCHANTS OF VISAS - LABOR IN SAUDI ARABIA

"Pay a man before his sweat dries..." a hadith of the Prophet Mohammed.

"Expatriates have already proven themselves a dangerous vehicle for the introduction of subversive and corrupt social values and behavior patterns in our society, not to mention the immense drain in resources they are causing both to the Government and their employers," **columnist Amjad Muhammad Ridah.**[1]

No Saudi is comfortable with over 4 million foreigners working for 6.5 to 7 million Saudis. The foreigners were needed for the massive effort to transform desperately poor, backward Saudi Arabia, into a modern nation. The Saudis were too few and too poorly educated to do the job alone. Further, since manual labor is considered beneath most of them, foreigners were needed for most of the dirty work. The need has since grown into an embarrassing dependency. The 1985 Five Year Plan wanted to cut 600,000 foreigners but the goal was not reached.

Most foreigners are determined to stay in the Kingdom as long as possible. They may dislike the treatment they receive, hate the curtailment of their rights, and despise the lack of religious freedom, but they love the money. Most earn much more than they could at home. For this reason, jobs in the Kingdom are eagerly sought, especially by persons from troubled Third World nations.

That almost changed on Jan. 4, 1988, when the government announced an expatriates-only income tax. It was bad enough that wages for the Kingdom's foreign workers had already plummeted 50 percent or more by 1988. Now, the government was going to tax what was left. Deputy Minister of Finance Saleh Al-Omair informed the Kingdom's stunned foreign workers that those making over SR60,000 a year ($17,000) would pay a 30 percent tax. Those that made as little as SR6,000 per year, would pay 5 percent. Salary, air tickets, accommodation and food would be included in the computations. Further, taxes applied to termination bonuses. SInce the average bonus is equal to half a month salary for every year worked in the Kingdom, long-term workers begged to be fired and paid off before the tax came into effect on Jan. 21.

Work slowed to a crawl at King Faisal Specialist Hospital where the despondent medical staff ceased work, lined up at the personnel office to file resignations, and packed their bags. "Go process your letter of credit yourself," one banker growled at a Saudi American Bank customer. He was too busy to serve customers; he was totting up his losses on a calculator.

The tax was designed to raise SR5 billion for a cash-starved government. The budget, released 4 days earlier, announced the first Saudi government borrowing in 20 years. Oil revenues were still down, so someone at the Ministry of Finance suggested the tax. Of course, expatriates, not Saudis, would be taxed; citizens would hate to learn their taxes are paying for new princely palaces. The tax would encourage expatriates to leave, which would free more jobs for Saudi workers.

The gambit succeeded beyond expectation. Businessmen complained that they were losing their executives. Bankers packed their bags. Hospital staffs made airline reservations. Fearing Libyan- style currency controls, Lebanese transferred millions of dollars abroad. The tax was the last straw for many. The General Organization for Social Insurance (GOSI) retirement plan was already a casualty of lower oil revenue. Most Saudi and non-Saud workers contributed to the plan, which offered a generous retirement package. The government decided the program was too expensive, and announced in 1987 that foreigners would no longer participate, and would have their contributions refunded. It was another sign that the good times were over.

Fahad scrapped the tax, but not before the episode shattered the illusion that the Kingdom's 15 years of Saudization, college education, and vocational training, had succeeded. The Saudis still lacked the self-confidence to run things themselves. Properly trained and motivated young Saudi males were too scarce. The Iraqi invasion of Kuwait exposed the weakness even more. Pay bonuses were promised to expatriates if they stayed on after a war broke out. The army had too little manpower to stave off the Iraqi threat, and foreigners were required to defend the country as well.

THE SAUDIS

"Incompetence I have discussed at length," wrote former British Ambassador to the Kingdom, Sir James Craig, in a valedictory note: ".... By incompetent I mean feckless, disorganized unconscientiousness. This quality is common throughout the Arab world but is to be found in particularly large measure among the Saudis, where it is compounded by two sub-features: arrogance ...and a consequent reluctance to admit the need for guidance and reform; and a disdain for any work which is not noble (Sharif). Most peoples shy away from work which they consider ignoble; Englishmen, for example, are reluctant to be waiters or dustmen. But the Saudi classification of jobs is extraordinarily strict. Not only do they reject all manual and menial work; they are also reluctant to undertake anything which is tedious or humdrum. Plumbing is manual and roadsweeping is menial: for these tasks they employ foreigners. But whereas taking decisions is noble, the work of preparing to take decisions is ignoble: so the collection of facts, the collation of statistics, the checking of references, the planning of timetables is skimped. The results are sometimes disastrous."

One need not rely on a British ambassador's word; Miss Sua'd Fathi, a young Saudi woman, wrote to the local Arabic paper, *Okaz,* "It is true that developing countries depend on skilled laborers who usually earn more money. Their skills ensure a secure and good life. Yet, I cannot marry one, lest my friends make a laughing stock out of me. Their views have not yet changed."

The hardest working Saudis come from poorer areas, such as the Asir, or disadvantaged groups, such as the Shia from the Eastern Province. These people were already accustomed to working for others. Work attitudes are also conditioned by slave-owning. Saudis claim, with some justification, that their slaves were like members of the family. Nonetheless, men and women were bought and sold up until 1962, when Faisal freed 20,000 slaves and paid their owners compensation. Stories of un-freed slaves possessed by Faisal's old wife, or descendents of the Sharif Hussein still float around, but they are impossible to verify. Many former slaves continued working for their old masters.

The most pernicious effect of slavery was that it made manual labor a thing done by "slaves" and not a "free" man. Bedouin tradition reinforced this. Noble tribes herded camels and practiced military arts. Lesser tribes herded sheep or goats, and earned more mundane livelihoods. The less manly townsfolk farmed and supplied necessary metal goods.

Further, there is a generation gap in work attitudes. Many older Saudis call the youth idlers without an appetite for hard work. In the pre-oil days, a proud scion of a merchant family, the Binzagers, used to empty his own septic tank. Unfortunately, the advent of wealth permitted young

Saudis the luxury of sloth. Sometimes, though, Western employers mistake family orientation for laziness. Saudis usually think nothing of taking a day or two off to deal with family problems.

The collapse in oil prices has generated more dislike of foreigners rather than a change in work attitudes. This resulted in intensified presure for Saudization, the official program to replace foreign workers with natives. This has become more important because the government can no longer afford to emplooy every Saudi who wants a job. A series of laws promoting Saudization were strengthened in the post oilboom period. The Labor law already required that 75 percent of every company's labor force should be Saudi, but during the boom nobody could comply, and few tried. The Ministry of Finance established bank Saudization targets but relaxed them after the oil recession bad loan problem cropped up.

Sponsorship rules were toughened to quicken the pace of Saudization. Saudi visa applicants now must prove that the job in question cannot be filled with an eligible Saudi. The Ministry of Interior hiked the cost of transferring Iqamas. In 1986, transfer of sponsorship was restricted to those with university degrees. Formerly, when one Saudi firm lost a cleaning contract, it would offer the winning firm its workers, who could, if they wanted, continue to work, although at lower wages. Now the workers are out of luck if their sponsor loses a contract bid.

In 1989, the Ministry of Commerce issued new laws against sleeping partner arrangements, under which foreign businessmen, usually Lebanese, run a business with a so-called Saudi partner. The partner, who plays no role in the business, simply takes a pay-off to use his name. The new law awards part of the heavy fines to the person who reports the transgression. This law is designed to push foreigners out. The Ministry of Labor and the Ministry of Information are also cracking down on advertisements for job openings that they feel are written specifically to exclude Saudis.[2]

The Ministry of labor has stepped up deportations of unemployed foreigners. Under its new rules, over 300,000 foreigners were deported for various reasons in the two years before Oct. 2, 1986. Getting rid of foreigners is easy, but replacing them is not. In the last Five Year plan, over $41 Billion was earmarked for manpower development in universities, vocational centers, and general training and education.

The Ministry of Labor established the General Organization for Technical Education and Vocational Training (GOTEVT) to develop manpower. GOTEVT runs 26 Vocational Training Centers, 8 Pre- vocational Training Centers, and 8 Technical Institutes. The Vocational Training Centers are for anyone between 18-45 years old with minimum schooling of 5th grade. Students receive a monthly allowance which is raised if the student passes 50 percent of the course. They also receive housing, transportation, materials, and allowances for food and clothing. Graduates receive cash bonuses with extra for excellent grades, plus a bonus after completing 6 months on a job. Once the worker spends some time in his field, the Saudi Credit Bank, gives them up loans start businesses.

The Technical Schools are the equivalent of high school or secondary school. They offer auto mechanics, electricity, machine trades, and architectural drawing. The Polytechnic Institutes are compArable to Two-year colleges. Again, the students are paid and get the other allowances. If the graduate enters the government, he automatically enters on the government as a Grade 6 employee. The Saudi government scale runs from 1 to 15.

To cover all of its bases, the Kingdom's vocational training program also offers Pre-Vocational Training Centers (PVCs). PVCs are meant to educate school dropouts, Graduates can enter a Vocational Training Center. Entrants receive the usual allowances and graduation incentives.

"Before, our training schools did not attract people," the Secretary General of the Greater Manpower Council, Dr. Hussein Mansour said. "Now the number of people coming to the training centers is greater than they can handle. The young Saudis are eager, and some of schools have begun raising their admission standards, from graduation from general school, to graduation from high school. They have also started asking for higher grades."

Despite these efforts, industries established by the Peace Shield Offset Investment program found inadequate numbers of Saudi skilled workers and management. Young Saudis got jobs despite their level of training during the oil boom because the government hired every graduate. Now, the government has frozen new hiring, and cut overtime and benefits. Some agencies slashed wages by as much as 25 percent. Military pay has wisely been untouched.

Just how serious is the problem of Saudi participation in the workforce? A look at statistics tells the story. Some 1.5 to 1.9 million Saudis comprise 27 percent of the total workforce. However, this includes the government, and government-owned companies such as Aramco, Petromin, the electric companies, and the Saudi Basic Industries Corp. Participation in the private sector on farms and small industries veers downward to 10 to 2 percent.[3] A visitor to a privately-owned factory will be hard- pressed to find a Saudi on the factory floor. Saudis may occupy white collar positions, but the actual blue collar work is almost invariably left to others.

Many companies have two sets of figures: *total* and *useful* Saudization. Total figures include teaboys, drivers, and "expediters," a breed of fixers hired to push papers through Saudi bureaucracy. Useful Saudization figures are always much lower. "I do believe there is a lot of hidden unemployment and underemployment among Saudis," former Saudi Investment Bank (SAIB) chairman Abdulaziz Al-Dukheil told *Gazette* reporter Theroux. "If you take the size of the economy and look at the modern age, where new technology minimizes the intensity of the labor force, you see the problem is not really the availability of Saudis. I think it's a question of discipline, of training, of habit, and of motives -- not a question of the volume of people. There are a lot of Saudis around doing nothing. In past years there's been a lot of money chasing a few Saudis -- it was very difficult to attract people to hard work or disciplined work. But the more the money dries up, the more interested people will get in serious work."

A few years later, after the oil downturn began to bite, Dr. Dukheil found little improvement. At a Businessman's Conference in Abha, he complained that Saudi firms were still not hiring any Saudis. Riyadh Businessman Abdul Rahman Al-Jeraisy, owner of Riyadh House Establishment, one of the Kingdom's largest computer and office machinery firms, concurs. "We do our best to train our Saudi employees. Our problem is that Saudis don't want to work in the private sector, but in the government."

"We try to hire Saudi people and try to train them, but most of them want to be in the top of the responsibility even without experience, but if you put him there without experience he will make mistakes. Then, after 2 or three years, he wants to leave and start his own business. The Saudi employee will not stay 11 years like I did with the businessman, where I gave back to him what he gave to me. We want these people to stay with us."

In the boom period, any Saudi could find a foreigner to serve as his manager, get a cheap loan from the Saudi Industrial Development Fund, (SIDF) and start a factory or business. He could also get a low-cost loan from the Real Estate Development Fund (REDF) and build property which he could rent out. Young educated Saudis were scarce, and could, through connections, soon generate business and operate their own firms. Those days are ended now, but the attitudes are changing much more slowly.

Even those youth with lowered expectations and improved work attitudes still face problems. Under pressure from oil revenue declines, employers have consistently shaved expatriate salaries. These have declined to a point that employers incur a substantial loss in employing their countrymen. No Saudi could hope to support a family on wages paid to many expatriate workers.

Saudi bosses prefer expatriates not only because they are cheaper, but because they are more pliable than their own people. This also explains a preference for workers from poorer countries. "Egyptians never discuss with you whether you are right or wrong," said one Arab diplomat. "It is always, 'yes sir.' This satisfies the Saudi. He likes to feel he's a people owner, not a sponsor."

Saeed Musfir, owner of a water tank factory employing 20 foreign workers, told *Okaz* newspaper "They are all foreigners. I pay them reasonable salaries and their work is satisfactorily good. Moreover, they are committed and dedicated and, unlike Saudi workers, they never look for excuses to absent themselves during work hours. I had experience with two Saudi workers. They were skilled but they used to absent themselves very frequently, were arrogant and never accepted directions, which they interpreted as insults."

Many young Saudi trainees claim they are harassed by foreigners who resent training someone to take over their jobs. "Sometimes the Saudi national is not trained enough, so he does not do the job properly," says Dr. Mansour. "This reflects badly on him, and causes him to dislike his work, which then creates a bad impression on the people who hired him. They won't give him full accreditation. This reinforces his dislike of the job, which he tells other Saudis who might be interested in the field. And the employers become reluctant to hire more Saudis."

There are economic constraints as well. Organization Resources Counselors, Inc., published a report stating that the cost of training in the Kingdom is prohibitively high. Dr. Mansour, argues "We have to start it on a sound training base so that the Saudi will not get the job based on his nationality, but because he is capable of doing the job."

This is not necessarily true. All firms with 100 or more workers must hire at least 5 Saudis. In the past, some Saudis would hire themselves out as "ghost" workers for several different companies. The "Ghosts" got training subsidies from the government for each program they enrolled in. The companies met their quota. Everyone was happy.

Now, because of lower oil revenues, the loophole is being eliminated through tighter controls. One is a labor certification program developed with assistance from the U.S. Department of Labor. Workers coming into the Kingdom will have to pass tests to be certified as competent plumbers, technicians, carpenters, or any number of other jobs. This will help employers by guaranteeing they will get properly skilled individuals. It may also force expatriates to understate their skills, and allow employers to save money, said a Labor Department consultant. The certification program will be run by some lucky, influential, private firm which will charge $80 per test. The tests themselves will cost $15 to administer.

WASTED RESOURCE

The Saudization problem would be less severe, if the Kingdom didn't squander its educated women. The post-Kuwait invasion statement of King Fahad supposedly addresses this. He called for Saudi women to join the medical services, and pledged to employ them in jobs that don't conflict with Islamic traditions. That is exactly what he has said before, although in a more forthright manner. Presently, girls schools offer the most jobs. Other opportunities are limited, particularly by the regulation that women work in all-woman environments.

A few women (mostly foreign) have been hired as secretaries by companies, because a woman is a status symbol. Aramco employed a few women, while Saudi American Bank at one time had numbers of women on its staff. Some Saudi women are entering the ranks of dentists and doctors. Few enter nursing because it is considered menial.

Saudi women could replace tens of thousands of Filipino and Pakistani clerks, teachers, and nurses. They would spend their money in the Saudi economy instead of sending it overseas.

Further, they are politically reliable. It was this reason that the Ministry of Interior considered hiring Saudi women to feed data into its Big Brother computer system.

FOREIGNERS

The expatriate worker habit developed from an early dependency on foreigners for technology. While poor Saudis sought simple jobs in Egypt, Palestine, and other countries, Turks operated the famous Hejaz Railway, and erected buildings and public works in the Western region. After World War I shattered the Ottoman Empire, Egypt supplied the Saudis with engineers, teachers, doctors, and technicians. Tragically, the Egyptians also provided the Saudis with their bureaucracy, the ill-effects of which are still felt.

Farouk Aslan, Egyptian Labor Attache in Riyadh, says the foreign worker flood began in 1970 after oil revenue increased. Some 200,000 Egyptians were part of the Arab first wave of expatriate workers. Soon, political radicalism made Arabs less attractive, and the Saudis turned to India, which already supplied workers to other Gulf Arab states. Pakistanis arrived, and served in the military as well as civilian sectors. Americans were hired by Aramco and large American contractors such as Bechtel. Khuwajja, a word which means outsider, or foreigner, came to mean Europeans and North Americans. Britons were hired by many firms, but other Europeans, such as the Swedes, Germans, and French, came with their own national companies.

It was only in the early eighties, that the Far Eastern Asians began to make a big impact. The Korean construction firms such as Hyundai had brought armies of Korean workers to build their new projects. But these workers soon became expensive, and their places were taken by other Asians, such as Filipinos, Thais, and Indonesians. India's market share was whittled away by cut-rate competitors, Sri Lanka and Bangladesh.

Few firms hire a homogeneous workforce. A group of mutually antagonistic nationalities remains too fragmented to challenge management. Those that do unite do not dare to stage a strike. Unions are illegal, and strikers are either deported or imprisoned. In 1953, 17,000 out of 19,000 Arab workers at Aramco went out on strike. Leaders of the strike were exiled, or jailed. In the 1970s, some Asians organized a strike for better wages and working conditions. The leaders were deported. Most strikes end up this way. Unionism is a long way off in the Kingdom.

Office politics, however, has reached a fine art. Indian, Lebanese, Pakistani, or Egyptian office "mafias" usually try to muscle other nationalities out, and achieve dominance in their particular companies. They compete through rumors, backbiting, and peddling favors. Sometimes fistfights break out, but usually national rivalries just keep office politics simmering.

The international mix of workers made English the Lingua Franca of the Kingdom. Would-be Arabic students find this disconcerting. In everyday life, drivers, bank clerks, and cashiers are more likely to speak Urdu or Tagalog than Arabic. This means nationalities with good command of English, such as the Filipinos, Indians, and Pakistanis, prosper. The Thais, for instance, are less expensive than the Filipinos. But for every ten Thais or so, a foreman who can translate into English must be hired. He will earn as much as 60 percent more than his fellows. This requirement erodes much of the savings in hiring Thais.

ECONOMIC PRESSURE

The government responded to lower oil revenue by delaying payments. Employers responded by cutting labor costs using methods that range from arbitrary, to illegal.

NUMBERS

Foreigners made up more than 59 percent of the workforce in 1985, a percentage that has not declined by much. A Ministry of Planning source said in 1988 that the number was as high as 4.5 million, with perhaps 1 million dependents. Although Ministry of Labor statistics do not make it clear whether domestics and drivers are included in the estimate, they are included in the Ministry of Planning figures.

The numbers below are not completely accurate; the Saudi Ministry of Labor and the Ministry of Interior know the true numbers. Embassies do not. The numbers below were obtained from embassy labor attaches and include dependents as well as workers. Women workers, who are included in the totals, are set aside in parenthesis when their number is known. Countries which send the Kingdom considerable numbers of maids, but do not give statistics will have a (?). A higher percentage of Europeans and North Americans bring families, but the total number of Arab families are higher. There are 60,000 Egyptian and 100,000 Syrian families in the Kingdom. The figures show changes in relative numbers of workers, but by the time of publication, it is certain that the number of Yemenis will decline, due to the change in labor regulations.

Illegal workers are not included in the estimates. these are men whose visas expired, or who stayed after perfomring Hajj. A sizable number of Pakistan's 69,000 annual Hajjis stay to work. Thailand estimates that perhaps as many as 30,000 of the Thais in the Kingdom came on Hajj visas and stayed illegally.

	1986	peak
Yemen	1.2 million	1.6 million
Egypt	450,000 (18,000)	800,000
Pakistan	400,000-600,000	600,000-700,000
Philippines	300,000 (70,000)	350,000
Syria	250,000	
India	175,000	400,000
Turkey	150,000-160,000	
Lebanon	150,000	360,000
Sudan	140,000-150,000	
Thailand	134,000 (10,000)	300,000
Bangladesh	100,000-120,000(?)	150,000
Sri Lanka	80,000 (20,000)	
Indonesia	80,000	
Ethiopia	80,000 (of this number 80 percent are Eritrean)	
Palestinians	80,000 (includes Lebanese, Syrians, Jordanians.)	
Somalia	50,000	
Jordan	50,000	
U.K.	30,000	
United States	30,000	70,000
S. Korea	30,000	140,000
W. Germany	12,000	
France	10,000	
Japan	2,500	

PAY

SR per month (plus housing and food)

	Doctor	Nurse	Maid	Teacher	Skilled-	Un-Skilled
USA	30,000	7,500	----	6,000	7,500	----
UK	20,000	6,000	----	5,000	6,000-10,000 -----	
Lebanon	10,000	----	----	----	3,0000	----
Egypt	4,000	----	700	----	800	-----
India	6,000	----	----	----	600-500	-----
Pakistan	6,000	----	----	----	600-500	-----
Philippines	7,500	2,170	671	----	1,400	725
Bangladesh	-----	----	----	----	800	375
Thailand	----	900	600	----	850	430

Sultan Younis, 28, of Madras, India, suffered from the common and cruel cost cutting method of withheld wages. As of March, 1987, the janitor and 111 other men inhabited the cramped former offices of their Saudi employer. They lived without electricity for 5 months and without running water for 20 days. The men, all except two of whom are Indian, sometimes fanned out in Riyadh, in the shadow of the Institute of Public Administration, washing cars for enough money to buy rice and bottled gas for cooking. At night, they lit cans filled with fat, and lay side-by-side in rooms, hallways, and on the roof. They filed a complaint with the Labor Courts, where the case languished since April, 1986, leaving them trapped in a strange country, unable to leave, nor permitted to seek other employment.

"My ambition was to come out here to earn enough to buy a house," Mirano Aziz Abu Baker, of Kerala, said through an interpreter. "I borrowed 16,000 rupees and have to pay 20,000 (Close to $1,700) to get this job. I still have a lot of problems at home, and now I am shattered and my hopes are finished."

Things could be worse. *Okaz* reported on March 5, 1987, that a Pakistani worker, Muhammad Alsam, 28, tired of wandering the streets without a job, seized a meat cleaver and cut off his left arm. It was sewn back on at King Fahad Hospital in Jeddah.

Other arbitrary methods for cutting labor costs included informing employees that they must accept pay cuts or quit. Many simply found their pay packets were thinner, if not delayed. Some new workers are greeted at the airport with an ultimatum: sign new lower contracts or go home. Flying home emptyhanded is not only embarrassing, but financially impossible for those who borrowed to get their Saudi job.

One Bangladeshi worker, called Saleem by the *Saudi Gazette,* signed a SR700 per month contract for 6 eight-hour days per week, plus a room. Instead, he is paid SR500, works 11 hours a day seven days a week and lives in an open field in Jeddah, stuffing his documents, money, and pictures of his wife and family under his bedroll. When he complained to his sponsor, the Saudi laughed, and said that if he didn't like it, he didn't have to work.[4]

A group of 78 Filipino women, 58 Filipino men, and 82 Indonesian and Indian recruits, worked for a Saudi cleaning firm at the the Maternity and Children's Hospital in Riyadh. The sponsor vanished after falling 7 months behind in wages. The workers were forced to live off of handouts from the hospital and underground Christian groups. Eventually the sponsor forced the women to sign away their rights in return for transferable Iqamas. These Iqamas were sold by the sponsor to other Saudis so the women could work as maids.

Lower oil wealth has increased the incidence of employee abuse. Unpaid wages has led to greater numbers of indigents. An article entitled "Employees Left in the Lurch go Begging," in *Al-Riyadh* reported that "Errant employers who leave their employees in the lurch are the main cause of beggary in the Kingdom." Mushaweh Abdul Rahman Al-Hawshan, Deputy Director of the Department to Fight Beggary, said these people are forced to beg to support themselves.[5]

Some employers fire older workers who received salary increases over the years. They are replaced by less expensive nationalities. This alters the makeup of the expatriate labor force. Britons replace Americans. Indians replace the Britons. Bangladeshis replace the Indians, ad nauseum. Salaries dropped as precipitously as the oil prices. The lowest case recorded by one labor attache was $41, or SR150, a month to a Bangladeshi. Since the petro boom petered out in 1983, wages have fallen by an average of over 50 percent.

How can the Saudis tolerate this widespread abuse? Part of it is arrogance about Asians, Africans and Indians. Further, employer attitudes are conditioned by recent slavery and Middle Eastern authoritarianism. This meant that while foreign workers might be viewed paternalistically, they are considered possessions, particularly if they are non-Muslim. Thus, when oil wealth decreased, foreign worker rights were given short shrift by the average Saudi. When Bangladeshi security guards at King Saud University complained that they were unpaid and were forced to sleep two and three to a bed, university officials countered by saying that Bangladeshis liked sleeping that way.

"The Labor market in the Kingdom has developed into a vicious circle." said Bangladesh Ambassador Hedayet Ahmed. "The worker will pay sometimes as much as $2,500 to an agent for his work permit and visa. After he arrives in the Kingdom on a multi- year contract, he is permitted to work only one year before being fired by the employer. The employer and labor agent then fleece another Bangladeshi worker while the other man flies home with barely enough money to cover the bribes paid to the Agent and the Saudi sponsor. "

"Our people are easily blackmailed. When they come here they are at the mercy of their sponsors and agents back home. If they come here and are told to sign a new contract, or aren't paid a month or two, they will do little. After all, they have 'invested' in their jobs. They have come here thinking that they would be treated fairly well as well as make a lot of money. For them to risk everything in complaining, or filing a labor suit, is a dangerous step." Saudi jobs are too valuable to lightly throw away. Americans make twice what they do at home. Britons take home almost 3 times, and Indians earn 8 to 10 times as much.

LABOR LAWS

The abuses take place despite by progressive labor laws. Workers are regulated under two sets of laws: the Labor Law, and the Residency Law. Labor law is administered by the Labor Courts of the Ministry of Labor and Social Affairs, which also supervises the various Saudization programs. It regulates benefits, overtime, and living conditions for almost all workers except domestics. A workman must not work more than 8 hours in a day, or 48 hours in a week, Termination of contracts without cause is forbidden. Employers must provide decent housing (Art. 146). Those in remote locations should get water and three meals a day. "Saudi labor law is favorable to the employee," says Islamic legal expert, Frank Vogel. "He cannot waive those rights given to him under the law. Typically, employees win in the labor court, and we have a lawyer in the Jeddah court who said he has never lost a case."

Employees are supposed to have the first crack in bankruptcy proceedings, he adds. In August of 1986, the Ministries of Labor and Interior passed a regulation that would bar a sponsor from leaving the country until wage disputes with his workers are settled. "That a worker should not have to wait months before being paid, is a general Saudi feeling," Vogel says.

That may have been the case when the oil boom was on, but it has changed. Most Third World workers have no idea of their rights under Saudi labor laws. If they do go to Court, they find it converses only in Arabic, is overworked, and slow. The workers first speak with a labor inspector who tries, within a week or two, to meet with the sponsor to work out an amicable solution. The Labor Courts prefer negotiation to coercion. If the inspector cannot solve the problem, it goes to the Labor Complaint Committee, a process which can take another few months. If no decision can be reached, the case goes to a high committee, with a judge from the Ministry of Labor. This process can take another 2 months. The whole process easily drags on 7 months or more. Workers are seldom, if ever, awarded sums to cover the time they wasted while seeking back wages.

"In other countries they have a written law. But here, it seems that every case is unique," said one Arab labor attache. "I can strongly put it that there is utmost casualness in dealing with people's problems." The waiting game is hard on the workers. A favorable ruling must still be enforced. "If you do get a judgment in your favor, and you have been awarded your rights, you are still not paid," said one Arab diplomat. "It is not important to have a judgment, it is important to have influence." Workers talk of friends who thought they finally won their battle, and were driven to the airport. Once they arrive, the sponsor presents him with much less than he is entitled to. By that time, the poor man is so sick of it all, he simply takes the money and goes, full of bitterness.

Whatever advantage a worker has under labor law is nullified by the Residency Laws, said one attorney. "The Labor Law is very fair, as good if not better than that in the United States. But what gives them (the sponsors) the advantage is the Residency Law."

The Residency Law gives sponsors tremendous discretion in the life of an employee. If the employee wishes to quit and work for another sponsor, he must get his employer's written permission. The employer can approve the transfer of the sponsorship document, the "Iqama" to a different Saudi or issue a "letter of no objection" to the worker's return to the country to work for somebody else. If he refuses to write either of these two letters, the worker cannot re-enter the Kingdom for 3 years. If the employer wants to, he can file a complaint which prevents the worker from ever entering Saudi Arabia again. None of these letters, by the way, can be appealed. They are strictly up to the sponsor.

Haidar Kazem, the business editor of the Jeddah's *Saudi Gazette*, learned about this the hard way. He finished his contract with the *Gazette*, went home to India, and then returned on a better contract with cross-town rival *Arab News*. The *Gazette's* vindictive publisher, Iyad Madani, was furious and called the police. Haidar was imprisoned until negotiations between the two papers resulted in his grudging release.

Some sponsors extort money for these letters, even though it contravenes a religious ruling by the Kingdom's Islamic scholars who called the practice "Morally wrong."

SPONSORS

Every visitor to the Kingdom, except pilgrims, must have a Saudi sponsor, called the "kafeel." The sponsor is personally responsible for his employee, including debts and criminal behavior. This system is based upon the Bedouin system of protection money extorted from caravans passing through their territory. The modern Kafeel system was toughened up after many unsophisticated Saudis were bilked or cheated by foreigners who then skipped the country. The sponsor now applies apply for work visas on either a "block" or individual basis. His request goes through the Ministry of Labor, which determines the validity of the request, and forwards it to the Ministry of Interior, which actually grants the visas. The sponsor takes the employee's passport, locks it in a safe, and gives the worker a government residence pass, called the "Iqama." The Iqama is brown for non-Muslims, and white for Muslims. Without it, a worker is subject to arrest.

The worker needs his Sponsor's permission to buy a car, install a telephone, travel from city to city, and leave the country. This allows unscrupulous Sponsors to hold foreigners hostage. Again, the Residency Laws provide no procedures to force a sponsor to produce his worker's passport, or grant permission to leave the Kingdom.

The arbitrary power of a sponsor gives some Saudis a slaveowner mentality. "Imagine how we feel when this Saudi comes in, and is angry at the worker, saying, 'She cannot do this, I bought her,'" a labor attache said, adding that one case involved a princess who "gave" some Filipina maids to a friend.

The Residency Law allows Saudis to take foreigners commercial hostage. By denying a man an exit visa, a sponsor puts the expatriate under virtual country-wide house arrest. Trapped in an unfriendly country with no way to earn a living, many foreigners cave in to Saudi employers.

Western managers of small Saudi firms are increasingly being jailed for economic failures, some of which occur because of late government payments. The Saudi partner or owner places the blame on his expatriate manager and then avoids the police. "The Saudis grab the highest ranking company official they can get, and toss him in jail," said Vogel.

Economic hostage-taking increased dramatically after the oil bust. In 1987, two German workers were held as commercial hostages by a prince who sought to coerce their parent company. After languishing in the Kingdom for several months, they tried escaping over the border into Jordan, but were caught. Imprisoned, they were freed only when German Foreign Minister Hans Deitrich Genscher personally appealed to Fahad during a state visit. The ambassadors representing the European Community (EC) presented Foreign Minister Prince Saud Al-Faisal with a demarche on the topic. Normally, he follows the Saudi custom of offering guests tea. The minute he heard the ambassadors were there to discuss commercial hostage-taking, he brusquely dismissed them. He didn't want to hear about it.

GETTING A SAUDI JOB

Unscrupulous sponsors form unholy alliances with Piranha-like companies called labor agencies to peddle jobs to Third World workers desperate for Saudi employment. These firms infest all of the labor exporting countries. Thailand has over 300 private labor exporting agencies, plus its official government firm. India has more than 1,100 licensed agents in Delhi, Bombay and Madras. The Philippines, Bangladesh, and other countries have both official and unofficial labor recruitment firms. These countries try to regulate the business without success.

The typical labor recruitment begins like this:

In Thailand, fictitious worker T. Princhampong lives in the impoverished Northeast, which furnishes most of Thailand's labor exports. Once he has decided to go abroad to make his money, he sells his household goods, or borrows from the local loanshark. He uses this to begin a wearying series of pay-offs. He could circumvent the whole expensive process by heading directly to Bangkok, but he does not know any better. He goes to his village fixer and pays perhaps $145. The fixer then takes him up a chain of fixers, numbering four or five, until the worker has laid out as much as $2,000 for his job. At least $100 goes to the Saudi who furnishes the visa.

This cycle of extortion is played out all over the Third World from Bangladesh to the Philippines. Indians borrow at 25 percent interest, to cover charges of up to 25,000 rupees ($2,187). This is in a land where per capita income is around $250. Some Filipino labor agents simply sell falsified passports and documents to the rural poor who arrive in the Kingdom to face immediate deportation.

Foreign officials are loathe to blame Saudis for the labor extortion rackets. When Bangladesh Ambassador Ahmed told newspapers that Saudi sponsors and labor agents collude to victimize laborers, the Saudis nearly refused to grant him accreditation. Cesar Averia, of EDI Staffbuilders, of Manila, says Saudi employers "go to the company in Manila and ask for a certain amount of money per worker they hire. It is usually about $100 per worker." The money does not come out of the agents' pockets; it is extracted from the workers.

Indian diplomats say Bombay is a frequent haunt of Saudi merchants of visas. These men take bribes and other favors from labor agencies or individual workers in Bombay. Syrians tell tales of vacationing Saudis offering visas to the highest bidders. The visas do not guarantee a job. Ethiopians and Sudanese workers bought visas from a Saudi, who mailed one genuine visa in a bundle of worthless photocopies. Ethiopia has begun demanding proof that the visas are genuine from the Saudi Chambers of Commerce and the Ministry of Interior. A Beirut-based Saudi diplomat was renowned for demanding gold and sexual favors for issuing visas to the Kingdom. Another was gunned down in Bangkok because he cheated on deals with Thai labor agents.

Despite horror stories, Saudi jobs are prized. The worker stakes everything on the chance to make enough to pay for family weddings, land, and perhaps a small business. Others come to escape wars at home. The Port of Jizan, just across the Red Sea from Ethiopia, receives a steady trickle of small unseaworthy craft carrying Eritreans fleeing the never-ending war of secession raging in Ethiopia. Boats sink and people die of exposure, but most arrive and are issued Red Cross refugee passports upon arrival (the Kingdom supports the Eritrean liberation movements). The refugees eventually make their way north to Jeddah. A trucking line owned by the Minister of Interior, Prince Naif, is the main transporter of the refugees to Jeddah. Eritreans, like the Lebanese and Palestinians, are subject to abuse because they are stateless and have no home to return to.

Illegal immigrants and other unskilled laborers gather every morning in Baatha in Riyadh, on Palestine Road, in Jeddah, and on other streets in other cities, waiting for a boss to stop in a pickup to hire them. The men, many of whom overstayed their visas, or came on the Hajj and stayed on to work, wait hopefully with picks, shovels, and trowels by their sides until the sun grows too hot. Many of these day laborers are organized in kinship units. An employer hires a group which contains the necessary skills. This system worked well enough in the boom period, when there was plenty of work, but today there are slim pickings.

Those without jobs are subject to deportation. When Deputy Minister of Labor Ahmed Yahya was asked by a reporter about unemployment among expatriates, he replied, "There is NO unemployment. You show me a man without a job and we will send him home immediately."

REACTION

Foreign diplomats are often remiss in defending their nationals. Former Filipino Ambassador, Dr. Mauyag Muhammed Tamano, whose relatives own labor export agencies, claimed reports of maid abuse were fabrications of the press. "They were attacking our Arab brothers in the Manila press. There were allegations of ill-treatment of Filipino domestics. Then I had to appear on the radio and television to refute those allegations."[6]

Third World embassies hate to anger the Saudis because their economies depend upon worker remittances. Bangladesh's second-highest source of hard currency is worker income. Exports in 1986 totalled $900 million, while her export laborers sent home $600 million. $190 million of that came from Saudi Arabia. At the height of the boom, the Filipinos sent back close to $1 billion annually. Their remittances were so important to bolstering former President Ferdinand Marcos' shrinking foreign reserves, that Filipinos were required to remit a large proportion of their salaries through the main Philippines bank. Naturally, the exchange rate was punishing. On each flight to Manila, Filipinos carried U.S. dollars on behalf of others, in what they called door-to-door banking. Thais in the Middle East generate $460 million in remittances. Pakistanis sent back $3 billion. Egypt's 3.5 million expatriate workers remitted nearly $3 billion a year, the largest source of foreign currency for that country. Just the workers from Kerala state in India remit nearly $470 million per year.[7] Each Lebanese expatriate worker supports 2 to 3 families. They are involved in all levels of the economy, but their numbers have declined since radical Shia movements have surfaced in that country. The Ministry of Interior has ordered companies employing Shia Lebanese not to renew their contracts. Strangely, the Saudis seem to trust Lebanese Christians more than they do Lebanese Muslims.

Saudi jobs also ease rural unemployment in Third World countries. "What would we do with all these people if they did not work in Saudi Arabia?" said one Asian diplomat. On the other hand, badly-needed professionals take lower level jobs simply to earn money. Teachers clean Saudi houses, and business school graduates work as clerks or secretaries.

Usually, the Third World countries get back individuals who are not only richer, but better trained than when they left. The Saudis talk of technology transfer, but it works out differently than they think. In private industry and agriculture, skills are learned by the expatriates who hold the jobs, not the Saudis who don't. These workers take their skills home when they leave. Others devote spare time to learning to use computers or speak new languages. The Kingdom is arguably the world's biggest vocational training center. Every two years or so, a new batch of workers comes in, while the old batch "graduates."

All these benefits breed competition for Saudi jobs. The Indian and Pakistani embassies launched a whispering campaign against the price-busting Bangladeshis in 1987. Rumors of Bangladeshi radicalization and unreliability reached such a pitch that the Saudi government clamped down on new Bangladeshi work permits. Bangladesh President, General Ershad, held talks with Saudi officials to dispel the rumor, particularly the one which said the Bangladeshis were Khomeini-loving Shia; the country is almost 100 percent Sunni.

Worker remittances don't satisfy all governments. The Filipinos raised a furor when the Aquino government, in March, 1987, tried to impose a 55 percent duty on the electronic goods and appliances Filipinos were taking home. Shipping companies do a healthy business shipping airconditioners, refrigerators, as well as high-priced stereos to Manila. Other countries with expensive restrictions on import of luxury goods find that a lot of money is remitted in the form of electronics. "I know of many of these poor guys who go home to their village with a television set," said one Pakistani executive. "The guy has no electricity, so he puts the TV on the oxcart and takes it down to his friend's village, where they have electricity, to watch programs. That is not a very intelligent use of money, if you ask me."

The United States, for many years, was one of the few that taxed its overseas workers. This was rectified in the early Eighties when American businessmen based in Saudi Arabia took their case to Congress. They pointed out that any income tax on an American expatriate is passed on to the employer and makes Americans prohibitively expensive. This harms American exports. Once Aramco started replacing Americans with Britons, British and not American products were purchased. American engineers specify American standards, and British engineers specify British standards. Add a little nationalistic pride, and one comes up with large shifts in consumption patterns. American expatriates spur American exports.

Western diplomats don't have as many problems as their Third World colleagues, because Westerners are at the top of the two- tiered Saudi labor system. Third World laborers, called TCNs, for "Third Country Nationals," are the bottom half. TCNs for outnumber the Westerners and live much harder lives. They get vacation once every two years, and are rarely permitted to bring their families. Families imply permanence and mean more security headaches. Every once in a while, the Ministry of Interior announces a relaxation of rules on allowing wives to come to the Kingdom, but it reneges once it sees the pent-up demand to bring families to the Kingdom.

When it comes to treatment of foreign workers, white Westerners fare the best; Asians, and Africans fare the worst. Pakistanis, Indians, and Bangladeshis do not fare much better than Asians. This sometimes spills over on Westerners of ethnic groups. Many Asian-Americans are handled rudely because they are mistaken for Filipinos. One black American was beaten by religious police who suspected he was with some "women." Their reply after the U.S. Embassy filed a protest was: "We thought he was a Sudanese."

WOMEN

Pity the thousands of women who, as domestic help, are not covered by labor law. There is no limit to the hours they have to work. There is no time off and no overtime. The Kingdom probably has more maids and domestic help per capita than any other nation. The Gulf region has hired a total of 1.5 million maids, a ratio of one for every 10 people. The Kingdom's newspapers are filled with cartoons, editorials, and articles about maids, who are blamed for "sneaking in Christian propaganda" and subverting the local culture. There is a genuine concern with the pervasive influence of Asian maids, but no desire to do without them.

A wealthy Saudi yelled at the American visa officer about Visa delays for his maid (the Saudis demand instant visas from other countries even though it takes months to get a Saudi visa). "I have to have those two maids. How do you expect me to manage with a wife and two children?" the man yelled at the officer.

The diplomat, with a wife and two children of his own, replied drily, "The same way I do." The Saudi got his visas. Like many Saudis who take Ethiopian and Filipina maids to the United States, he was shocked when his maids skipped off to become illegal aliens in America.

Life in America is preferable to the daily grind of working for many families. Maids are usually hired on two-year contracts. Most cannot leave their employer's house, unless they are travelling with the family. They must be up at the crack of dawn and don't retire until their employers go to bed, which for nightowl Saudis is usually past midnight. The maids are sometimes locked in their rooms at night. Worse, they are often sexually harassed or raped.

The Sri Lankan embassy relates how one Saudi reported his maid had died of "natural causes." An autopsy revealed she had been raped to death. Another Sri Lankan sent home after being raped by her employer, was raped by the policeman taking her to the airport. A Filipina maid shattered her ankles when she leaped from the second story of her employer's villa to avoid rape. Other women, locked up at night and blocked from any contact with the outside world, despair of the beatings, sexual assault and overwork, and commit suicide.

Many maids, unsurprisingly, become pregnant, are accused of improper behavior, and find themselves in prison. The *Gazette* editor spiked a story about the large number of babies found in Jeddah's trashbins, most of which are half-eaten by the legion of half-starved cats. Many of the Babies look half-Asian, and officials suspect they come from maids or Saudi women who slept with Asian drivers.

Some women flee their employers. The Philippines Embassy on April 16, 1987, had 53 escaped maids cowering in the compound, begging for airfare home. Unpaid and mistreated, they had enough of the Saudi dream. A Bangladeshi diplomat watched as a Saudi employer chased a servant down the street and beat her.

When problems occur, most embassies in Riyadh are reduced to following up complaints through the Ministry of Foreign affairs. The Egyptians teamed up with Saudi charitable societies to establish *Al Bait Al-Riyayah Bal Arab* "House for Looking After the Foreign Woman's Good." When an Egyptian maid escapes her sponsor, she can stay in the house for 1 to 10 days while discussions take place. The house was paid for by Egyptian contractors concerned about their countrywomen. It is under control of the Saudi police. "Servants we do not encourage, because they have too many problems here," says the Egyptian Labor attache.

To avoid these problems, many countries bar the export of women. The main suppliers are Indonesia, India, Sri Lanka, Egypt, Philippines, Eritrea/Ethiopia, Pakistan, Bangladesh and Thailand. The Saudi Ministry of Labor decided that women below the age of 40 should not be allowed to work in the Kingdom to reduce incidents of sexual harassment. Pakistan has raised its minimum to 45 years, but women wriggle around the age limit anyway.

The outcry on maid abuse was such that the Philippines considered a ban on maids. The Saudi ambassador in Manila immediately threatened, "If you deprive us of the comfort of having the comfort of a Filipina domestic helper, we will retaliate."

Finally, in March, 1988, the ban was imposed. The Saudis struck back by refusing permits for any more Filipino workers. Desperate for worker remittances, the Aquino government groveled, and rescinded the ban without securing any extra protection for its maids. Even after the episode was finished, the Saudis refused to help the women.

OTHER FEMALE WORKERS

Single female workers, such as nurses or teachers, also live with Saudi sexual apartheid. Filipinas at Riyadh's Al-Hammadi Hospital are only allowed out until 11 p.m., and then, just twice a week. Western female doctors and nurses have curfews, but can get an extension to 3 a.m. if they ask permission. If they break curfew, the may lose their jobs and be deported, or have a bad morals notation in their files. If they are in danger of breaking curfew, most women find it is better to stay out all night and come in the next morning.

Some Western women are unaware of the problems faced by fellow females. Author Summer Scott Huyette, sat in her lovely home and called women who complained about Saudis ignorant. She never had any problems with Saudis. Her husband, a former Citibanker, had status and high income. Summer had a driver, a maid, and powerful friends. She was isolated from the mainstream of either Western expatriate life, (which is light years above Third World expatriate life) or lower middle class Saudi life. She dealt with ministers, not bedouin. She never had the experience of an Egyptian American friend who, properly garbed, was walking alone in the souk when a Saudi grabbed her buttocks. She turned around and slapped him. He punched her in the mouth.

CONCLUSION

The Saudis have a saying, "Every man is a prince." Unfortunately, the Saudis have too many princes and not enough workers. The same wealth that made development possible, gave the Saudis the luxury to indulge these attitudes. In the meantime, seeds of bitterness are being sown among many foreigners over their treatment in the Kingdom. Iraqi propaganda feeds on that resentment.

Saudis are hurt and angered by what they consider an ungrateful attitude by foreigners who earned good money in the Kingdom. Expatriates often leave angry over broken promises, religious oppression, and deliberate isolation from the Saudi culture. There are many who love Saudi Arabia and its people, but they tend to be from the upper echelons of society, where they are insulated from the problems faced by the vast majority of Third World workers. The bitterness is a sad commentary on a nation which has given so many people a chance to earn good incomes and which has, at the same time, derived great benefits from the labor of these people.

But, there are just too many men whose sweat dried before they were paid, and up until now, there are too few Saudis willing to take those men's places. This is a problem that will worsen as growing numbers of young Saudis graduate from school. Sure, oil supplies will last another 100 years, but what of the Saudi people? Their role is far from established.

9

PETROLEUM

"Let us let those countries that are expanding their production flood the markets. They may have this temporary satisfaction, and then their resources will be exhausted and they will leave the market to us for a long time to come....It is not the Seventies that are the Golden Age for Arab oil, rather we expect that it will be in the nineties...," Oil Minister Ahmed Zaki Yamani [1]

"There is no Saudi grand design to exercise arbitrary control on oil output or prices..." Oil Minister Hisham Nazer. [2]

Iraqi tanks did in 24 hours what Saudi oil policy failed to achieve during the decade of the Eighties: it boosted prices AND Saudi oil production. Spot prices hit $40 per barrel (bbl) and production increased from the OPEC quota of 5.58 million barrels per day (mbd) to over 7.5 mbd. In dollar terms, daily Saudi oil revenue nearly doubled to $262.5 million.

Before the invasion, Fahad vainly sought a formula that would increase his production and, at the same time, secure higher prices. Former oil minister Ahmed Zaki Yamani argued that Fahad sought the impossible, and was eventually sacked because of the policy's failure. Yamani's replacement, Hisham Nazer, fared no better on world oil markets, but had a defter political touch with Fahad, and retained his job.

Yamani, known to world as "Mr. OPEC" was a realist. In 1979, after spot oil prices hit $39 bbl, he told journalists and disbelieving Saudi students that, the Kingdom's production would fall from 10 mbd to below 4 mbd by the end of 1981. Spot prices soon edged slightly over $40 a bbl, but by mid-1981, prices fell to the $32-36 bbl range. OPEC tried to cut production, but Iran and Iraq pumped more crude to support their war. Nigeria and Iran quietly offered $4 per barrel discounts. The October OPEC meeting agreed on a price freeze of $34 per barrel until the end of 1982, but could not agree on a target quota of 18.5 mbd. They ended up with a quota, (excluding the Saudis) of 23.5 mbd. Yamani argued, as he always did, that higher prices discouraged consumption.

Eventually, the Kingdom agreed to OPEC's plan to cut production to prop up prices. The Saudis became the swing producer who lowered production during low demand periods, and made up the difference when demand picked up. In practice, when the Saudis cut production as planned, Nigeria, Iran, and others increased output and cut prices. After OPEC agreed to cut prices to $29 during March, 1983, Nigeria soon secretly offered discounts of $3. Saudi oil production swung lower and oil prices kept falling. Meanwhile, oil barter deals, such as the Kingdom's $1 billion deal for Boeing jumbo jets, put increasing amounts of crude on the market.

Saudi production fell to 2.3 mbd and the Kingdom was feeling the economic strain when Yamani persuaded Fahad to strike back. To avoid the onus of breaking prices, Yamani created netback pricing in August of 1985. Netback deals essentially guaranteed the buyer a profit by taking into account market value of refined products, and subtracting transportation and refining costs.

The price war lasted nearly nine months, and knocked prices from $27 bbl to around $10 bbl. Saudis liked the new tougher policy on OPEC cheaters, but foreigners did not. Then Vice

President George Bush visited the Kingdom and voiced U.S. concern. The Iranians made threatening noises, claiming the price war was was aimed at them, since the Saudis and Kuwaitis made up the shortfall of Iraq's revenue. Iran had no allies with deep pockets to turn to.

The Iranians confined their attacks to Yamani, whom Fahad used as a convenient scapegoat. The King ordered his minister to secure a higher price AND a higher quota at the October 1986, OPEC meeting; Yamani, predictably, failed. He learned via Saudi television that he was sacked on Oct. 29, 1986. The oil price war was over.

Yamani privately bemoaned Fahad's premature termination of the price war because it should have lasted six more months to obtain lasting benefits. He said oil prices had to remain under $15 bbl for an entire year to kill off all alternative energy programs, and end further exploration for new sources of oil. Yamani's scenario may have been wrong after all. One economist, Dr. Michael D. Williams, argues that due to the price war, costs for exploration and drilling actually declined relative to the price of oil. The price war bankrupted many exploration firms that then auctioned off equipment at ten cents on the dollar. The number of drilling rigs remained the same, but now cost their owners one- tenth as much to buy. Further, technological advances reduced some of the other expenses associated with exploration. Williams says that Yamani could have achieved his aims only if oil fell to, and remained at, $2-$3 per bbl.

Post-Yamani oil policy is more tailored to domestic needs, because Fahad is more concerned with problems at home than those abroad. His dismissal of Yamani proves Saudi oil ministers do not "make" policy; kings do. The ministers try to sell their monarch a program, but let him make his decisions himself. Saudi oil strategy has not changed much since the first oil minister, Abdullah Tariki, argued for national control of oil prices, and the establishment of OPEC. His radical tendencies and aggressive behavior eventually earned the enmity of Faisal. He fled the country, returning decades later, partially broken, unrewarded after playing such an important role in the Kingdom's oil development.

Yamani, his successor, engineered the nationalization of Aramco, and sought a stable oil market with a fair share for the Kingdom, and reasonable profits for everyone. This attitude, shared by others, made Saudi oil policy conciliatory toward the West. They saw no point in damaging the world economy for short-term profits. During a May 24, 1977 Washington visit, Fahad said, "Oil will not be used as a weapon," and pledged to help the U.S. build a 6-month strategic petroleum reserve. The only beneficiary at the time appeared to be the United States, which would then have a cushion against any future oil embargoes. Fahad was criticized at home and in the Arab world, but it turned out that the millions of barrels he sold to the Americans were, up until the Iraqi invasion, worth less than half the price the U.S. paid for them.

The Minister of Planning, Hisham Nazer, replaced Yamani, but not his oil policies. The biggest change involves style. Nazer has proven more adroit than his predecessor in dealing with Fahad. He wisely took the King's nephew, Prince Abdulaziz bin Salman, as a protege. The Monarch wanted more of a role in oil policy than Yamani was willing to concede and resented it when Yamani overruled him during Faisal's reign and, in effect, forgot that he was a mere commoner. Yamani's only hope is that Abdullah becomes king, and restores him to his ministry.

Most oilmen subscribe to the idea that Yamani excited royal envy by being seen as the "leader" of Saudi Arabia by the Western world. Nazer has always kept a much lower profile than his predecessor. Nazer lets Fahad make mistakes in oil policy, assuming, correctly, that the King is a fast learner. Nazer acquiesced to Fahad's decision to assume (unofficially and very quietly) the role of swing producer for a short period of time. When that proved counterproductive, the King moved back toward a market share strategy. The 4th quarter of 1988 was another rough spot, due to cheating. Fahad told Nazer to put pressure on OPEC by raising production above 6 mbd.

OIL IS WHAT IT'S CRACKED TO BE

Too often, the public treats oil as if it is a "special" commodity subject to its own laws of supply and demand. This is not so. Oil is composed of hydrocarbons, the same sort of molecules that make up not only coal and gas, but our living tissues as well. It is the raw material for wax candles, Kevlar bullet proof vests, or fiberglass surfboards. If it is burned, it provides energy for heating or transportation.

Petroleum comes out of the ground as a mixture of light and heavy hydrocarbons. The lighter types form gasolines. The heavier ones might be wax, or tar. Heavy crudes have proportionally more of the thick ingredients, such as asphalt, while lighter crudes have more of the lighter products such as gasoline, per barrel.

These hydrocarbons can be broken apart and reassembled. A "Cracker" breaks apart the heavier materials into lighter hydrocarbons. Suitable technology can do the same thing with coal, the way the Germans did during WW II. Other technology can combine lighter hydrocarbons into more complicated molecule chains, such as those found in plastics.

Oil is replaceable, either directly, by turning coal into gasoline, or indirectly, by burning coal instead of oil. Nuclear power, solar energy, hydroelectricity, or coal can generate electricity. Energy conservation cuts petroleum use. Drive less. Turn more lights off, use thicker insulation, and build more efficient machines. By 1989, passenger jets were 30 percent more efficient than they were during the Seventies. A 1990 American five-liter V-8 car gets nearly the same mileage that a 1.6 liter Volkswagen achieved in 1970. Higher fuel prices meant better-insulated houses and more efficient heating and power generating systems.

Replacing oil DOES take time and money. It takes years to build nuclear power plants, dams, and coal plants. It also takes time for people to replace gas-guzzling cars with efficient sub-compacts. Airlines and shipowners can't retire their fleets overnight. Finding and extracting oil is expensive and time-consuming.

This means that classical economics of supply and demand suffer a time lag in oil. On a temporary basis, demand for oil seems inelastic. By this, the economists mean that you can raise the price tremendously without affecting demand much. People need oil, can't easily use something else, and therefore pay the extra cost.

But the opposite is also true. Once demand falls, it is hard to boost it quickly, even with radical price cuts. No matter how low oil prices are, nobody will rip insulation out of his roof. More energy-efficient machines will continue to be used.

This explains why the oil glut was not retribution on evil price hikers, or (as some Middle Eastern conspiracy lovers believe) the result of a plot by the industrialized countries. It was the result of simple economics. Once prices rose to a certain level, people conserved, and switched to new energy sources.

High prices encouraged oil companies to develop new oil supplies. Countries from Angola to Yemen began exporting oil. Drilling crews braved the icy North Sea and Alaska's North Slope to exploit new fields. Technology squeezed additional barrels out of "exhausted" wells in Texas.

More oil hit smaller, more efficient markets and prices fell. The United States shifted its buying to its neighbors, Canada and Mexico. This should not let Americans feel complacent about the Middle East. If Middle East crude stopped flowing, where would the Europeans and Japanese go? They would turn to Mexico and Canada, and start bidding up prices. This is precisely what occurred during the panic following Iraq's invasion of Kuwait.

Aramco released news of new oil finds to emphasize the point that the Kingdom could keep such production levels up. OPEC temporarily fell back in line.

NEW CONCERNS

Though OPEC is important, Fahad has re-oriented oil policy from an international to a national focus because, even if the Kingdom has limited control over the world oil market, it must try to ensure it receives a reasonable income. Fahad knows that low oil revenues cause domestic trouble. This explains moves made to guarantee a market for Saudi oil production and to streamline and improve the domestic hydrocarbon industry.

Fahad's concern with domestic oil policy was a factor in choosing Nazer. He worked with Nazer in creating the industrial cities of Yanbu and Jubail, and knew Nazer shared his interests. Nazer announced his agenda soon after Fahad confirmed him in his new position.

Nazer announced he would reorganize the domestic hydrocarbon industry, consisting of Aramco, the oil producer, Petromin (General Organization for Petroleum and Minerals), which is responsible for refined products, mining, and Liquified Petroleum Gas (LPG) sales, and the Saudi Basic Industries Corp. (SABIC). SABIC uses hydrocarbons as feedstock to produce petrochemicals, fertilizer, and plastics.

REORGANIZATION

Nazer approached reorganization carefully, using a study prepared by Arthur D. Little. All he wanted to do with Aramco was finish nationalizing it. Petromin was a greater priority because it was disorganized. Petromin's Governor, Abdul Hadi Taher guided the company through the hectic expansion of its first 25 years. Petromin made the country practically self-sufficient in lubricants, and nearly so in refined petroleum products.

Critics claim Taher was made wealthy by Petromin and say corruption was responsible. Like his boss, Yamani, he ended his career worth millions of dollars. Both men say their business acumen, plus royal gifts of land accounted for most of their wealth. Taher's career ended soon after Yamani's, but he was allowed to retire, "forcibly," he said.

"We were in the entrepreneural stage," Taher said, explaining the disorganization that beset Petromin. It handled all hydrocarbon-related industries until SABIC was formed. In fact, the first SABIC company, SAFCO, was started as part of Petromin.

At the time of Taher's retirement, Petromin consisted of over 20 firms, each of which operated independently. Petromin operated one lubricant base oil refinery, three domestic refineries, three joint venture export refineries, two joint venture lubricant blending plants, and one wholly-owned lubricant blending operation. Petromin made state-to-state crude oil deals using expertise gained marketing princely crude, and handled LPG sales to foreigners, and sales of gas to SABIC companies. Petromin's best profits were earned by sending crude abroad for refining, and re-importing it.

Many Petromin projects were profitable, but some were losers. The Petrola-Petromin Refinery at Rabigh, which began as a deal between the secretive Greek Financier John Latsis and Fahad was over 3 years behind schedule, plagued by bad planning and construction delays. It is Petromin's largest refinery, with a capacity of 325,000 bpd, but is, well, "primitive." Each barrel of oil run through Rabigh produces mostly fuel oil, which was selling in the eighties for almost less than crude oil. The Mobil and Shell joint venture refineries use sophisticated technology to produce "slates" that emphasize lighter, more profitable petroleum products such as gasoline. Petromin has since demanded additional units to improve Rabigh's slate of products.

"We felt that if things fell apart, Petrola is not, let us say, the equal (in complexity) of the joint venture refineries with Mobil or Shell," Taher said. "...We ourselves did not feel comfortable with taking the burden of a refinery so complex. We always played the game that if nobody wants to participate with us, then we can do it on our own; maybe not do it as big, but still do it alone."

Another embarrassment was the 1,200 km East West Petroline when Aramco was awarded management of the Petromin project. Taher says that once an expensive management contract with Mobil ended, Petromin did not have the internal capability to take over. Aramco, which already tends the parallel gas line, was awarded management.

After its capacity was raised to 4.8 mbd, throughput was barely 2 mbd until Iran and Iraq began bombing each others' tankers. That conflict proved the strategic soundness of the project. It allowed the Saudis to ship oil from the Red Sea, and locate industries on two different coasts. Iraq thought it was such a good idea, that it hooked a 500,000 bpd spur onto the Petroline, and then built an additional parallel line. These pipelines were turned off by the Saudis after the Kuwaiti invasion only with United Nations approval.

REORGANIZATION

Nazer decided Petromin's inefficiency was unaffordable during the oil downturn. Earlier, in 1985, financial troubles forced Petromin to cancel the Ashuqaiq and Qassim refinery projects. Reports said that cancellation penalties for the Qassim refinery were so high, Petromin could have finished it to a lower specification for the same amount as the penalties. Taher disagrees. Although towers, vessels, and pipes were on order, they were not yet delivered. As to cancellation penalties, all he says is that they were considerable. Nazer found a need for greater cuts. Nine months into the reorganization, a high level official admitted that none of the dead wood had been trimmed off, but "At least we now know how many we have, and what they are supposed to be doing." Petromin retained its LPG business, but handed crude sales to Aramco. Nazer then broke Petromin into three divisions: Saudi Arabian Marketing and Refining Corp. (SAMARC), Petrolube, and a vaguely defined Minerals Division.

SAMARC absorbed every refinery except the Petromin Mobil joint venture lubricant base oil refinery, Luberef I. Petrolube was originally a 71-29 joint venture with Mobil. It blended lubricants for Petromin, Mobil, and 9 other companies, using the base oils supplied by Luberef I. Before the reorganization took place, Petrolube had built Petrolube I in Jeddah, and Petrolube II in Riyadh. A planned Petrolube III in the Eastern province was scrapped. Instead, Petrolube bought out the new wholly-Petromin owned Jubail Saudi Lubricating Oil Co. (JSLOC) plant in Jubail. It was the first plant in the Kingdom to make grease as well as oil. Petromark, a marketing company, was also absorbed into Petrolube, in which Mobil continues to hold a 29 percent share. Luberef's integration has been stalled over disagreement on the value of Mobil's shares in the refinery.

The reorganization made an oil-glut casualty of a planned sister plant to Luberef I, Luberef II. It had once reached the stage where Chiyoda Petrostar had done engineering design on the plant. However, economic considerations forced cancellation. Chiyoda Petrostar, which was said to have close connections with Taher and Yamani, offered the Saudis a good deal to complete it in 1988, but continuing falls in oil prices killed it.[3] To increase the amount of base oil production, Petromin will debottleneck Luberef I. They estimate that this will boost production by 30 percent, to around 1.9 mbd, or enough to be completely self- sufficient.

Because Petrolube is profitable, the government wants to privatize it. By early 1989, the company had already printed up share documents. But even if it goes public, privatizing the rest of Petromin will have to wait. Petromin sources say that it will be impossible to privatize SAMARC, because it depends upon government subsidies to make a profit. Petromin's mining activities will be spun off, possibly as a shared government-private sector company. Nazer is creating a passive holding company out of Taher's independent empire.

ARAMCO

Although the Arabian American Oil Company (Aramco) was "nationalized" in the Seventies, the final paperwork had never been finished, and this hobbled efforts to buy Texaco's assets in the United States. This prompted Nazer to officially finish the deal that Yamani had made more than a decade earlier. Papers were filed to complete the legal transformation of the Delaware-based corporation into Saudi Aramco.

Once it was nearly complete, the Saudis astounded the world by announcing they paid $812 million for a 50 percent stake in Texaco, including three modern refineries, 1,400 Texaco stations, and 10,000 franchised stations in a 23 state area. The deal is an insurance policy during periods of low oil demand. When crude prices are low, refineries make better profits. The Texaco retail outlets provide a permanent market for 00,000 bpd of crude.[4]

"Yamani felt that downstream was the right policy, but that the nation had to solve its OPEC relationships first. It had a shortage of people, and budgetary priorities were such that it was not the time to commit money to such a venture," one oilman said. Nazer examined the success enjoyed by Kuwait, which moved downstream in Europe. He wanted a strategic acquisition in a major market, such as the United States, Europe, or the Far East. With the low dollar, American firms looked most tempting. Texaco, crippled by a $11 billion court judgement in favor of Pennzoil, was fighting off corporate raider Carl Icahn and was vulnerable.

Aramco, or more properly, Saudi Aramco, continues to explore for, and produce crude oil. Though Nazer is changing little at the firm, it is evolving from its days as an American enclave. Women were specifically granted the right to drive within the Aramco compound by King Abdulaziz. Unlike the rest of Saudi Arabia, the homes were not surrounded by walls. Green lawns, softball fields, and mixed schools made Aramco's compound seem more like San Diego from the early Sixties than Saudi Arabia in the Eighties. Aramco made other unheard of concessions to its American workers. Because many of the oilmen were in danger of going blind by producing moonshine, Aramco produced a small booklet on distillation entitled "The Blue Flame." One litigious American was arrested for selling alcohol (in strict violation of policy) and is suing his former employers. Gradually, more restrictions have been imposed on Americans working and living on the Aramco compound. In 1989, the pork ration was ended. The women's right to drive looked endangered, but is hardly likely to end now that American female soldiers are tooling around in jeeps. One can assume that an inevitable religious crackdown has been delayed as well.

When the oil glut began to bite, Aramco was straining to produce 10 mbd. Its first reaction was to slow down all exploration efforts, and resort to simple wellhead maintenance. Later, in 1987, the firm was granted a revised charter to explore outside of its original concession area. This is what led to finding a new oil field at Al-Hawtah, 190 km south of Riyadh. The new oil fields have increased Saudi reserves by 20 percent, and reduce the nation's absolute dependence upon the Eastern Province for oil. The new discoveries mean the prospect of the Kingdom running out of oil has become even more remote. At a 5 mbd production rate, the Saudis can pump oil for over 150 years.

The reduced activity of the oil glut led to personnel reductions. The number of Americans Kingdomwide declined from a high of 75,000 (most of whom worked for Aramco) to about 30,000. Saudis have replaced many Americans. Ali Naim became the first Saudi to head the company. Aramco's Saudi executives tend to be higher quality than their compatriots in other high positions because many had to work their way up the ladder at Aramco. In many ways, Aramco was the first Saudi university, for its alumni serve throughout the Kingdom in government, business, and industry.

Aramco also did well by the despised Shia, who, having no social standing to begin with, were less reluctant to undertake low-level jobs for the company than their Sunni compatriots. Aramco also employed Saudi women as engineers and analysts. But this promising start has not been maintained, because of increased conservatism.

At first, it was assumed that Aramco would be broken up and incorporated in Nazer's vision of a National Oil Company. It appears at this point that Aramco is the National Oil Company he was talking about, and has survived intact.

SABIC AND THE MASTER GAS SYSTEM

SABIC will be discussed more thoroughly in the chapter dealing with industry, yet, briefly, we can say SABIC was the offspring of a Petromin-inspired project, the Master Gas Collection System. The collection system was built at a cost of $20 billion to provide gas for industrial use. The gas also powers the big desalination and power generating plants. Taher said the only barrier to building it was the cost of gas. Once prices rose, the gas system was built.

The lighter Arabian crudes occur in the ground mixed with natural gas. When crude is pumped out of the ground, the gas must be separated. Before the collection system was built, the only option was to burn the gas, called a "flare off." It was a terrible waste. Thus, the collection system was a triumph for efficient use of natural resources and for a cleaner environment. "Before they built it, if you drove to Dhahran at night, you saw the desert lit up by all of these flares, burning orange in the darkness," one long-time resident told me. "There were so many burnt hydrocarbons in the air, that the atmosphere was hazy. At sunset, you never really saw the sun hit the horizon because of the haze. Today, it is much, much clearer."

During 1985 and 1986, Yamani excused his floating storage plan as a method of ensuring oil production stayed over a certain level. If production of Arabia light slipped too far, he said, associated gas production would be insufficient to provide for petrochemical, power and fresh water needs. Most of this was untrue. The low production did make it difficult to fulfill LPG contracts, but sources said it was unlikely production would slip low enough to endanger the domestic supply of gas. After the Khuff non-associated gas field came on line in the mid- eighties, then the danger was nil.

However, the tanker storage was part of a bigger strategy. The gross worldwide oversupply of supertankers made it cheaper to rent tankers than to build storage tanks. Floating storage gave Yamani oil already pumped and ready to move onto markets, and was a gun to the heads of other producers. All Yamani had to do was radio instructions to a tanker captain, and the oil would be on its way.

MINING

Although oil gets all the glamor, King Abdulaziz signed a gold mining agreement before he signed an oil concession. The Ministry of Petroleum and Minerals says that non-petroleum mineral wealth will make an important contribution to the Kingdom. Though some deposits are large, and may be commercially viable, experts and banking officials believe mining activity will be limited. Mines require new infrastructure and ore processing often uses prodigious amounts of water. Manpower is another bottleneck.

The most promising Saudi mines are the gold mines at Mahd Adh- Dhahab, and Sukhaybarat. The best-known of the two is Mahd Ad Dhahab, said to be King Solomon's mines. There is evidence of intermittent mining activity for several thousand years. The mine has an estimated life of 12-15 years, producing roughly 2.8 tons of gold per year from 120,000 tons of mined ore.

The most promising other discoveries are large deposits of zinc, copper, and iron, but world metals prices are depressed. Low revenues mean the Saudis will find it hard to justify the huge expenditures required by mine development. Further, Saudi deposits tend to be either large, with low-grade ore, or small, with high-grade ore.

The iron deposit at Wadi Sawawin, about 340 miles northeast of Medina may have 300 million tons of low-grade ore, to supply the Saudi Iron and Steel Co.(HADEED) iron smelters in Jubail. Although preliminary ore extraction has taken place, development slowed down significantly after oil revenues plunged. As early as 1985, most additional mineral exploration was put on hold due to budgetary problems.

Other important discoveries include coal, though the abundance of oil makes it unlikely the coal will be mined. The Ghurayyah deposit near Wadi Sawawin contains large amounts of tantalum, columbium, tin, and uranium. A report by Watts, Griffis, and McQuat says Ghurayyah could add 34 percent to the world's identified tantalum deposits, and 8 percent to columbium. A zinc deposit at Umm Ash Shalahib was being developed by Shell Minerals Exploration, but has been abandoned. Shell decided the mine would not be commercially feasible.

In 1989, new mining permits were granted for raw magnesium near Zirghat, 160 kilometers southwest of Hail. Estimated reserves are 4.5 million tons of ore. Another possible magnesium mine may be near Jabal Al-Rukham, 190 kms southeast of Medina. Some 12 million tons of ore have been found there.

One of the more promising mining areas lies on the floor of the Red Sea. The Jeddah-based Saudi-Sudanese Red Sea Joint Commission has performed tests that indicated ocean-bed mud-pumping extraction can yield commercial quantities of copper, zinc, cobalt, and silver.

Stone quarrying has the best potential. Granite is quarried near Taif, Yanbu, and Medina. Limestone is quarried near Riyadh. Government "buy local" contract requirements has spurred use of Saudi stone, but fewer contracts (victims of lower oil revenue) and the Saudi preference for imported decorative stone has not helped.

The major use of Saudi minerals probably lies in quarrying material for Saudi cement plants. Thus, more gold is earned digging sand and lime than in mining gold itself.

10

INDUSTRY

"...We naturally regret these new and more aggressive attempts to control the amount of SABIC exports to the EC," SABIC Managing Director Ibrahim Salamah upon learning of stricter EC duties on SABIC petrochemicals.

A reporter was taken to see Riyadh's new Wooden Door factory while its expatriate manager touted it as another Saudi industrial success. Its modern machinery and disciplined workforce churned out quality, tasteful products. Certain questions surfaced. Since the Kingdom has no timber industry, does it use any domestic materials? No. Even the glues are imported. Does the factory employ Saudi workers? Excluding an executive, no. Managers were Americans, and the workers were Thai. Does the factory make a profit? Yes, if one discounted the fact that it was built on government-provided land using subsidized loans, or that it depends upon subsidized electricity and water.

The last question, "what's the point?" concerns the value of the Kingdom's industrialization policy. Fifteen years of oil revenues took the country from rudimentary crafts to petrochemical industries. Industry was expected to reduce dependence upon oil exports, reduce manufactured imports, and provide jobs. Saudi businessmen approached industrialization with enthusiasm, but most have the traditional Saudi merchant mentality. They look for quick returns and prefer making deals to making products. Lower oil revenues revealed that Saudi industry became, not self-reliant, but addicted to government subsidies and imported labor.

The Kingdom's most successful industries are capital-intensive, use domestic raw materials, and require relatively few workers. Refined oil products, Petrochemicals, and cement fit in this category. yet, just when the government is seeking increased foreign and domestic investment in such ventures, its policies, combined with the oil downturn, have made this more difficult. The crisis in bank lending has hampered long-term financing. The Saudi Industrial Development Fund (SIDF) has tightened its low-cost credit unless the borrower has the right "connections." Stock market policies make it more difficult to float new offerings or to trade existing shares. Bureaucratic regulations hamper licensing, registration of new firms, and securing visas for workers and executives. Skilled Saudi manpower is in short supply, yet employers are pressured to increase the percentage of Saudi workers. Profitable joint ventures get taxed in Saudi Arabia and at home, because the Kingdom has not signed double-taxation treaties with many of its trading partners.

OFFSET INVESTMENT

The Peace Shield Offset Investment is one project that should have avoided bureaucratic pitfalls. American companies were ranged agaisnt eachother to build the Command, Control Communications, and Intelligence (C3I) system that tied the Kingdom's new AWACS jets into a unified air defense system. Since the 30 percent rule had recently been promulgated, Saudis thought that, somehow, a percentage of the big defense contract should go to local firms, and therefore, help offset the overall decrease in government projects. The Offset Program, designed to promote high technology investment by the winners of the contract, was labeled a national priority. A high-powered Offset Investment Committee was formed, headed by Prince Fahad bin Abdullah bin Mohammed. The joint ventures were offered Saudi Industrial Development Fund (SIDF) loans, tax holidays, and all the usual subsidies.

The program started in 1983 when the government told bidders for the $3.94 billion defense project that they would have to invest a percentage of the contract award in Saudi-based joint ventures. The Peace Shield contract winners, Boeing and Westinghouse, formed the Boeing Industrial Technology Group, (BITG). BITG and General Electric, which won the radar contract worth several hundred million dollars, agreed to establish several ventures. By 1990, none of the proposed companies had started production. Only one had even moved into a building.

The joint ventures were mostly aviation-oriented. The Saudi Propulsion Center (SPC) is a jet engine overhaul center. Pratt & Whitney and General Electric of the United States are expected to participate with Saudia, National Industrialization Company (NIC) and Gulf Investment Corporation (GIC) in the project. If Rolls Royce enters the project, it means all of Saudia Airline's jet engine suppliers will be involved. Rolls Royce also supplies engines to other regional airlines and to the Tornado fighters.

Other ventures are an airframe maintenance center, an avionics electronics maintenance center, and an aircraft hydraulics and subsystems maintenance center. These will be built at King Khaled International Airport. The Advanced Electronics Center, (AEC) is buying up to $300-$400 million worth of military radio kits over a ten-year period from Racal. Racal is supplying AEC with design and manufacturing technology. Computer Science Corp, a joint venture partner in the consortium, pulled out of a proposed computer software joint venture, leaving Boeing to fill the gap. Other investments include bioengineering, and medical products.

The Americans stumbled over red tape in securing licenses from the Ministry of Industry and Electricity and commercial registrations from the Ministry of Commerce. The SIDF was slow in approving loans. The firms even had problems getting permission to move into their industrial park. The government refused to promise business to the Offset ventures, even though Royal Saudi Air Force contracts are required to guarantee success. BITG discovered a dearth of market information. The Ministry of Labor concealed the high cost of Saudi labor and the scarcity of qualified Saudi workers.

Finally, Saudi businessmen preferred talking about the program to investing in it. Saudi Advanced Industries Company (SAIC), was established to provide smaller businessmen a vehicle for investing in Offset, but the flotation had to be extended, and considerable government pressure applied, before the SR100 million ($26.7 million) offering was successful. However, the private sector National Industrialization Co. (NIC) has taken shares in some projects.

The British have an even harder time ahead of them. When Sultan signed the first Al-Yamamah contract worth $7.5 billion, he grandly announced that it would be subject to an offset program. This played well in the Kingdom, but the British, caught unawares, were astonished. An Offset Investment clause was not included in the arms deal contract, and Thatcher's government could not legally coerce British Aerospace into cooperating. The British dithered until a figure for investment was reached. The Saudis dropped their insistence that all the Anglo-Saudi joint ventures be high tech, and the British grudgingly agreed to invest nearly $1.5 billion. If BITG had problems finding decent investments for $500 million, one can imagine the difficulties facing the British as they comb through the leftovers to find profitable ventures for three times that amount. If the Saudis expect offset investment on the second Al-Yamamah contract, valued at $15 billion, the problem becomes mind-boggling. Sources say the British could offer to co-produce part of the 90-helicopter deal with Westland, and possibly build a petrochemical plant to fulfill their offset investment obligations.

JOINT VENTURES

If the Offset Investment companies ran into such problems despite abundant official backing, then what of lesser joint ventures? The government has tried to bludgeon unwilling foreigners into joint ventures, but most have demurred. A great deal of pressure was applied to the Japanese to build a pickup truck factory in the Kingdom. The Japanese replied that they see more investment potential in the United States, Asia or Eastern Europe than the Middle East. The local market is considered too small, though the Saudis argue that 7 million affluent Saudis and 17 million GCC residents constitutes a viable market. They used to throw in 9 million Yemenis, 27 million Iraqis, and 50 million Egyptians as additional markets, but the Kuwait invasion has upset those calculations.

When a foreigner decides to invest, he encounters other hurdles. His proposed petrochemical plant cannot get the required license from the Ministry of Industry, because the government-owned Saudi Basic Industries Corp. (SABIC) holds it, has not used it, and still refuses to relinquish it. Commercial registration and industrial licensing drag on, sometimes because a prince wants a piece of the action or the proposed venture will compete with an official's relative. Dr. Abdul Rahman Al-Zamil, the energetic deputy Minister of Commerce disputes this, and says his office quickly processes applications.

Foreigners complain that they are prey to Saudi commercial hostage-taking. Visa approval is glacial, even though Saudis easily gain entrance to other countries. There is no protection for technology. The Kingdom was long known as a pirating paradise, and only recently passed rudimentary copyright protection. Customs slows down shipments of necessary supplies. A company has no guarantee that prices on subsidized electricity, water, rents, and feedstock won't be arbitrarily hiked.

The one organization expected to champion better business conditions, the Chambers of Commerce and Industry, has come under fire by its own members because its poor performance. The Chambers are quasi-governmental bodies that regulate most day-to- day functioning of the business community. The Chamber provides Saudi businessmen a collective voice. Several nation-wide conferences have been held by the Chamber, and many of their recommendations were adopted, including: lower port fees to encourage exports, a publicly-held firm to promote industrial exports, and a 1983 regulation requiring that 30 percent of every government contract to go to Saudi firms. The 30 percent requirement can be met by either buying materials locally, or sharing the contract with local Saudi firms. The Ministry of Industry also holds trade exhibitions to showcase Saudi output, and supported extension of some tax holidays.

The biggest problem, and the one least amenable to government intervention, is the scarcity of Saudi manpower. The Iraq invasion underscored this weakness. Though the government subsidizes training programs, industries are hard-pressed to hire locals because Saudis cannot afford to live at the wages paid to a Bangladeshi worker.

A firm has to consider the following before it builds a plant in the Kingdom and hires Thai workers to operate it. The cmopany would not only save on construction costs by building the factory in Thailand; it would save on labor, since it is less expensive to pay Thais local wages than fly them to the Kingdom, provide room and board, and pay them higher salaries. This labor problem undercuts all Saudi industry, but has its heaviest impact on manufacturing. Lastly, Thailand has a bigger market (approximately 50 million) than the Kingdom.

REFINING AND LUBRICANTS

Lubricant manufacture is the most successful Saudi industriy because it is capital intensive, uses local raw materials, and has a large domestic market. The Kingdom was in the embarrassing position of having to import refined products until Aramco established the first refinery at Ras Tanura to supply the Kingdom's needs. Subsequent investment in Petromin refineries and lubricant plants continued the path of downstream industrialization.

By 1990, the Kingdom was self-sufficient in most refined products, particularly in lubricants. Saudi lubricant manufacturers dominates the large domestic market. One reason the market is so large is that Saudi automobile owners change oil every 2,000 kilometers. Saudi lubricant manufacturers export their surplus throughout the region, and meet all international standards. Petromin has even moved into grease manufacture. The size of the domestic market has created a demand for downstream suppliers. Exxon built a factory to supply lubricant additives. Another factory makes steel drums. One firm has even been established to recycle used oil.

While the quasi-governmental Petromin-Mobil joint venture dominates, private joint ventures involving Shell, Total, and Gulf, compete in blending and marketing lubricants. The three largest-selling brands are Petromin, Shell, and Mobil. Shell's diesel engine oil has so dominated the market that truck drivers call any diesel engine oil by Shell's brandname, "Rotella."

SABIC

The best-known of the Kingdom's export-oriented industries is SABIC. It was established to build the primary industrial base for further Saudi development. It suffered during the oil downturn because low oil prices eroded its cost advantage vis a vis the Europeans. European petrochemical plants use the naphtha by-product from refining operations as feedstock. SABIC uses natural gas. Cheap oil means cheap naphtha, and therefore, more competitive prices for European petrochemicals.

On top of this, the Europeans, Americans, and Japanese erected tariff barriers against SABIC petrochemicals, plastics, fertilizer and steel. The Saudis and their GCC brethren bitterly protested since they allow foreign products to enter their countries virtually duty-free. Of course, the GCC disingenuously neglected to mention its own protective duties of 20 percent on cement, steel cables, and on several other domestically-produced industrial goods. "They always like to say they are a developed country until it comes to trade talks," complained one U.S. diplomat. "Then it becomes, 'You ought to give us a special break because we are a developing country.' I'm sorry, but if you look at their per capita income, they are living a lot better than many 'Developed' countries such as Greece."

As of this writing, the GCC and EC are holding trade talks, and have not resolved the tariff problem, nor, for that matter, the lesser issues of economic hostages and political and religious rights. SABIC products ran into American tariffs after a 1986 lawsuit filed by small steel producers against SABIC's Hadeed Iron and Steel, after a small 10,000 ton shipment. The verdict was that SABIC is subsidized more than other Saudi industries because its low-cost Public Investment Fund (PIF) loans cover 60 percent of a project while the SIDF loans to other industries only cover half.

SABIC's cautious entry into the world chemical market won an apologetic editorial from *Chemical Week* about its earlier alarmist stance on SABIC. "Quite clearly, the Saudis, and others in the Mideast, had been aiming at becoming respected players and partners in the world chemical game from the outset. And quite frankly, why anyone would have thought otherwise, I find troublesome," wrote editor Patrick McCurdy.[1]

SABIC's entrance was cushioned by increased world demand for plastics. American and Japanese complaints are muted because many of the sales in those countries were handled by joint venture partners. To head off European criticism, European partners were sought for a Methyl Tertiary Butyl Ether (MTBE) plant. The Italians and Finns were brought into the SABIC family. MTBE is an octane-enhancing compound used in unleaded gasolines and is aimed almost entirely at export markets. SABIC now plans to establish plants in Europe to overcome export barriers, although this hardly helps to establish a basic industrial base in the Kingdom. SABIC downplays its exports' impact on world markets because it accounts for only a small portion of total world production. Since SABIC exports a greater percentage of its output than most companies, it affects markets more than the firm admits.

Sabic's first company, the Saudi Arabian Fertilizer Co. (SAFCO), was established in 1970 by Petromin, to convert associated natural gas to make urea fertilizer. SAFCO's serious teething problems taught the Saudis that foreign partners are needed for operation and marketing. SABIC was capitalized with SR10 billion and incorporated in 1976. It absorbed SAFCO, Jeddah Steel Rolling Mill (Sulb) and Hadeed Iron and Steel. The steel firms were initially economic flops, but have done well recently. SABIC has even expanded Hadeed's capacity. The success is deceptive. Hadeed prospers because it sells in a protected market, produces steel using heavily subsidized energy, and is provided with bulk material conveyors to and from the port. Saudi planners hope to use Saudi iron ore in the future. At present, the plant makes do with imported ore, and at long last, the Kingdom's abundant supply of wrecked cars. In a related development, Saudi investors are ignoring the relatively poor profits from Bahrain's aluminum smelter and want to build a 214,000 ton per year aluminum smelter in Yanbu. Without government-subsidized energy, the smelter could not survive.

SABIC and Petromin enticed foreign partners with oil "entitlements." Multi-national firms were promised a certain amount of oil, at OPEC prices, per million dollars invested in the projects. Partners figured it is better to invest some money in a project that MIGHT make money now, than risk being cut off from oil later. Investors soon learned that standard government incentives and low feedstock prices are more than offset by increased construction costs.

Shell and Mobil invested in both Petromin and SABIC projects. Exxon joined SABIC. The Japanese, through a consortium headed by Mitsubishi, invested in two projects. The Taiwanese invested in a fertilizer plant. Texas Eastern, Celanese, and later, Korea's Lucky Goldstar, Finland's Neste Oy, and Italy's ENI, established joint ventures.

Dow Chemical, of the United States, backed out of its agreements, and rumor has it that SABIC chief Ibrahim Salamah extracted excruciating concessions from Dow before it was permitted to break its contract. For a time, SABIC projects failed to meet projected goals. Eastern Petrochemical Co. (Sharq) was the most glaring example. This polyethylene plant had many problems, some of which were legal. When auditors checked Sharq's books, they found that Sharq's chief accountant had invested in Yen futures to hedge against currency fluctuations. The Yen fell, and Sharq lost money. The unsophisticated Saudi police grew suspicious and placed him under virtual house arrest for over nine months. Sharq Chairman, Dr. Mahsoun Jalal, was taken off an international flight. The accountant inadvertently became enmeshed in a investigation of the Royal Commission for Jubail and Yanbu. The Royal Commission was responsible for supplying industrial infrastructure to the SABIC companies, and its chief, the Egyptian-born Farouk Akdar, was accused of extorting money from companies in return for supplying them with plots of land and utility hook-ups. He was never convicted, but had to resign his job. Some sources in the Ministry of Planning say Akdar, a friend of then planning minister Hisham Nazer, was innocent. Others say a proper investigation could never be carried out because Sharia law doesn't cover examination of bank records for suspicious money transfers. Akdar was cleared of charges.

SABIC's charter promised privatization, but this has fallen behind schedule. The company has now sold thirty percent to the private sector. The government says it will eventually sell 70 percent of the company to the public. In 1988, the firm provided shareholders a 35 percent return on the face value of their stock. Overall, the firm has been an industrial success story.

These achievements cannot obscure SABIC's failure to deliver on downstream industrialization. The planners had a flawed concept. "They are doing it backwards. They think that by supplying the material, such as basic plastics, they will generate business, but if you look at the plastic industry historically, it does not work that way." one expert at SIDF said. "Plastics are used in substitution for other materials." In other words, the Kingdom would need assembly, or manufacturing businesses which substitute plastic for existing metal parts. There is only so much demand for extruded plastic buckets, water cans, and hangars.

Secondary downstream firms, which use SABIC output to make new chemicals and plastics, are few because SABIC charges too much for its output. "SABIC wants to sell at world prices, but most of these downstream companies would need a 40 percent discount to be profitable," an expert said. It is less expensive to export SABIC output to another country, manufacture the downstream product there, and re-import it to the Kingdom than it is to build the factory in Saudi Arabia. He said SABIC must offer concessional rates to local firms.

SABIC's critics say that firm itself is an obstacle to private industrial participation. During the initial phase of expansion, SABIC was awarded exclusive rights to manufacture most petrochemicals in the Kingdom. SABIC refuses to surrender the un-used licenses because, senior SABIC officials say, it considers the private sector incapable of handling such big jobs.

PRIVATE SECTOR PETROCHEMICALS

When over 25 of the Kingdom's business heavyweights formed the Saudi Venture Capital Group (SVCG) to invest in secondary and primary industries, its consultants claimed that SABIC was a roadblock. Eventually, SVCG was awarded three licenses, and began moving ahead with its projects. Long before SVCG was formed, Dr. Mahsoun Jalal, a former academic and banker, launched the National Industrialization Co. (NIC), a sort of private sector SABIC for joint ventures in downstream industries. The government was going to take a share, but backed out at the last minute and endangered the flotation. The firm was capitalized at SR600 million, but subscribers only paid half in the beginning. NIC was a new concept, and investor response was lukewarm. NIC is involved in disposable diapers, a much-needed steel recycling plant, and holds a share in SABIC's Ibn Hayyan PVC plant as well. It is building the Kingdom's first hazardous waste disposal plant, and is part of the Offset Investment Program. NIC is not terribly popular with investors, because it was slow to begin paying high returns, said Dr. Jalal. This forced cancellation of plans to ask for the second half of the capital. A new avenue for financing was opened when NIC bought 10 percent of Saudi Investment Bank. Dr. Jalal has also considered an Islamic profit- sharing investment deal.

CEMENT INDUSTRY

A third major industrial sector, Cement, is proof that a capital-intensive industry using local raw materials, benefiting from subsidized energy and catering to strong domestic demand, is not always successful. Saudi cement producers suffered from over-enthusiastic government funding. They accounted for SR3.4 billion, or 24.5 percent, of all SIDF loans through 1987. This naturally led to overcapacity.

By 1985, the glut had not yet occurred. The Kingdom consumed 14 million tons of cement. In 1986, total consumption of cement in the Kingdom fell to 11.5 million tons; there were no complaints yet, because 8.2 million tons of that came from domestic producers. The next year, total demand dropped by 2.5 million tons, and the cement producers began to panic. Demand sank toward 7-8 million tons per year, yet the 10 domestic producers now had a combined capacity of 14,500,000 tons of cement per year. [2]

Saudi Kuwaiti Cement Company's Chairman, Ahmed Al-Tweijeri, led a battle against cement importers headed by Ghaith R. Pharoun, head of REDEC. They claimed the importers dumped cement on the Saudi market. Sensitive to criticism and eager to avoid a damaging fight, the importers offered the producers a deal in 1987. They would stop importing if they got exclusive rights to sell Saudi cement. The producers spurned the deal, and launched a price war. The big importers, REDEC, Rolaco, Arabian Bulk Trading, and Rashid Abdurahman Rashid, fought the producers, but were forced out. The producers then secured a 20 percent tariff against "dumping." Some, such as Southern Cement Co., boosted their exports as well.

OTHER INDUSTRIES

Saudi firms prove more disappointing the farther one moves from capital-intensive industry. The National Automotive Industries (NAI) was founded by Juffali to make the ubiquitous Mercedes heavy trucks. It started with great fanfare, but production never hit an economic level. Sources at the plant said it never made a profit, and production has steadily been scaled down. A Riyadh bus factory also operates below capacity. It is no wonder that the Japanese rebuffed Saudi pressure to build a joint venture pickup truck factory.

Air conditioner joint ventures, on the other hand, have prospered. Freidrich, Gibson and York, of the United States, and Daiken of Japan have formed joint ventures. For the most part, the Saudi plants are more involved in assembly than actual manufacture, but they benefit from "buy Saudi" laws. Besides, the Kingdom is one of the world's largest markets for window units. Central air conditioning hasn't caught on, mainly because house construction is still unsophisticated.

Other large firms include cabel manufacturers. These supply the needs of the Kingdom's rural electrification program. Jeddah's Saudi Cable Company (SCC) has been aggressive, but cried out for protective tariffs. A second plant, built in Riyadh by the Shamsan group, planned to make a tidy profit behind the government's 20 percent tariff shield.

CONSUMER INDUSTRIES

Successful domestic industries are those that make consumer disposables needed in the Kingdom. The high birthrate supports several disposable diaper manufacturers. Paper tissues sell well in the dusty, sneezy Saudi environment. Wahib Binzagr's soap factory is a success story. Soft drink bottlers and Omar Aggad's processed food factories serve the Saudi sweet tooth.

Saudis buy a lot of medicine. The Saudi Pharmaceutical and Medical Appliances Co. (SPIMACO) was awarded sole rights to manufacture a wide range of drugs in the GCC. Because of "buy local" regulations, it is guaranteed a monopoly on government sales. Consequently, drug manufacturers reluctantly licensed production of their more popular medicines. "We were faced with a choice," said an official with Ciba-Giegy. "We either hold on too long and risk losing our entire market, or we go along with it, and keep something."

HISTORY OF SAUDI INDUSTRIALIZATION

Ayman Al-Yassini says the oil industry has minimal impact on an economy because it is self-contained and requires few skills that are transferable to other industries. Drilling oil wells requires peculiar skills. Further, oil exploration and drilling usually takes place in remote areas, which discourages transfer of technology.[3]

These observations are not meant to condemn oil; oil funded Saudi industrialization. But it means that oil did not automatically lead to further industrial development the way, say, toy assembly did, for Singapore.

The Americans to their credit, encouraged development in the Eastern region. Aramco established an office giving loans and assistance for new local industries. Industrialization began in earnest during the construction boom of the Seventies. The first factories were low-tech affairs that supplied cement, bricks and cinderblocks. These industries were founded with loans from the SIDF. In 1974, it approved SR150 million of loans; the next year, loans topped SR1.18 billion. Over the years, SIDF policies create production gluts because it never thought to slow down approvals before a glut occurred.[4]

Fund advisors monitor the projects, but they don't always follow things closely enough. Westinghouse's licensee, Middle East Circuit Breaker Co., secured SIDF loans with the proviso that a certain percentage of each breaker would be locally-made. During a formal factory opening, SIDF and other government officials watched workers industriously spot-welding sub-assemblies on machines the Author saw covered by tarps a week before. "We had to dust them off for this visit," a factory official explained. The firm actually buys the subassemblies pre- assembled. Nonetheless, Middle East Circuit Breaker scored significant export orders, including the sale of several thousand units to the United Kingdom.

CONCLUSION

Though the range of goods the Kingdom is producing is growing, the hardest thing for a factory to make in the post oil boom period is a good profit. It is harder yet to find the Saudi workers necessary for true industrialization to take place. Labor and dependence upon government subsidies are the weak points of Saudi industrialization, and must be addressed if the Kingdom hopes to continue its drive toward an industrial future.

11

INFRASTRUCTURE

"At Timon's villa, let us pass the day, Where all cry out, What sums are thrown away." - Alexander Pope

It seems incongruous. A sign in the bathroom of a sparkling new Saudia Airlines 747 tells passengers to sit on the toilet, not squat with their feet on the lid. But that's what you get when you yank a pre-industrial society into the Twentieth Century. The Kingdom has spent billions to transform the country into a modern 20th century state. Fifty years ago, even the cities of Medina, Mecca and Jeddah, had little in the way of roads, electricity, or running water. The population was 99 percent illiterate and had no industrial tradition. When the oil glut hit, the Saudis had nearly completed their physical infrastructure, but their human infrastructure was unequal to the task of maintaining it.

DEVELOPMENT STRATEGY

The first development projects tried to tie the newly conquered provinces into a single state. Roads, communications, and an airline started the process. King Abdulaziz asked Aramco to build a railroad to from Dammam to Riyadh, which achieved little economically, but made the Saudis feel like they were now a "developing" country. The same logic was probably behind the later construction of the Hadeed steel plant.

Soaring oil revenues in the Seventies allowed the government to expand its infrastructure in a serious fashion. Most of the development followed the general guidelines of the Five Year Plans published by the Ministry of Planning. Internal logic explained some outrageously expensive projects. Why string power across hundreds of miles to isolated villages or build huge highways up the treacherous Western escarpment? Such projects provided work and money to the isolated regions, and made them feel a part of the Kingdom. The facilities bound them to the government, and facilitated control as well. It is also less expensive to build a road to the rural Asir now than to fight a guerilla war later because the region was neglected economically.

London's "Economist" disagreed. A cover story in 1987 said the Saudis squandered their wealth on overambitious infrastructure and industrialization projects. The Kuwaitis, it said, invested its surpluses overseas to provide the country with a trust fund. In the late Eighties, Kuwait earned more from investments than oil. The comparison is unfair. Kuwait is a city-state while the Kingdom is a nation covering a vast area. Further, Saudis cannot be blamed if they want to do more than live off the fat of petro-investments.[1]

Some Saudi investments were foolish, due to inexperience, enthusiasm, and over-reliance on well-paid Western "experts." The best-known of the white elephants were the billion dollar Rush Housing Projects erected in Jeddah, Riyadh, and Dammam. The multi-story apartment buildings were supposed to provide cheap public housing. Instead, the spacious, modern apartments stood empty for more than a decade because officials said Saudis refused to live stacked up like animals in cages. One glaring fault was the absence of separate elevators for men and women. At long last, spurred by a need for revenue, the Real Estate Development Fund (REDF) announced it would award apartments in the buildings in lieu of new loans. Saudis tired of the interminable wait for an REDF loan were becoming less reluctant to live stacked up like animals. Distribution of the apartments would generate a little cash flow at long last. Few, if any apartments had been doled out by the time the Iraqis invaded Kuwait. Now they are filled with Kuwaiti refugees.

Costs during the Boom Era were high because of primitive facilities, the need to import everything, graft, and finally, because the Saudis were willing to pay top dollar to have things built NOW. Ghaith Pharoun, Adnan Khashoggi, and other fixers made millions as "cultural translators" because they could speak English and knew enough about Western business to serve as go-betweens for traditional Saudi princes and officials.

The most critical squeeze occurred at the ports. Helicopters ferried cement off of freighters backed up outside of Jeddah. Port delays were nightmares until a quirky, irascible individual named Fayez Badr was appointed head of the Ports Authority. Badr whipped the Ports Authority into shape, reorganized procedures, and rammed through a building program to end the backlog.

With profit margins of 45 percent on contracts, it took phenomenal ineptitude, plus bad luck, to lose money. The government made initial payments worth 20 percent of the contract. Officials at the Franco-American joint venture Bouygues-Blount, said a well-run firm could almost finance an entire contract off of its initial payment.

When revenues began falling, the government cut initial payments by half to 10 percent. A royal decree required open bidding. This cut some project costs by nearly 50 percent. The government's Buy Saudi requirements forced foreign firms to purchase more locally-produced goods. Some contractors circumvented the rules with false bills of lading, or by paying a Saudi to certify that a foreign product was made in his particular factory. Margins shrank to five or ten percent, and over-extended contractors collapsed. Late government payments damaged well-run firms and killed off the inefficient. New projects grew scarce.

HIGHWAYS

"How many highways and airports do we need anyway?" asked one government official. In 1954, the Kingdom had a total of 327 kms of road, or approximately 200 miles. By the middle of 1988, the Kingdom spent SR110 billion ($29.3 billion) on road construction. Over 81,500 kms (51,000 miles) of roads were built, of which over half were high grade roads. Another 3,500 kms of expressways were built.[2] Spectacular roads were built up and down the Tihama escarpment near Abha and Taif, while the difficult mountainous terrain south from Taif to Abha was crossed with a highway. The $564 million Bahrain Causeway was built to link Dhahran and Bahrain, 25 km off shore. The project includes an additional $90 million artificial island near the center of the 5 spans that cross the Gulf.

Maintenance of these new bridges and roads has proven more expensive than expected. Road wear is caused by intense sunlight and heat which prematurely age and soften asphalt surfaces. Some roads were poorly designed, and others shoddily built, but by far the biggest threat to Saudi roads and bridges is overloaded trucks. The Riyadh Ring Road was not open a year before the surface was so deeply rutted by trucks that it needed resurfacing.

The bedouin's favorite truck, the Mercedes 1924, is so durable that he calls it "The Conqueror of the Desert." The trucks, painted in lurid colors depicting sailboats, lakes and forests, carry twice their rated capacity. Their ability to break up roads and bridges makes them "the Conquerors of the Highways."

The Ministry responded to overloading by establishing weight limits in 1985. As of 1989, the weighing program was still not fully launched, most likely because of resistance to government regulation. At the same time truck weighing was announced, the government established the Vehicle Periodic Inspection (MVPI) program. MVPI was more successful than the weighing program because it was handled by private enterprise. Automated car inspection stations were built all over the Kingdom. In 1989, the government announced that it was going to assume control over the stations, a victory for bureaucracy over businessmen.

Alarmed at the Kingdom's high accident rate, Deputy Minister of Communications Suliman Al-Saloum. consulted a U.S. Department of Transportation expert. The American suggested a ban on wearing Saudi ghutra headdresses while driving. The hanging folds of the ghutra function like blinders on a horse, eliminating peripheral vision. Saloum responded by sacking the American.

The one deterrent to traffic fatalities is the "Blood Money" a man must pay if he causes the death or severe injury of another in an auto accident. The amount now stands around $30,000 for a Muslim man, and half that for a Muslim woman. Even if a pedestrian threw himself under the wheels of a car, barring exceptional evidence of deliberate suicide, the driver of the car would have to pay blood money.

The Ship of the Desert, the Camel, is particularly nasty in collision. Once its long legs are knocked out from under its bulky body, the entire animal comes crashing down on top of the vehicle. One acquaintance at Westinghouse turned his large American car into a convertible when he struck a camel at night. At the last second, he ducked, sparing himself decapitation. Although the bedouin never seem able to monitor their animals to keep them off the highways, they appear with alacrity to collect money for those killed by cars. Finally, in July, 1989, the government re-wrote the laws. Car owners would no longer have to pay for killing a stray animal. Second, and more important, the owners of the animals will be held responsible for death, injuries or damage resulting from an accident with their animal. Camel fences line major roads, and special camel tunnels and opverpasses have been built.. One firm proposed fastening reflectors to the camels' legs and necks so they can be seen at night.

CITY STREETS

One source of never-ending amazement to foreigners is the Saudi predilection for ripping up roads. Even in these hard times, a city street is built, ripped up to put in sewer pipes, resurfaced, then torn up a few months later to lay in power lines, and then repaved. Next, it is gouged open to lay telephone lines. Later, it is time to repair the sewer lines. The Diplomatic Quarter, beneficiary of pre-planning and unlimited budgets, has seen its 2-year-old streets shredded for various reasons. One city official said this was due to poor planning, though a more cynical answer would be that continuous contracts afford more opportunities for "baksheesh."

Another mystery is why, after spending hundreds of millions on city streets, so many have no names. Most in Jeddah were informally named after the statuary that adorns the city. Bicycle Turnaround is a traffic circle surmounted by the world's biggest bicycle. Fist Road has a giant bronze fist protruding from the Earth. Riyadh's roads are only now being named, as part of a contract. Unfortunately for Riyadh's expatriate drivers, Riyadh Governor Prince Salman has decided that all signs shall be solely in Arabic.

RAIL

Lower oil revenues derailed plans to expand the Kingdom's one railroad, the Saudi Government Rails Organization (SAGRO) which runs from Dammam to Riyadh. Officials looked into the possibility of reviving the old Hejaz railroad of Lawrence of Arabia fame. The rail lines and facilities still exist. Rusty locomotives and bullet-riddled rolling stock sit abandoned at various sites. After reviving the Hejaz line, they planned to lay track to Riyadh. Hussain Mansouri, Minister of Communications, announced that oil revenue problems forbid implementation of the project. Plans still exist to build spurs to the Riyadh Oil Refinery, and up to the gas sweetening plants of Shudgum and Othmaniya. This will take the existing Riyadh-Dammam line north from Dammam to Jubail.

Railroads are less expensive to maintain than roads, and use fewer people to carry more cargo than trucks. That is a major the problem. Truck driving is one of the few jobs the bedouin take, and the government likes to keep them occupied.

The existing line terminates at the Riyadh Dry Port, a facility that allows container cargo to bypass customs in Dammam, and enter in Riyadh. The dryport was built to boost Riyadh's economic importance. In 1986, the government completed a modernization program that cut the rail trip nearly in half, to 4 hours, which made traveling that way more popular. New track was laid, and rolling stock was improved. Elaborate railway stations were erected as well.

TAXIS

Private Saudi taxi drivers nearly disappeared during the oil bust, though not as a direct result of oil revenues. These avaricious souls multiplied to such an extent that the government limited, in the early eighties, the importation of more schoolbus yellow taxis. The government also ruled that henceforth, only six cylinder cars could serve as taxis. This was designed to spur auto sales.

Around 1983, the first of the Saudi "Limousine" services were established, using big American cars and foreign drivers. By 1989, the yellow cabs were verging on extinction, and the government ruled that foreign drivers will have to be replaced by Saudis, who now, ironically, earn less for driving than when they were independent.

Customers prefer limos because they give a guaranteed price, and their drivers speak some English. Despite the new ruling, most of their drivers are Pakistanis or Filipinos. Limousines tend to be safer for foreign women than the yellow cabs. Those who try to find the cheapest prices catch illegal taxis in Jeddah and the Eastern Province, where expatriates break the law by picking up passengers.

BUSES

Many Women ride Saudi Public Transportation Co. (SAPTCO) buses. When the orange, white and blue buses pull over, the women dutifully get in the special back compartments reserved for women. There, they are supposed to place the fare in a box. "You would think these good Muslim women would pay us, but they do not. It is stealing from us," a Saudi SAPTCO manager said, but added, "I think they are Egyptians. Saudi women would always pay, but they probably don't ride."

SAPTCO, established by Saleh Kamel, is guaranteed a profit by the government. This became increasingly expensive, which led the government in the early eighties to double fares from SR1 to SR2. It still loses money. SAPTCO runs bus lines in the major towns and cities and operates a service connecting the urban centers. Its prices are reasonable, but distances are so far and airfare so inexpensive, that only the very poor take the bus.

One reason SAPTCO loses so much money is that small privately-owned buses called "coasters" ply the busiest avenues and steal the company's customers. Coasters are popular because their fare is half of SAPTCO's and they run more frequently. They are also a menace to traffic, since the drivers dart in and out of traffic as they leapfrog eachother to grab the maximum number of passengers.

AIR TRANSPORT

The interior of Riyadh's King Khaled International Airport is possibly the most beautiful in the world. Huge columns support spacious open ceilings which represent stylized palm groves. The terminals contain flower gardens and fountains. The light, airy atmosphere bespeaks luxury and taste, unless one's eye drifts to the central column in the domestic terminal. There, like a polyester vest on a British banker, stands an enormous plywood palm tree. The tree is decorated with the smiling visages of Fahad, Abdullah, and Sultan. The palm tree, erected on a temporary basis for the opening of the airport five years before, remains. Nobody dares remove the portraits.

For the same reason, Saudia didn't dare refuse the royal "gift" of 10 oil barter jumbo jets. The expense of maintaining the new jets made the airline plunge deeper in the red. The Jumbo Jets are part of a fleet composed of Boeing 747s, and 737s, Airbus A-300s, Fokker F-28s, and Lockheed L-1011s. The average age of its planes is low, but the variety creates training and maintenance problems.

This airline, part of Prince Sultan's Ministry of Defense and Aviation, is a money-loser. Saudia's unprofitability is doubly damning because all of its fuel is subsidized. The only time Saudia planes take on non-subsidized fuel is when they tank up for return flights from overseas. It loses money because of its bloated payroll. Employees have quasi-civil servant status, which makes it difficult to terminate the inefficient and incompetent. Its Special Flights division is expensive. Luxuriously appointed Gulfstreams, Boeing 737s, and the King's 747 ferry the Royal Family around the world. Further, a Prince or Princess can board any flight, bump off paying customers (even if those passengers have already taken their seats), and fly for free.

Saudia charges low domestic fares, and tries to make its profits off of overseas flights. Although its no-alcohol policy keeps flights free of drunks, foreigners want planes serving liquor. Saudia has used government connections to force people to fly its white, green and blue aircraft. It once sent an official letter to private sector companies threatening the loss of government contracts if their employees did not fly Saudia on foreign trips. Diplomatic complaints finally forced the Saudis to rescind the order.

Saudia has tried to cut costs. It cancelled a maintenance agreement with TWA and has stalled on paying bills. It ran up a tab of over SR5 million alone in Riyadh to hotels putting up its ground crew.

Saudia operates out of an extensive series of airports. The newest, King Fahad International Airport in the Eastern Province, was nearly a casualty of lower oil revenues. It was not necessary, but there were commissions to be made, and yet another monument to Fahad to be erected. It is the third of the three International Airports. The others are Jeddah's King Abdulaziz International Airport, and Riyadh's King Khaled International Airport (KKIA). KKIA was finished in 1983, the product of the boom years. It is arguably the most beautiful airport in existence, and is equipped with every modern facility. It has, as do all the airports, a special terminal for Royalty or state visitors. Excepting Jeddah, for which a special Hajj terminal was built, the airports are underutilized. One of Riyadh's 4 non-Royal terminals has yet to be used.

The airports often have dual military and civilian roles, and because of this, they are run more like military bases than civil transport centers. Efficiency is a low priority. That is why, astonishingly, Jeddah permits the Egyptian queue, a herd of people 8 abreast, 8 deep, all clamoring for seats on an already-filled aircraft. Human chaos inside a modern shell is the best way to describe Jeddah's airport.

Air travel is popular now, but Abdulaziz was careful about introducing it. During World War II, he allowed the Americans to fly to a dirt airstrip far outside of Jeddah. Every two weeks, the American pilots returned to Cairo swearing that the airport was moved closer to Jeddah. By the time the airstrip was placed adjacent to the city, Saudi officials admitted that the biweekly shifts were meant to gradually expose the people of Jeddah to foreign aircraft.

HOTELS

During the boom years, hotel rooms were at a premium and businessmen slept in lobby chairs. Those days have ended with lower business and an increased number of hotels. The Ministry of Commerce's Hotel division scaled back on hotel permits too late. Hoteliers resorted to discounting. Many Saudi partners are now refusing to put more money in the properties, which leads to deterioration. Many international firms have checked out. Kuwaiti refugees have filled many hotels for the first time since the boom.

The government has tried to compensate by encouraging in-country tourism. This keeps Saudi money in the Kingdom, and foreign ideas out. Half Moon Bay in the Eastern region will cater to Saudis who might want to drive over the causeway by day to Bahrain, but remain in the Kingdom at night. For stay-at-homes, there are plenty of amusement parks. Saleh Kamel is still talking of a Disney amusement park in the Western Region, which, if it is built, will certainly be a winner.

ELECTRICITY

The government raised electricity rates to cope with lower revenues, but citizen anger forced it to scale back the hikes. Saudi citizens have never seen the need for conservation. Electricity is subsidized by over 25 percent, but utilities stockholders do not suffer; the government guarantees a return on their investment.

When electrification first began, European systems dominated the West, while American systems ruled in the East. Houses still have any of a number of different sockets, and either 240 volt or 120 volt electricity. The government consolidated the small firms into regional electricity companies, the SCECOs, which invested prodigious sums in power generation. The SCECOs received the bulk of their loans from the SIDF.

The Saudis pioneered the use of the easily built, but not terribly efficient large gas turbine generators. Later installations use the more efficient steam turbine generators. Many are powered by gas, but others use fuel oil or treated crude.

As power lines reach remoter villages, the small diesel generator packs used in the outlying towns are then sent off to still more remote regions. While driving off the tracks on the Tihama plains, two of us chanced upon a small village, whose rumbling diesel generator powered strings of lights in the central square.

The Kingdom has finished a large transmission line that ties the Central Province with the power grid of the Eastern Province. The GCC is planning a regional grid that could reduce generating costs for all the member states. Desalination plants that use thermal processes for desalinating water use the excess heat to generate electricity. In 1988, the Saline Water Conversion Corp. (SWCC) produced 20.1 million Megawatts of power. New plants will add over 400 MW of additional generating capacity.[3]

Despite so much power, the Kingdom has done extensive experimentation in solar energy. Three villages are powered by the world's largest photovoltaic power plant. Solar power is used for remote microwave transmission sites and on pipeline anti- corrosion systems.

TELECOMMUNICATIONS

"Gosh, those phones sound good," friends overseas say to those calling from Saudi Arabia. Saudi telephones and telex machines work great, and put most European systems to shame. The oil glut, though, is affecting the quality of service, and has made it difficult to get a telephone installed. A six-month waiting list in popular areas has created a telephone line black market.

Saudi Telecom cannot afford to install new phones because its revenues go to the Ministry of Finance, which has not released enough money to fund expansion and maintenance. As a consequence, the phone company has resorted to cannibalizing equipment to keep strategic gear operating. It would help if princes paid their bills, but that has not been forthcoming. Until then, or until oil revenues pick up, Saudi phone service will have to make do.

ROYAL COMMISSION

The Royal Commission for Yanbu and Jubail was established to build developed the industrial cities of Jubail, on the Gulf, and Yanbu on the Red Sea. Since the construction of fully integrated industrial centers entailed desalination, electric power, roads, ports, and housing, all of which are under the supervision of different ministries, Fahad established the commission to break through ministerial in-fighting.

The results are impressive. Gigantic industrial complexes stand on what was formerly bare desert, and export petrochemicals across the globe. The cities not only provide impressive industrial infrastructure, they also contain complete communities with shopping centers, mosques, schools, and hospitals. Planners expected population to grow rapidly, but this has not taken place as quickly as expected. Workers are unenthusiastic about moving away from their families in other cities to the Jubail and Yanbu.

The head of the Royal Commission is the urbane Prince Abdulaziz bin Faisal bin Turki. He oversees the gradual transfer of responsibility to other ministries. Some facilities have already been transferred to the Ministry of Industry and Electricity, and others to the Ministry of Health. The Commission is working itself out of a job.

Industrial Cities have also been built in the major cities of the Kingdom, but are unrelated to the Royal Commission. These industrial parks all provide infrastructure, subsidized rents and utilities. The most important are located in Dammam, Riyadh, and Jeddah.

MEDICINE

The baby cried before she was put to sleep and laid on a bed of ice. Like antiseptic techno-vampires, doctors drained her blood from her body. The heart monitor went blank as her temperature dropped. There, in the operating theater of Riyadh's Military Hospital, a baby had technically died of cold. Saudi heart surgeon, Dr. Mohammed Fagih, said the infant was ready for surgery.

After suturing a hole in the tiny heart's ventricle wall, and closing the little chest, Dr. Fagih allowed technicians to introduce heated blood into the child's veins. Minutes later, as her body temperature rose, a faint blip on the cardiograph screen showed life. The operation was a success..

Dr. Fagih, who later performed the Kingdom's first heart transplant, epitomizes Saudi successes in the medical fields. Today, he, other Saudis, and expatriates, provide medical care ranging from cancer treatment to organ transplants. Just thirty years ago, Saudi medicine consisted of herbs, branding, and camel's urine. Teeth were pulled by the barbers. Saudis suffered from Malaria on the Tihama Coastline, and Bilharzia, Trachoma and other blinding diseases.

Oil revenue permitted the government to send the seriously ill abroad for care. At least one family member was sent at government expense to accompany the patient. The hospital construction program was oriented to big, showy hospitals, not the plain primary healthcare clinics which could have lowered the Kingdom's high infant mortality. The curative approach to medicine has been criticized by some Saudi doctors who say preventative medicine saves more lives at lower cost.

The stumbling bloc is that big hospitals and advanced equipment are sexy. The Kingdom already has more of the advanced Nuclear Magnetic Resonance Imagery machines per person than Great Britain. Lower oil revenues forced the Ministry of Health to reconsider and start building more Primary Health Care clinics, but did not change its penchant for big hospitals. Thus, it pressed ahead with Riyadh's latest and largest agglomeration of hospitals, the King Fahad Medical City.

The cash squeeze did result in some cost-cutting, mostly in the field of operations and maintenance contracts. For example, Whittaker Corp., an American defense contractor, was paid $1.4 billion to run 4 MODA hospitals for 3 years. The advent of competitive bidding cut the same contract by two-thirds. Hospital operators responded by replacing expensive American nurses and doctors with Britons, or Third Worlders. In most hospitals, the quality of care has declined, although it is still far superior to that in most developing countries. Government contracts try to prevent the slippage by specifying the minimum percentage of Western doctors and nurses that are required to meet standards.

The Ministry of Health is not the only organization providing hospital care. The ministries of Health, Defense, Interior, and the National Guard all operate large hospitals as a means of dispensing patronage to the average Saudis. Two more hospitals were built under the personal patronage of the Royal Court. The biggest is the King Faisal Specialist Hospital, in Riyadh, where Crown Prince Abdullah went for care after his heart attack. The other is the King Khaled Eye Specialist Hospital, also in Riyadh. Both hospitals can be entered only by special approval from a senior prince.

Despite free government hospitals, many Saudis patronize private facilities. The Ministry of Health provides special loans and an annual subsidy based on the number of beds that are provided. The latest business fad in 1985 was private health clinics. These hospitals and clinics provide the bulk of care for foreigners, but list many private Saudis as patients. Some Saudi women rent private suites to permit assignations, a private hospital physician confided. A husband or family will not question an illness. Anyone can come up for a "visit" as the woman "recuperates."

Not all private hospitals are built on a profit basis. Dr. Nasser Al-Rashid, a wealthy contractor, used land donated by King Fahad to build a $20 million hospital for the treatment of children suffering from leukemia and other cancers. Dr. Al-Rashid's young son nearly died from leukemia until he was treated at St. Jude's Children's Hospital in Memphis Tennessee, which had been founded by another Arab, the comedian Danny Thomas.

All the money thrown at treating diseases will not solve one of the Kingdom's fundamental medical problems: an inordinately high ratio of birth defects. This occurs because of constant in-breeding and first cousin marriages. Even Saudi medical professionals ignore the problem, because first cousin marriages were sanctioned by the Prophet.

EDUCATION

When Jamal went to school thirty years ago, he simply walked to the local mosque. There, if he were lucky, he would join other boys in memorizing the Holy Koran. He might learn a bit of the Arabic Script as well as simple subtraction and addition. Only a very few students had an opportunity in those days to attend the handful of schools in the the Kingdom.

Today, Jamal's son attends computer science courses at Riyadh's King Saud University, gets paid a monthly salary, and is provided with free housing. Further, if Jamal is still interested in learning to read, he can take adult education classes.

Over one and a quarter million Saudis are enrolled in over eight thousand schools across the country. All education is free and is obligatory from elementary through high school. There are large numbers of dropouts. Vocational schools and universities pay students wages.

The Ministry of Education, the Presidency of Girls Education, the General Organization for Technical Education and Vocational Training, and the Ministry of Higher Education teach the Kingdom's youth. Two of them, the Ministry of Higher Education and the Ministry of Education will be merged for efficiency's sake.

Boys and girls attend Kindergarten together but are separated from First Grade on. They are assigned a teacher who stays with them for the first six years of primary education. This promotes continuity and a strong bond with educators. Next come come three years of intermediate school and then three years of secondary school.

Active boys join the various sports clubs in their towns. There, they can play soccer, swim, or work out in gymnasia. Unfortunately, many students do not avail themselves of these facilities and vegetate in boredom.

Harder times, plus the generally high social status of education has improved Saudization in the schools. The government says Saudis account for 67.34 percent of primary, 43.58 percent of intermediate, and 27.61 percent of secondary teachers. Saudization is more advanced in girls' schools than in males' schools, mainly because teaching is one of the few avenues available to working Saudi females.

The best of the four main universities is the newly renamed King Fahad University for Petroleum and Minerals. It and the King Faisal University are in the Eastern Province. King Saud University is in Riyadh, and King Abdulaziz University is in Jeddah. Additionally, there are several Islamic Universities. The biggest, Imam Mohammed bin Saud Islamic University, is in Riyadh. Women have separate branches in the "secular" schools, but their equipment is usually substandard.

The universities are not producing the kinds of graduates the country needs in this era of lower oil revenues. There are too many liberal arts majors, and too few engineers and business majors. As detailed in the Labor chapter, the vocational programs are trying to attract enough young men to provide skilled workers for industry. Happily, the tougher economic environment has encouraged young men to apply themselves to more practical studies.

GOVERNMENT INFRASTRUCTURE

Abdulaziz ruled, as desert sheikhs before him did, through his own authority, and deputized followers to handle particular tasks. As life grew more complicated, he and his successors created the ministries on the following dates:

Ministry of Foreign Affairs 1930
Ministry of Finance 1932

Ministry of Defense 1946
Ministry of Interior
Ministry of Education
Ministry of Agriculture
Ministry of Communication
Ministry of Commerce and Industry
Ministry of Health   All 1951-1954
Ministry of Petroleum and Mineral Resources
Ministry of Labor and Social Affairs
Ministry of Pilgrimage and Waqf
Ministry of Information Ministry of Justice   All 1960-1962
Ministry of Public Works and Housing Ministry of Industry and Electricity Ministry of Posts, Telegraph, and Telephone
Ministry of Municipal and Rural Affairs
Ministry of Planning
Ministry of Higher Education
3 ministers without portfolio (1975)
Independent Bureaus include:
General Personnel Bureau
Central Planning Commission
The Grievance Board
The General Department for Intelligence
The Advisory Council Committees for Propagation of Virtue and Forbidding Evil
National Guard (has direct access to King).[4]

The Council of Ministers meets regularly. Ministers possess autonomy only if they also happen to be royals. The Ministers' bureaucratic machinery is weakening the role of tribal and religious authorities. If a man wants a house or entrance into a government hospital, he can bypass the traditional sheikh and go to an official. If the bureaucracy frustrates him, he may still go through traditional channels to get action.

The one ministry that seems almost superfluous is the Ministry of Planning. Every five years, it puts out the detailed Five Year Plan, which is trotted out for foreign visitors, but largely ignored. This is unfortunate since the government has no other long-range planning group.

The Ministry of Urban and Rural Affairs is responsible for municipal governments. The town's police, however, answer not to the Municipality's mayor, but to a princely governor, who reports to the Ministry of Interior.

It is possible to delve further into the government organizations, but after a point, it becomes pointless. The Saudi governmental structure has grown more complicated and its regulatory nature has increased over time, but this has not been a result of the oil glut.

THE LEGAL SYSTEM

A bedouin told Abdulaziz a prince had struck him. "The King called on his children to come to his court. He asked the plaintiff to point to the one who hit him. So the man obliged and pointed out the guilty. With a strange vibrance in his voice, his Majesty asked the child, "Did you hit him?" The son was quiet and did not answer. The just father realized that his son had committed the act. So he looked at the bedouin and asked him, while his features showed anger and deep hurt, "With what did he hit you?"

"With a stick," the bedouin replied.

"Get up and hit him! Get revenge from him. Get up!" The King said.

Whispers of anxiety and anticipation filled the air. The man answered, "I cannot!"

"God enlighten you, get up, old man, and do not be afraid. Justice has equated between you and him, but you are greater than him because Justice is on your side, and he is younger than you are. He is the guilty one. Get up and hit him."

"Excuse me! This is sufficient from you. Justice has erased the guilt of your son. What you have done is the best reward for me. I decline my right completely."

At this stage, everyone thought the matter had been solved since the plaintiff dropped his complaint. After this symbolic compromise, which the plaintiff did not even dream of, all of a sudden Abdulaziz stood up, angry and screaming at his son in with a strong voice, "You hurt him and you do not fear God. Do you think that your belonging to me gives you the right to transgress, or that you will escape punishment?" He then hit him, hit him hard, and he ordered that he be taken to the court and be imprisoned alone.

This event led him to make the following pronouncement which was distributed throughout the land:

"From Abdulaziz Bin Ibn Saud to the people of the Arabian Island: every one of our people who feels that injustice befell him , must come forward with complaint. Everyone that comes with a complaint should send it by telegraph or the free mail, at our expense. Every employee of the post or telegraph must receive the complaints from our subjects even if they were directed against my children, my relatives, and the people of my home. Let it be known to every employee who tries to dissuade our people from presenting a complaint, no matter what it is, or try to influence the plaintiff so that he will minimize the impact of its language, we will punish him severely. I do not want to hear in my life of a single one oppressed, and I do not want God to have me carry the burden of oppressing anyone and not helping an oppressed or extracting the right of an oppressed. This is made known, so God is my witnesses."[5]

After a drug-using young prince was bested by a commoner from the Al-Harb tribe in the sport of maniacal Riyadh driving, he shot the youth dead in the desert. The family tried for months to see justice served, but Fahad demurred. In desperation, the boy's mother passed a message through tribal sources that she would march naked to Fahad's palace to demand her rights. Only then, did Fahad order the prince to be executed. The woman accepted her victory in principle, and took blood money in lieu of the prince's life.

Saudi law is under pressure from the demands of a modern economy. New problems such as automobile accidents, or construction contracts appeared before the government, and it was not long before Abdulaziz realized that changes were required to handle the grievances and complaints. He established Summary Courts, Sharia Courts, and the Commission on Judicial Supervision in 1933.[6] The Summary Courts handled misdemeanors, discretionary, and statutory punishment. Sharia Courts handled all other cases. This was fine, and is still reasonably good for general civil and criminal law. Sharia law, as related in the Religion Chapter, is based upon the Koran, and the Sunna, or doings and sayings of the Prophet Mohammed and his companions.

The King's new Commission on Judicial Supervision drew members from the Ulema. It supervised courts as well as reviewed decisions. Abdulaziz allowed judges to use whatever Islamic school of jurisprudence they felt was applicable. Later, the judges were instructed to emphasize the stricter Hanbali interpretations.

Concern with law never led to formation of a constitution, because conservatives consider divine law sufficient, and the Royal family wants no formal limits on its power. The only time Saudi kings mentioned constitutions was when they thought it would help them get through a crisis. Abdulaziz promised one after he conquered the Hejaz in 1926 to placate world Muslim opinion, and again after he created the Kingdom of Saudi Arabia in 1932. Faisal made similar announcements after a coupe attempt and the Yemen troubles. The statements were intended more for foreign than domestic consumption.

"Whether Saudi Arabia is really in need of a written basic law can be argued either way. This issue, however, is not a burning one." [7] The problem is whether Sharia law can be adapted to the needs of a modern society. Conceptual differences between Sharia and Western law makes it difficult to combine the two. Western law says something is either legal or illegal. Religious law, one Arab attorney explained, has different shades. "There are 5 to 6 different levels in Sharia, ranging from 'Forbidden,' to 'Discouraged,' to 'Neutral,' to 'Encouraged,' and, finally, 'Necessary.'"

Further, Sharia law cannot be scrapped like other law; it is eternal. "It's not two different legal systems, but two different sources of law, and hence, two separate legal systems," one attorney said. Synthesis of Sharia with modern law is being attempted outside of Saudi Arabia. Sharia scholars in the Kingdom have not been formed into a law commission or any sort of body to attempt this. Instead, the Ulema goes over laws to determine the Islamic nature of the regulations. On purely regulatory matters, the Islamic judges give the government wide leeway. A judge in 1967 ruled that drivers in accidents can be dealt with by traffic courts. Sharia only applies, he said, to determining damages.

"More and more, Saudi authorities are trying to limit the application of the Sharia, the attorney added. "They are trying to squeeze Sharia into a corner." When the Grand Mufti of Mecca died in 1970, Faisal refused to fill the vacant position. He took advantage of the vacuum to created the Ministry of Justice and the Supreme Judicial Council, and usurp the Grand Mufti's judicial functions.

"This is a Gulfwide phenomenon. Kuwait, Bahrain and the others, over the past 20-30 years, have tried to do this. After all, even Conservatives know that Sharia cannot deal with circumstances of modern commerce. None of its rules are specific enough.... You can't quarry Islamic texts for rules."

This, then, is the difficulty confronting the Kingdom in establishing a legal infrastructure. The problem has been compounded by the economic hard times, because it sharpened the need for bankruptcy hearings, and the need for legal measures for the banking system. Yet so far, all efforts have been half-hearted.

"On paper this is a pure Islamic state...in terms of its constitution and legal structure," said Islamic law expert Frank Vogel. "On the other hand, of all the Islamic states, it is the wealthiest, and the state which has been thrust most vigorously and quickly into the Twentieth Century...When you have traditional Islamic structure and a booming economy, you have the worst of both worlds."

CRIMINAL LAW

Sharia law is hard on crime and decrees death for murder, rape, armed robbery, adultery, and apostasy. Amputations, which are rare, take place after multiple convictions. It may be crude, but it works; Saudis do not fear crime the way New Yorkers do.

The criminal justice system starts with the police investigation, in which everybody involved tends to be arrested. This applies more strictly to foreigners than Saudis. Though the practice of setting a bond is increasing, generally the only way to get out is to have a relative pledge security for you. If you skip town, your relative is put in jail until you are produced.[8] There is no right of habeas corpus. This is ameliorated by deduction of time held in detention from the jail sentence.

Crimes are considered an offense against a person, unlike the West, where a crime is an offense against the state. It is up to the survivors or victims to grant clemency to a murderer, and at rare times, they do so. Normally, the police pursue cases only at the insistence of the aggrieved party; there is no public prosecutor. [9] Still, police have been urged to pursue some cases even if the original plaintiff of action wants to drop them.

Once the investigation is finished, it goes to the court. There are no juries. Procedure, for both criminal and civil matters, consists of the judge listening to the complaint of the plaintiff, which is recorded. The defendant then presents his refutation, which is also recorded. If witnesses are brought by the plaintiff, they are first judged to be of good character. The defendant than has the chance to refute the testimony of witnesses, though not necessarily to confront them. After this, the judge makes a decision.

In criminal law, the judge asks the defendant if he is satisfied with the judgment. If answer is no, then an appeal may be filed within 10 days. A system of judicial review was started when the Judicial Commission was established in 1967. A lower court's judgments can only be overturned by the King, because it can refuse to recognize the commission's order of retrial.[10]

CIVIL LAW

The biggest problem for civil law, says Solaim, is that officials cannot rewrite laws without fear of reaction by "the Ikhwan with all their puritanical zeal."[11] Thus, rather than overhaul the basic law, i.e. Sharia, the government added "extra-judicial" bodies. These were empowered to render binding legal judgments, but were considered outside of, yet subordinate to, Sharia law.

The first, in 1954, was the King-appointed Grievance Board (Wilayat al-Mazalim) which has roots in traditional Islamic jurisprudence. The Board handles complaints against the government. "The central position which the board occupies in the system of justice in Saudi Arabia has been the product of the extreme difficulty involved in digesting and incorporating the ever-growing administrative and other regulations into the Sharia, and consequently, into the Sharia court system," says Solaim.[12]

The second body was the Committee on Cases of Forgery, established in 1960, again with some Islamic precedents. It was combined with another body in 1966, to pursue forgery cases. The Commission on Cases of Bribery was set up 1962. This hasn't been very active. The Commission on the Impeachment of Ministers has never met. The Supreme Commission on Labor Disputes (regulations were first published in 1947) was formally established in 1963. The Commercial Courts combined the Commission on the Settlement of Commercial Disputes, established in 1965, and the Commercial Papers Committee.[13] The Committee for Settlement of Commercial Disputes was transferred to the Grievance Board in January, 1988. Earlier, jurisdiction over banking loan cases was transferred to the new SAMA Committee on Banking Disputes.

The first echelon of the Civil Courts consists of the Notaries Public, who perform the judicial role of approving the legality of the documents they attest. Cases then go to the judges, who, like all other judicial and quasi-judicial officers in the Saudi legal system, require all documents and arguments to be made in Arabic.

The Ministry of Justice is requiring a university education for new judges. Most come from Saudi universities, and then go to the Institute of Public Administration. Most of the present generation of judges have not gone abroad. Civil judges are considered fair, but are easily swayed by the status and nationality of the parties in the dispute.

HOW IT OPERATES

The Saudi courts, like their cousins around the world, are expensive and time-consuming. Legal costs are not recoverable. The party who wins, bears his own costs. "An average is from one year, if you are lucky, to five years if you are unlucky," one attorney said. "The run-of-the mill case takes 3 years to judgment, and then enforcement can be totally open-ended."

Foreigners find Saudi law is more oriented to reconciliation than proving one or the other party is wrong. "There is a tremendous incentive to settle," said a different attorney. "In all courts and committees and tribunals, they make big efforts to get parties to settle. Either send them out, or drag it out until parties reach a judgment. Even during a judgment, they try to split down the middle." This is an Arab trait, to avoid having either party lose too much honor over the dispute. Also, the less power a court has, the more likely it is to push compromise. The SAMA committee invariably urges "deals," while the Grievance Board issues a number of clear cut rulings.

Despite the Saudi love of cutting deals, foreign arbitration has been rejected out of hand ever since arbitration over border disputes went against the Kingdom. For that matter, a foreign judgment against a Saudi cannot be enforced without going through the whole case a second time in the Kingdom.

If a foreigner persists and wins an award against a Saudi, he has only won a third of the battle. "Getting enforcement is the difficult part," said a lawyer. It helps if one's opponent has no influence, and the compromise was worked out with the Governor's office. Otherwise, the Saudi avoids the police, so the judgment cannot be delivered. Many Saudis play this waiting game until the exhausted foreigner caves in. Princes simply ignore court rulings.

Before oil prices went sour, these problems were not severe. Enough money floated around to keep most people happy. Withheld wages from foreign workers, deliberate loan defaults by the wealthy, and other problems arose mostly because of the slower economy. The resulting increase in litigation highlights the shortcomings in the Kingdom's legal infrastructure. The response has been to cobble together ad hoc solutions, such as the Banking Disputes Committee.

The weakest element in the legal system is the fact that the 10,000 members of the royal family are essentially above the law. Sharia law treats rulers and commoners equally, but the police forces do not. There is no ruler of the caliber of Abdulaziz who beat his own son for breaking the law. A system of laws needs good laws, a system of men needs exceptional men. Post oil boom Saudi Arabia has neither.

12

FINANCE

"The Prophet, (Peace be Upon Him) said, 'A Dirham of Riba (interest) which a man receives knowingly is worse than committing adultery thirty-six times,'" - *as related by Abdallah ibn Hanzalah.* *Mishkat Al-Masibih, Kitab Al-Buyoo, Bab Al-Riba.*

If the Prophet hated interest so much, who could blame a devout Saudi businessmen who refused to pay his bank loans? The Kingdom's courts certainly didn't, and ruled against any bank that tried to collect from debtors. The bankers were furious.

"In any other country, there is a moral stigma attached to not paying your debts," a senior banker said. "Here, if I go to a party with Saudis who don't know who I am, you can hear them bragging about how they screwed this or that bank. They do this because they can get away with it."

"What we have is a moral breakdown," the new Saudi French Bank General Manager Yves Max told the Saudi Gazette in an interview that enfuriated the central bank, the Saudi Arabian Monetary Agency (SAMA).[1]

Saudi banking's problem is simple: it operates on interest, yet interest is forbidden by the state religion, Islam. This fundamental conflict was papered over with petrodollar profits during the oil boom; profit margins were 20 or 30 percent and nobody had financial problems. The oil recession and late government payments unearthed the problem. Once borrowers defaulted on their loans, and the banks tried to collect, the courts not only ruled against the banks, but in some cases, ordered them to refund interest paid on earlier loans. In the rare instance where a bank won a favorable ruling, the police refused to enforce it.

Most Islamic scholars say interest-based modern banking and Islamic law are impossible to reconcile because the Koran expressly condemns the paying or receiving of interest. They dismiss arguments by a minority that Mohammed meant "Usury" not "interest." Interest attempts to circumvent the will of God by guaranteeing the lender a profit no matter what happens. Christian Europe wrestled with this dilemma during the Middle Ages, but decided the Bible attacks Usury, not interest itself and escaped the present Islamic deadlock on the issue.

Once borrowers realized the banks were powerless, they quickly defaulted; soon over 25 percent of bank loan portfolios went sour. Saudi provision-to-reserves ratios averaged near 2.3 percent, compared to a world standard of under 1.3 percent. The Kingdom's largest bank, National Commercial Bank (NCB) reported zero profits in 1986, 1987 and 1988. Saudi Cairo Bank, 40 percent owned by Banque Du Caire, lost millions after bank officers speculated in precious metals. Managing Director Baghat Khalil, and Foreign Department Director, Ahmed Abdul Baseet Bajneeb, both Egyptians, lost the money in 1979 during the Hunt Brothers' attempt to corner the world silver market and falsified the 1980 and 1981 annual reports to conceal mounting losses. After SAMA finally investigated, the men were both fined $2,840, and jailed one year. Saudi Cairo lost SR408 million ($105 million), or two and a half times the bank's capitalization.[2] The prison sentence did not seem to dent Khalil's career. He surfaced again, as a financial advisor in the Albarakat Islamic bank. After a SAMA-picked replacement was removed for making questionable bad loans, Saudi Cairo's capital was doubled. It was doubled yet again in 1988, by the Public Investment Fund (PIF).

At one point, five out of the Kingdom's 12 commercial banks were reporting losses. All reported sharply lower profits. Thus, while the government urged the private sector to invest in the economy, businessmen could get no credit, because banks were leery of loaning money. Loans and advances fell 3.3 percent alone in 1986, after the steepest declines were already registered in 1984 and 1985.[3]

The worst borrowers were the princes, some of whom assaulted bill collectors. At one time, banks prized their royal borrowers; today they loathe them. When Bahrain's royal family, the Al-Khalifa gained a reputation as deadbeats, the ruler, Shiekh Isa Bin Khalifa, offered his country's bankers a deal to pay 75 percent of his family's collective debts.[4] Some Bahrain-based banks were unhappy with the deal, but Saudi bankers looked on with envy; the Saudi royals refuse to admit a problem even exists.

Saudi newspapers accused the banks of greed; some said they should happily write off existing bad loans because they made big profits during the boom. These attitudes were aggravated because bankers are considered un-Islamic Westerners.

Part of the bad loan problem was self-inflicted. Loan-making policies were sloppy during the go-go period of the boom. Insufficient paper work was done, few loans were secured by collateral, and financial background checks were non-existent. Loans were made on a name basis, and princes were supposed to have the best names around. Some sources say corrupt bankers took pay-offs to approve loans. When questionable loans were made, it was hard to determine what was the reason it was made. One officer at a joint venture made such a disastrous series of loans that the bank had to write off 30 percent of its portfolio. He later established a bank overseas with a list of founders who closely resembled the bank's list of bad borrowers. When a Saudi banker was brought in to clean up a troubled joint venture, he was removed by SAMA after approving loans to select individuals above regulated limits.

Foreign bankers focused on short term results, particularly since the managing directors who doled out easy credit had climbed further up the corporate ladders by the time the loans went bad. "I think that you can always look back and say, 'Boy, was I dumb,'" said Mike Callen, the first managing director of Citicorp's joint venture, Saudi American Bank (SAMBA). He said the banks did not overlook the clash between interest-based banking and Islam, and had every reason to expect the boom would continue. "We had lots of analysts, and nobody predicted that the price of oil would go down. We had the head of a major oil company say oil was going up to $100 a barrel."

A few banks salvaged bad loans creatively. Al-Bank Al-Saudi Al- Fransi (Saudi French Bank), a joint venture of Banque Indosuez, came up with several interesting solutions to bad loans. When the Beta Group fell into arrears, (its chairman, Abdulaziz Zaidan, was also chairman of Saudi Cairo Bank!) the bank took Beta's share in a Riyadh building which was then used as a temporary headquarters building. To help the Korean contractor, Hyundai, work off debt built up by stalled government payments, Al-Fransi awarded its new headquarters construction contract to the firm. Hyundai built the building as payment for its debt.

Others were spooked and tried to bail out of the Kingdom's joint venture banks. USCB, created in 1983 out of Lebanese, Iranian, and Pakistani banks, experienced the first defection. Banque Du Liban de Outre Mer, sold its 10 percent share in 1986. Chase was one of the last banks to enter the Kingdom, and was one of the first to bolt when things got rough. Chase sought to unload its 20 percent share in Saudi Investment Bank (SAIB) as early as 1986, and was permitted to sell 5 percent to Dr. Mahsoun Jalal, former chairman of USCB, who also bought the five percent share of Germany's Commerzbank. Chase has tried to interest Gulf Investment Bank (GIB) of Bahrain in its remaining shares. SAIB's Chairman Dr. Abdulaziz Al- Dukheil, resigned in protest at the sale of the Commerzbank holding. He had not been properly informed of the deal, he said. "Approval of the sale tells these foreign bankers that it is OK to leave when things get rough after taking all the profits during the good times," he said.[5]

Little Bank Al-Jazira's 35 percent partner, National Bank of Pakistan, tried to sell its shares to a consortium of Saudi buyers headed by a member of NCB. The deal was signed, but blocked by the central bank. SAMA tried to stifle news of these defections, and forced some banks to "doctor" their balance sheets. Bank Al-Jazira lamely claimed a SR7 million profit in 1987, when it really drained SR100 million, out of a total of SR340 million shareholders funds, to make provisions.[6] This balance sheet sleight of hand was made with approval of SAMA. SAIB sources add that SAMA ordered them one year to adjust the balance sheet to show at least a small profit. These ploys failed to reassure foreign bankers, for they were evidence of a lack of internal banking controls which made the Saudi financial market more risky.

PRIVATE CAPITAL

Even during the grimmest period of the loan crisis, private Saudi investors were wealthy. Their estimated $60 billion overseas holdings were nearly equal those of the government. Saudis keep most of their money in Europe and the United States; the worldwide stock market crashes of October, 1987, only slowed the outflow of cash. They, and the large Lebanese business community, shift funds out of the country with little urging. The invasion of Iraq caused a capital stampede away from the Kingdom.

International creditors were already beginning to avoid the Kingdom because of unpaid bills when foreign lenders increased the business risk rating of Saudi Arabia. This alarmed the Ministry of Finance since it was secretly planning to begin borrowing. It started by issuing Bankers Secured Deposit Accounts (BSDAs) on a discounted basis. This means a buyer pays less than its face value, but is paid the full amount when the note is mature. This way, the government avoids paying "interest." The government faced greater resistance in 1988 when SAMA officially began borrowing by unveiling a $8 billion offering of "Development Bonds." The bonds, based upon the "cash flow" of un-named projects, yielded returns suspiciously similar to those of U.S. Treasury bills. SAMA said the yields were based upon "profit" instead of Islamically-forbidden "interest."

Shiekh Bin Baz, the stern head of the Religious Board of Scholars, was not fooled. How can an Islamic government pay interest on loans? he asked a source, who added that the scholar personally took credit for killing the proposal. However, nothing is so persuasive as necessity. Oil revenues in 1988 were still lower than projected. Fahad supposedly told Bin Baz that the first budget cuts would go on the Mosque expansion projects. Consequently, on June 11, SAMA cautiously started offering bonds to banks and government financial institutions. The cash-rich General Organization for Social Insurance (GOSI) and the Civil Service Pension Fund were tapped for the first, quiet issue of the bonds. In 1988, the two funds held up to $30 billion of the Kingdom's total $65 billion of reserves. The offerings were generally unsuccessful because the rates were not competitive in light of the relative illiquidity of the bonds. There was no secondary market, for instance, and the government only grudgingly gave permission to sell them to larger private investors, or include them in privately-held investor funds.

Abalkhail responded to decreasing confidence in his financial sector by extending foreign partners' tax holiday on bank reserves to 1991. His difficult task was to devise a system to bridge the gap between Islamic Sharia Law and Western banking practices. The practice of using euphemisms such as "commissions" for interest payments, was no longer sufficient. SAMA Governor Hamad Sayyari, and SAMA Director of Banking Control Jammaz Suhaimi, came up , with a solution they called The Banking Disputes Committee during March, 1988.

THE BANKING DISPUTES COMMITTEE

Abalkhail approached some U.S. diplomats at a function and said, excitedly, "Wait till you see what we have done." He unveiled his masterpiece at a banker's luncheon in the new SAMA building, a five-story marble building with huge, intricately patterned, bronze doors. Abalkhail said Fahad issued a Royal Decree transferring 500 outstanding loan disputes from the Commercial Courts to the new committee. Cynical bankers complained, privately, that the new committee would give debtors a 6-month holiday while it was being formed.

SAMA named a three men panel consisting of: Deputy Minister of Commerce for Technical Affairs Dr. Muhammed Hassan Al-Jabr; Dr. Ali Al-Johany, former dean of King Fahad University of Petroleum and Minerals; and Dr. Abdul Aziz Al-Guweis, chairman and managing director of Saudi Consolidated Electric Co. (SCECO) of the Central Region. The committee meets 3 to 5 times a week.

The Committee was given coercive powers to block bad debtors from leaving the country, freeze their bank accounts, attach their assets, and request government agencies from doing any further business with them. In a country where almost all contracts flow from the government, the last is a heavy threat.

The Committee avoids clashes with Sharia by blocking appeals to Sharia courts. The decree states that appeals of the Committee's decisions must be taken to the Royal Court alone. This alone should discourage further appeals, considering the sn speed of the Royal Court in deciding anything. So far, appeals to Sharia courts, princely Majlis halls, and the Ministry of Justice have been consistently rebuffed.

The Committee is not a court, because it reaches decisions, not by law, but by compromise. It tries to hammer out binding accords between banks and their borrowers. "It is like the old Majlis, where they work to establish a compromise, even if right is completely on your side," one disgruntled banker said.

"We are not getting all we want, but even a little is better than nothing," a different banker said. The committee has reached decisions on nearly 500 cases, but has shown a disinclination to use its coercive powers. When it does bare its fangs, its teeth are not particularly sharp. Its first ruling, against a Saudi client of AlBank AlSaudi AlHollandi, went over a year and a half without enforcement. After a Jeddah businessman's assets were reported frozen and his passport seized, he was spotted traveling overseas.

ISLAMIC BANKING

In the final analysis, the Committee is a compromise, and not a solution to the problem of operating a Western banking system in a country based on Islamic law. Some experts argue that the Kingdom should stop trying to cobble together a hybrid, and simply develop a complete Islamic financial system. There is a lot of grassroots support for such an attempt. "If I thought there really was a way to bank without interest, I would quit this job and bank that way," said a Saudi Cairo Bank branch manager. SAMA's only Islamic Banking expert, a naturalized Saudi citizen of Pakistani origin, Dr. M. Umer Chapra says, "The predominant portion of the population would favor Islamic banking. Circumstances force them to use them (regular banks) and over the years, some of them have degenerated (in response to economic pressure)," he says. He argues that 80-85 percent of the Saudi and Muslim depositors held non-interest-bearing demand deposits. Now, Chapra says, only 60-65 percent hold demand deposits. SAMA figures show the number of people holding interest-bearing deposits is about 44 percent, up from only 10.6 percent ten years before.[7] Certainly, the depositors' Islamic fervor dimmed as the economic crunch started to bite. Low-cost demand deposits are a boon to banks

Dr. Chapra has written *Towards a Just Monetary System*, which spells out the arguments for an Islamic system. He contends that interest-based economics encourage unsound lending to maximize profits. Western banks loan money as long as they feel the borrower has sufficient assets to pay back the loan, and do not care if the money is going toward frivolous or financially sound purposes. Since Islamic banks do not loan as much as "invest" for a period of time, they are concerned with viability. He says interest-based banking encourages wasteful over-lending, and over-consumption.

The decline in oil revenue has spurred an increase in religious feeling, and this has made itself felt in banking. This grassroots support for Islamic banking does not help Dr. Chapra. His office is a lonely one, seldom visited by SAMA's leaders. The Ministry of Finance is not only NOT interested in Islamic banking, he says, but is actively opposed to it.

SAMA, for instance, has refused to license Islamic banks. Prince Faisal's Dar Al Mal Islami (Islamic House of Gold), Saleh Kamel's Albarakat (The Blessings), and other Islamic banks owned by Saudis and other Muslims have unofficial offices in the Kingdom. None are permitted to open actual branches in the Kingdom. Albarakat, which has offices in other countries, maintains its headquarters in Jeddah.

"SAMA is acting as if they (Islamic banks) are affected with leprosy," Dr. Chapra says. The obvious reason SAMA resists Islamic banking is because even one "Islamic" bank raises two questions, "Are these other banks Islamic? and "What are non-Islamic banks doing in Islamic Saudi Arabia?"

"We know that Saudi Arabia is the heartland of Islam. Some of these banks are questionable,(one of Egypt's largest Islamic banks collapsed soon after the interview) and in any case, it is a very new thing they are trying. We cannot allow everyone to simply call their business Islamic, because that is like granting it religious approval. We are conscious of our religious responsibility, and we cannot experiment lightly with Islam," a high-ranking SAMA official said privately.

MONEY EXCHANGERS

The most Islamic and certainly most indigenous part of the Saudi financial system is the group of companies called money exchangers. These were founded by men who changed currency for pilgrims and later, for foreign workers. Michael Field, area journalist and author of two books about the Gulf, interviewed Suleiman Al-Rajhi, founder of the largest money exchanger, Al-Rajhi Company for Currency Exchange and Commerce. When Suleiman and his brother wished to transfer gold bullion between their Jeddah and Riyadh offices, one would travel to the airport, and hand a passenger gold bars with the instructions, "Give these to a man named Al-Rajhi at the other end."

"We never lost a bar," the old man said.[8]

Ahmed Hamad Al-Gosaibi, founder of Ahmed Hamad Al-Gosaibi & Brothers, provided $1 million in silver coins, because the Saudi workers would not accept anything else. He scoured the Gulf for big silver Maria Theresas, or the silver rupees of the British Raj, and brought them to Al-Khobar by Dhow and a caravan of 100 camels.

As years passed, the exchangers grew wealthier. Their low overhead allowed them to offer the best exchange rates. Banks closed before most laborers were finished with work, while the exchangers were open in the evening. Some even sent men out to labor camps for door-to-door banking. Exchangers thus captured 80 percent of the remittance market of over 4 million guest workers.

Al-Rajhi established a branch network bigger than NCB's with assets and profits that placed it among the top three or four banks in the Kingdom. He would later convert it into the Al-Rajhi Banking and Investment Corp. (ARABIC) a bank that made more profits than the four largest banks in the Kingdom put together. Jeddah-based Injaz, which means "Accomplishment" owned by a Saudi woman, Amouna Jamal, is typical of smaller firms. Her late husband founded the company in 1978 and opened five branches, with 3 in Jeddah, 1 in Mecca, and 1 in Al-Khobar. From 25 to 40 different exchangers sprouted up. Almost half were based in Jeddah. During the Hajj in Mecca, the number of exchangers balloons to handle the pilgrims. However, with time, five companies grew to dominate the sector. Al-Rajhi Company for Currency Exchange and Commerce, founded by Suleiman and three brothers, was as large as the rest put together. Two of the other top firms are owned by members of the Al-Rajhi family. The remaining two are owned by Al-Gosaibi, and by Kaki. Number six is probably Al-Subaie.

The profusion of Al-Rajhi money exchangers is confusing to the public and irritating to the four elder Al-Rajhi brothers. The fifth Al-Rajhi brother, Abdul Rahman Al-Rajhi, established his own firm, although his brothers disapproved. Based in Jeddah, the firm is named the Alrajhi Commercial Group for Currency Exchange. Sons of the original brothers founded two other companies. The Abdullah Salih Al-Rajhi Establishment was founded by Abdullah Salih. His brother, Abdul Rahman Salih Al-Rajhi established the Dammam-based Al-Rajhi Trading Establishment.

With time, the exchangers offered quasi-banking services. The 1966 Banking Control Act forbade this, but was ignored. Al-Rajhi and the others gave overdraft facilities and took deposits. These deposits are tremendously profitable. One exchanger privately confided that the money is placed overseas with banks, where, against Islamic injunctions, it earns interest. Most exchangers do this, but deny it. SAMA ached to control these exchangers, and finally got its chance with the collapse in July, 1982, of the Abdullah Salih Al-Rajhi Establishment.

Abdullah Salih Al-Rajhi's company collapsed after he speculated in silver, leaving debts of $300 million. Workers held worthless drafts. SAMA took advantage of this disaster to finally implement the long-ignored controls on the exchanger. SAMA announced that money exchangers would have to cease taking deposits. The big Al-Rajhi firm was to go public and be converted into a bank. Exchangers had to keep 20 percent of their capital on reserve with a SAMA-approved bank. The exchangers were also required to submit monthly statements to SAMA.

Implementation of the decree was uneven. Five years later, officials at Kaki reported that they took deposits as usual. So did Al-Rajhi Trading Establishment and Al-Gosaibi in the Eastern province. SAMA officials said they could not touch the original five, since their licenses came from the Ministry of Commerce before the Ministry of Finance became involved. Smaller exchangers were forced to obey, and bitterly complained that the big offenders could ignore the new regulations.

Al-Rajhi delayed their conversion while other exchangers examined their options. For a while, Dammam's Al-Rajhi Trading Establishment thought about merging with 9 other exchangers to become a bank. Al-Gosaibi, which had a small branch network but high technology, was already the house bank to the Al-Gosaibi trading and industry conglomerate, and wanted to become a merchant bank. Abdul Rahman Al-Rajhi sought a banking license, and applied for an Offshore Banking Unit (OBU) license from the Bahrain Monetary Agency.

The smaller exchanges awaited the transformation of Al-Rajhi into ARABIC, a move resisted by the Al-Rajhi brothers, who saw no need to share their profits. The brothers began stripping non-banking assets, such their unprofitable building materials factories and real estate. The SR322.5 million offering hit the market in 1988 and was oversubscribed within ten days. The offering was oversubscribed by over 7 times when it closed 30 days later. Al- Rajhi collected over SR2.5 billion in deposits for the shares, which it kept for the four months it took to sort out share distribution. Al-Rajhi disingenuously replied that profits gained from holding the deposits would eventually benefit all shareholders, so there would be no point in rapidly returning the deposits. These deposits were added to the SR12 Billion ARABIC already held in interest-free deposits. Against this, the bank had zero bad loans, and was therefore wildly profitable. Its first partial year of operation, pulled in over SR500 million profit, which was more than the next three most profitable banks put together. 1989 profits were close to SR1 billion.[8]

STOCK MARKET

By all criteria, a stock market is the ideal Islamic investment vehicle; investors share in the fortunes of the companies, and stocks are an accepted and well-understood investment. None-theless, government regulations tend to restrict the Saudi stock market, mainly to avoid a repeat of Kuwait's Souk Al-Manakh market crash. The Kuwaiti stock market lost some $90 billion due to use of post-dated checks. Though caution is laudable, Saudi financiers criticize the government's ambivalence about developing a strong capital market.

The government dealt a blow in 1984, when it eased out the old trader network in favor of the commercial banks, and required new procedures taking days or weeks to complete a deal. The next change was the 1987 opening of the Central Trading Hall. Investors were thrilled with the opening of a modern centralized stock market. One month later, the Saudi Big Board was dead, victim of a turf battle between the Ministry of Commerce and the Ministry of Finance. The Ministry of Commerce registers companies, and staked a claim to controlling stock transactions. The Ministry of Finance argued that the stock market is a financial organization and under its jurisdiction. Meanwhile, traders bitterly complained. Open bidding put too much pressure on their margins because the computerized system made it difficult to manipulate stock prices. Share trading reverted back to the banks. Sayyari said in 1988 that the hall would remained closed.

The irony is that the hall was closed just as the markets shook off three years of inactivity with major new offerings. Stocks for four major firms were floated. One of these was the giant money exchanger, Al-Rajhi. The flotations showed that Saudi investors were again looking for local opportunities. Yet, a lack of standardized reporting procedures, slow trading, and domination of the market by several dozen big traders, has retarded the market's development.

BANKS

The Western banking sector consists of 9 foreign joint venture banks and 3 Saudi banks: NCB, Riyad Bank, and ARABIC. The first Western banks arrived to provide services for pilgrims from French and Dutch colonies. Banque Indosuez and Bank Allgemene opened offices in the Western Province. The Mahfouz, Abdulaziz Kaki and Musa Kaki families formed a firm which became NCB in 1953. NCB was the Kingdom's bank until SAMA was formed, and was the third Arab bank after Palestine's Al-Hamemed Shoman (Arab Bank) and Egypt's Bank Misr.

British Bank of the Middle East, subsequently part of the Hongkong Bank group, opened offices in Jeddah and Al-Khobar in 1950. Next, the Al-Degaither, Sharbatli, Al-Souwailem, Abu Dawoud and Binzagr families started Riyad Bank in 1957. The bank racked up serious problems by the early Sixties and was bailed out by SAMA, which took a 38 percent share. Two Lebanese banks, Banque Du Liban et d'Outre Mer, and Lebanese Arab Bank were permitted to operate. Saudi investors happened to own large share in Lebanese Arab Bank. Pakistan was represented by United Bank of Pakistan, and National Bank of Pakistan. Korea Exchange Bank set up an office to service Korean contractors, but there were no Japanese or German banks. There was a total of 14 banks compared to over 40 in Abu Dhabi, and 50 in Dubai. The dominant banks were NCB and Riyad Bank, that got 60 percent and 20 percent of deposits, respectively, during the 70s. [9]

Citicorp opened the first joint venture bank branch in Riyadh. Chase, Industrial Bank of Japan, and Commerzbank of Germany, opened what would later be called the Saudi Investment Bank (SAIB) in a late attempt to enter the market. The newest joint venture bank, United Saudi Commercial Bank, (USCB) was established in 1983 by merging several banks. The transformation of the Al-Rajhi money exchange firm into a bank in 1988, gives the Kingdom 12 banks. Sayyari said no new banking licenses will be awarded.

When business was good, the Ministry of Finance enforced Saudization of the Kingdom's banks. Abalkhail recalled, "Some banks, like the Dutch, made the response immediately, but Citicorp was very resistant to the idea." [10] Eventually all of them caved in because the Saudi market was so lucrative; Citicorp's joint venture, SAMBA, paid Citicorp's investment in its first year of operation.

SAMBA touts itself as the leader in Saudi banking technology, even though it made one of the biggest computer purchase errors of any of the Kingdom's banks. It rejected IBM for a shocker: Perkins-Elmer. Perkins-Elmer computers are excellent machines, but they are primarily industrial process machines. Because of this, the bank's computer programming department has been forced to reinvent the wheel over and over, as it adapts normal banking peripherals, such as terminals or Automatic Teller Machines (ATMs) to the Perkins-Elmer machines. SAMBA is one of the best-run and most profitable foreign banks.

Arab National Bank is also a top performing bank, but follows a different path to profits. The joint venture with Arab Bank Ltd., of Jordan, sticks to low technology basic banking. It handles the government's Civil Service Pension account, which provides a huge low-cost deposit base. The only liability is that the bank must open branches even in uneconomic areas. ANB takes deposits and makes few loans; this policy earns good profits. However, when the bank applied to SAMA for permission to double its capital, the central bank refused. ANB's assistant managing director said the capital increase was approved after loans increased the next year.

Ironically, most of the banks are following ANB's lead. Loan less money and funnel funds overseas. This subverts the whole purpose of maintaining a Western banking sector; they are supposed to provide loans to bolster the economy. However, in the absence of payment guarantees, bankers extend credit grudgingly.

THE FINANCIAL SECTOR

The banks, money exchangers, and stock market are controlled by the Ministry of Finance and National Economy, which started life as the private treasury for King Abdulaziz. Today it is a sophisticated organization overseeing SAMA, the customs department, a statistics department, and the department collecting the 2.5 percent religious tax, called *Zakat*. In addition, the Ministry is the primary member of the five specialized credit agencies which have provided billions of dollars of subsidized loans to Saudi citizens. These agencies are the Saudi Industrial Development Fund (SIDF), the Real Estate Development Fund (REDF), the Saudi Agriculture Bank (SAAB), the Public Investment Fund (PIF) and the Saudi Credit Bank (SCB). These banks have billions of dollars in outstanding loans, and played an important role in disbursing petrodollars and in encouraging economic growth. The SIDF provides up to 50 percent financing for private industrial projects and the power generation companies. The REDF provides up to $80,000 in ten-year no-interst oans for homes or commercial buildings. The SAAB provides low-cost loans for machinery, seed, livestock and land. The PIF was established to provide 60 percent of the financing for large petrochemical plants and refineries, but was used to bail out Saudi Cairo Bank by doubling its capital. The SCB is the smallest of the five, and provides loans for miscellaneous needs, including wedding dowries. The generosity of all five has decreased along with oil revenues. The Ministry is only awarding loans out of repayments, and delays new loan approvals for months at a time.

The man who oversees all of this is a man of uncommon rectitude and shrewdness: Mohammed Abalkhail. The pro-American minister's family, like that of the Al-Saud, hails from the Nejd, and most of his appointees come from his hometown of Qassim as well. Some joke that the abbreviation H.E. Minister of Finance, does not mean "His Excellency" but "Hejazis Exit."[11] When the Hejazi former SAMA Governor Abdulaziz Al-Quraishi retired, his Hejazi deputy, Ahmed Abdul Latif was expected to replace him. Latif, descended from some long ago Asian pilgrims, was rejected in part because he looks "too Asiatic." Sayyari was selected instead, though it took almost two years to install him as full SAMA governor. Abalkhail's men tend to resemble him in brains and stature. He, Sayyari, Suhaimi, and most of the other Finance officials are both intelligent and short.

Abalkhail took over the Finance portfolio from Prince Musaid bin Abdul Rahman in 1975. That was at the beginning of the oil boom. Foreigners worried that oil-rich Arabs would wreak havoc with the world's financial system. Instead, the Saudis maintained a conservative investment policy, advised by Britain's Baring Brothers, and America's Merrill Lynch. Investments were made quietly in coordination with the central banks of the affected countries.

Contrary to Media reports, the Kingdom did not try to control the West's economic system and kept most investments relatively liquid. "Equity or real estate were never really attractive to us; it was always under 5 percent of the total. That was a very rigid rule," Abalkhail said. "We were not trying to use our investments to gain influence here or there. It was never political."

"We always felt that the surpluses had a very temporary nature...I was never taken in by the idea that we would be rich forever...The decline in oil revenues and the surplus happened in a way that was not only unexpected, but very difficult. It was impossible for us to make a very short-term focus in our investment strategy....we tried to take the uncertainty into consideration, to be conservative, to reduce the forecast of the Oil Ministry to be on the safe side. But we were still surprised. I was working with Shiekh Zaki (Yamani) a lot then. We were working with the same uncertainties. It was beyond the control of anyone in the government."[12]

Abalkhail has preserved himself through the highs and lows of the Kingdom's finances by competence and a low profile. The Riyadh Intercontinental Hotel, owned by the Ministry of Finance, was preparing to open a new complex. Its banquet halls are named after various Saudi towns, and the largest new room was called "Buraiydah." At the last minute, Abalkhail's office and ordered, "Change the name." The bewildered hotel management learned later that Buraiydah was Abalkhail's birthplace. "He didn't want anyone to think he was glorifying himself," an extremely smooth Lebanese hotel executive said, marvelling at Abalkhail's subtlety.

SAMA - THE SAUDI ARABIAN MONETARY AGENCY

Some call SAMA a mere messenger boy for the Ministry of Finance, not an independent central bank. SAMA Director of Banking Control Suhaimi is peeved that critics call SAMA a "quasi" central bank because it cannot serve as a lender of last resort. "What else are we then?" he asks, adding that SAMA regulates banks and manages the Saudi economy.

In the good old days, the Saudis regulated the economy and money supply through government spending. More government projects and subsidies boosted the money supply. Less spending trimmed it. That was the extent of it. Now, by offering better rates on BSDAs and the "Development Bonds," SAMA can attract more riyals. Those riyals which buy bonds and BSDAs are taken out of circulation and placed with SAMA. Thus, the central bank now has the means of adjusting the monetary supply by shrinking it.

This is a long way from SAMA's humble beginnings in 1952 when it was located in Jeddah. High on the list of SAMA's tasks was to introduce a novel concept: paper currency. Up until then, the accepted currency was the silver riyal. An American advisor was the father of the Kingdom's first paper currency: Pilgrim's Receipts.

SAMA issued Receipts to save pilgrims the burden of lugging purses full of coins. They were a temporary measure designed to educate the populace about paper money. Instead, they remained in circulation for 8 years until the first paper riyals were issued.

Saudis use cash. Old men feel secure enough to several hundred thousand riyals in plastic bags. Saudis do not trust checks, particularly those written by fellow citizens. One crafty fellow opened checking accounts at all of the Kingdom's major banks by depositing money. As soon as he was issued checks, he closed the accounts and bought a rubber stamp reading, "Certified Check." He then bought expensive watches, gold, and other goods. Merchants, wary of bouncing checks, refused, until he told them he was giving them "certified" checks. The merchants knew certified checks are a guaranteed form of payment, but weren't sophisticated enough to detect a con job. Their shock upon trying to cash the checks was considerable and the banks had to show the angry merchants what real certified checks look like. Dislike of checks, and the arrival of credit cards and ATM machines means the Saudis will probably leapfrog the check stage, and go straight to plastic money.

CONCLUSION

The Saudis might bypass checks, but not Islam. ARABIC's popularity indicates the Saudi grassroots support for Islamic banking. Islamic banking is fine for the average man, but has not demonstrated an ability to rechannel money back into investment and loans. The Western banks can do this, but stiffed by Saudi creditor ethics, and handicapped by Saudi law, they are no longer supplying the credit needed to sustain economic growth. It seems as if the halfway measures enacted so far help keep the ship afloat, but not get it moving.

The private sector, however, may work around some of these problems. Dr. Jalal's National Industrialization CO. (NIC) is seeking Islamic investment partners for some projects. One small firm has tried to capitalize on the average Saudi's need for personal credit . It buys and holds title to the item, a car for example, that is purchased. The borrower then pays "rent," until the price, plus "commission" is paid.

As interesting as these experiments are, they do not solve the big problem of the Kingdom's financial sector: how do you operate a modern interest-based banking system in a country based on Sharia law? Nobody in the Saudi government has come up with an answer.

13

AGRICULTURE AND WATER

"The Righteous (will be) amid Gardens and Fountains (of clear flowing water)," —*"Al-Hijr"*
Sura XV, Verse 45, The Koran

Sometime in 1985, a wizened old Qassimi farmer confronted the Saudi agriculture dilemma. Officials encouraged him to produce wheat by offering large subsidies, but months after he delivered his harvest, the government failed to pay. He stamped impatiently into the office of bureaucracy responsible for buying wheat, the Grain Silos and Flour Mills Organization.

"Where is my money?" he demanded. Every request for payments was met by delays, excused by low oil revenues. The clerk grimaced at the small man with dirty thobe and ghutra. "Go to hell," he said harshly.

"I planted my wheat, by God, and I brought it here, and I was told we would be paid."

"Go talk to the one who told you to plant the wheat," the clerk said, and dismissed him. As the farmer climbed into his battered Toyota pickup, he decided to see the man who told him to plant: the King. He attended the next Majlis of the Custodian of the Two Holy Harams and repeated the conversation he held with the Grain Silos clerk. Fahad smiled and blandly promised to help. Later, the monarch exploded, "Why aren't the farmers being paid on time?"

Minister of Agriculture, Dr. Abdul Rahman Al-Sheikh, authorizes unneeded agricultural projects because the Ministry of Commerce pays the Grain Silos' bills, he was told. Fahad then transferred the Grain Silos to the Ministry of Agriculture. The Minister of Finance, Mohammed Abalkhail, who opposed wheat subsidy payments, and Minister of Commerce, Soliman Al-Solaim were glad to drop the problem in Al-Sheikh's lap.

A SENSITIVE ISSUE

I was nearly thrown out of the Kingdom because of a story about the wheat program. The Ministry of Agriculture had sent a circular to the biggest wheat growers saying that, the next year, the Ministry would buy only 60 percent of the present year's crop. A Reuters story went out based on mine, but erroneously said the government would only buy 60 percent of the PRESENT crop. Al-Sheikh happened to be in Rome, headquarters of the United Nations' Food and Agriculture Organization (FAO). He read the article and was furious, not only because of the error, but because it pointed out that wheat payments were way behind schedule. My editor informed me that that King Fahad was also angry over the story. The fact that the Ministry had actually sent out the circular was no defense. My company talked the government out of deporting me, but ran my stories without bylines for the next couple of months to keep me out of sight. Several farmers later thanked me, because the article prompted the Ministry to finally pay for the wheat. Late wheat payments were chronic during my years in the Kingdom, and a great source of irritation to the agribusiness community.

AGRICULTURE AND WATER

Saudi agriculture policy is captive to the rhetoric of self-sufficiency. The government pays money it can no longer afford, to grow wheat surpluses it doesn't need, while consuming water it can't replace. The new realities of the oil glut still have not forced the Saudis to address this problem. In 1988, Deputy Minister of Finance Saleh Al-Omair told the BBC's Barnaby Mason that all agricultural subsidies would be removed within a year. The Royal Court sharply rebuked him. When former U.S. Secretary of Agriculture John R. Block visited the Kingdom in May, 1983 he said it was "Crazy" for the Kingdom to pursue agricultural self- sufficiency when it could buy wheat at low prices from the United States. He touched a nerve.

"Is it crazy to make the desert bloom?" shrieked an editorial in the now-defunct *Saudi Business* weekly magazine. "Farming is a most expressive means of patriotism," thundered Al-Sheikh.[1]

Self-sufficiency, income distribution, and rural employment motivate the wheat program. Saudis feel vulnerable to food embargoes even though wheat keeps for years, and is available from many sources. The subsidy redistributes oil income to provide small farmers a decent income. The Saudi rulers believe it is healthier for people to earn recycled petrodollars by farming than simply collect welfare checks. Finally, the government wanted to avoid the usual Third World problem wherein the countryside empties into giant cities full of underemployed, potentially volatile masses. Agricultural subsidies and rural development give Saudis an incentive to stay in the countryside.

The agricultural program did not work as intended. The rush to the cities may have been slowed, but not stopped, because many farmers hire foreigners to do the work. The Egyptians list farm laborers as one of their larger categories of expatriate workers. Further, most of the farming subsidy is collected, not by small farmers, but by princes and wealthy businessmen who established expatriate-staffed farms to reap the subsidies.

The wheat subsidy began as a guaranteed price of SR3,500 or about $1,000 per metric ton of wheat. That was five times the world wheat price in those days. When experts added the impact of other subsidies, such as electricity, diesel fuel for the pumps (2.7 cents per liter), low-cost loans, etc., the subsidies were worth 15 times the world price.

Farmers soon produced harvests in excess of the estimated 800,000-900,000 tons the country uses per year. From 3,300 tons in 1978, the harvest reached 3.6 million tons in 1989. Yields surged just as the oil glut began to bite. The 1984 harvest of 1,346,930 tons cost $1.3 billion. All this money went to just 15,911 farmers, according to Dr. Ahmad Shinawi, head of the General Organization for Grain Silos and Flour Mills (Grain Silos), which buys the wheat, stores it, and grinds it into flour.[2]

The main beneficiaries are large publicly-held agriculture companies. In 1986, five publicly-held firms alone accounted for 30 percent of the harvest. These firms are: National Agricultural Development Co. (NADEC); Tabouk Agricultural Development Co. (TADCO), Hail Agricultural Development Co. (HADCO), Qassim Agricultural Development Co. (QADCO), and the Eastern Agricultural Development Co. (EADCO). Another new publicly-held firm, Al-Jouf Agricultural Company (JACO) was established in 1986.

Princes are big shareholders in these firms, and the regional governor is usually the company chairman. Prince Miqren Bin Abdulaziz, the governor of Hail, is most visible of these as he directs operations of HADCO. But participation of princes is not restricted to publicly-traded companies. They hold shares, together with wealthy Saudis, in another 20 or so firms, that account for an additional 20 percent of Saudi wheat production. Ironically, Saudis imported wheat even while the surplus mounted. At that time, farmers grew soft wheat, while Saudis prefer hard wheat.

The surplus forced the Grain Silos Organization to embark on a crash construction program. Storage capacity rose from 900,000 tons in 1983, to 1.5 million tons in 1986. Larger farms were ordered to store wheat on their property. Delayed payments caused an outcry until Fahad ordered the Organization to pay the farmers in 1985.

The government then cut the wheat purchase price to SR2,000 ($533) per ton. By then, momentum had built up, and the next harvest was 1.7 million tons. Farms had already installed their irrigation systems and continued raising additional wheat. By 1986, the wheat harvest weighed in at 2.3 million tons, and cost the Kingdom over $1.26 billion. The harvest cost nearly as much as it did before the subsidy was cut.

The Ministry decided, in September, of 1986, to attack both the wheat surplus, and a different agriculture program that was going haywire: barley. A price war between Europe and the United States drove barley prices down to $69 a ton, yet the government still paid a barley import subsidy of $80 per ton. That year, the Kingdom imported nearly 5.5 m tons of barley for livestock. This was far more than Saudi animals could eat.

The government decided to phase out the import subsidy, and encourage barley cultivation with a SR1,000 ($266.66) per metric ton guaranteed price. The public agriculture firms were required to plant a third of their area in barley. In 1988, the government reduced the wheat subsidy to big farms to SR1,500 ($400) per ton but kept the old subsidy for smaller farmers. It also resumed its habit of delaying payments. As farmers hauled the 3.6 million ton 1989 wheat harvest to the silos, the large farmers contemplated the fact that while the small farmers were paid for the 1988 harvest, they were not. The government was nearly $1.3 billion in arrears. Meanwhile, the Kingdom began exporting wheat. Several million tons were sold, but the most were shipped as foreign aid to Syria, Jordan, Egypt, and Bangladesh.[3]

OTHER AGRICULTURE SUCCESSES

The desert's traditional staff of life, the date, has been cultivated in the Kingdom for centuries, but under subsidized support, production has soared. In 1986, the Food and Agriculture Organization (FAO) listed the Kingdom has the world's number one date producer. Saudi dates are exported commercially and as foreign aid. Subsidies have changed Saudi farming output. Sorghum

---

SAUDI WHEAT PRODUCTION (From SAMA 1980 Annual Report)

1978 - 3,297 tons
1982 - 239,690 tons
1983 - 674,631 tons
1984 - 1,346,930 tons (subsidy reduced)
1985 - 1,700,000 tons
1986 - 2,000,000 tons
1987 - 2,600,000 tons (Barley Subsidy introduced)
1988 - 3,300,000 tons (Two-tiered subsidy introduced)
1989 - 3,600,000 tons

crops dropped by one half to two-thirds. Maize production fell by half. Millet production stayed even, while sesame increased a trifle.

Subsidies are just one of the many Government supports for agriculture. Through 1985, farmers have been given 713,965 donums of land by the Ministry of Agriculture. This is equivalent to 71,396 hectares, or 171,350 acres. In 1985 this grant land accounted for 10.2 percent of the total land under cultivation.[4]

The Saudi Agricultural Bank (SAAB) provides low-cost loans for machinery, fertilizer, and equipment. By the beginning of 1986, SAAB had outstanding loans totaling SR12.5 billion ($3.33 billion). It had already disbursed SR16.96 billion ($4.52 billion). The loans cover well drilling, fertilizer, vehicles, fuel, irrigation systems and pumps, plus construction, ploughing, and leveling. Project loans accounted for 38.1 percent of loans in 1405/1406, ending on Oct. 14, 1985. These projects are approved by the Minister of Agriculture.[5]

The other source of soft loans is the Saudi Industrial Development Fund (SIDF). Although SIDF is mainly industry- oriented, it makes loans for portions of large integrated food operations, such as dairies, fish processing plants, and big poultry operations. It provides loans for coldstores, and other parts of the Kingdom's food handling infrastructure. Downstream food processing is a high priority for Saudi planners, so these schemes get SIDF loans. SIDF has provided 106 loans for food projects worth SR991 million ($264.3 million) as of 1986.[6]

Influential individuals find other avenues. Tareq Abdul Hadi Taher, son of former Petromin Chief, Abdul Hadi Taher, obtained a SR270 million loan for his chicken operation directly from the Ministry of Finance because SAAB limited loans to SR20 million.[7] Since the Saudis eat more chicken per capita (31 kilos per year) than almost any other country, poultry operations received a good deal of aid.

Saudi poultry and egg producers compete fiercely amongst themselves and with big chicken exporting nations such as France (Chicken ranks in the top three of its exports to the kingdom.) After disbursing more than SR381 million for 103 broiler projects and SR196 million for 55 egg laying operations, SAAB found that poultry projects in 1983 were producing at only 50 percent of capacity due to chicken imports. By 1986, 267 broiler projects were producing 186,246,563 chickens weighing an average of 1 kilo each. Broiler chicks formerly were shipped into the Kingdom. By 1986, 24 hatcheries supplied enough chicks to meet domestic needs.[8]

Domestic poultry farmers have difficulty in marketing their output. One entrepreneur, Abdul Rahman Fakih, established over 400 small shops throughout the Kingdom in which a customer could select a bird to have it killed and mechanically plucked before his eyes. Saudi consumers like their birds fresh. Today, greater numbers of customers are buying chilled chicken.

Meanwhile, the Kingdom's egg-laying operations feel the effects of competition, despite a 25 percent imported egg tax. Egg prices fell 30 percent. The number of egg-laying operations peaked at 187 in 1984, with production at 2.4 billion eggs. In 1985, total egg production rose to 2.5 billion, but the number of projects declined to 168. Layer chicks are being produced by 4 local firms.[9]

Saudi agriculture proves most efficient when it receives the least government assistance. Greenhouses benefit only from general subsidies, and compete with imported produce. They tend to be energy and water efficient. Saudi tomatoes, cucumbers, and other vegetables are good quality. Greenhouse farmers were also helped by two events in the mid-eighties. The first was a decision in September, 1985, to ban foreign refrigerated vehicles from entering the Kingdom. The Ministry of Interior said smugglers were concealing drugs in the copper tubing of condenser units and in the insulated walls of the truck bodies.[10]

Another reason for banning foreign refrigerated trucks, was that it gave Saudi truckers more work. Unfortunately for consumers, truckloads of fresh Turkish, Lebanese, and European fruit and vegetables rotted in the heat as the cargoes were transferred to Saudi vehicles. The higher cost of imported fresh fruit helped Saudi producers. The Chernobyl nuclear accident resulted in the temporary banning of most European produce. Even without these windfalls, Saudi greenhouses have proven themselves competitive. In highly publicized instances, the Saudis have actually exported flowers to Holland and vegetables to Great Britain.

Some ventures are duds. Eastern Province farmers raised bumper crops of good quality potatoes, but the people eat rice, not potatoes. Consequently, the Ministry of Agriculture is encouraging construction of a frozen french fry factory.

Dairy farming has done well. Firms first imported powder for reconstituted milk, but fresh milk soon displaced these products. Swedes, Germans, Americans, and Irishmen provided dairy expertise adapted to the harsh Saudi environment. Cows live under sprinklers which keep them cool.

"We found that the wives were not taking our milk home to drink," said a surprised marketing man for Masstock Saudia. "We found they were taking it home to make Laban with it." Laban is a faintly sour-tasting cultured milk drink. It was originally made by the bedouin as a way to keep milk drinkable for three days or so without refrigeration. The Saudi dairies went back to their farms, experimented, and soon were putting Laban on the shelves. Today, almost 85 percent of fresh milk sales are Laban, though the proportion of fresh milk is rising slightly.

The Saudi Agricultural and Dairy Company (SAADCO) proved that extensive subsidies do not guarantee success. SAADCO was founded as a partnership between two Lebanese brothers, Prince Abdullah Al-Faisal, and Alfa-Laval, of Sweden. With close to 10,000 cows, it was expected to become the Kingdom's flagship dairy operation. Instead, it ran up huge debts and had to reschedule its loans with Saudi Investment Bank.

The camel, the traditional dairy animal of the desert, has earned a spot on Saudi milk counters. The first modern camel dairy, Al-Mujahem Co. for Camel Production, was founded by members of the famous camel-owning Al-Oteibi tribe. Several Al-Oteibi brothers, who work as bankers, police officers and computer operators, never lost their affection for camels. The dairy was their way of preserving the economic utility of the beast. Camel milk is more nutritious than cow milk, but camels do not lend themselves to mechanization. Their teats are different shapes, and a recalcitrant she-camel can withhold her milk. Twice a day, the camels are milked by hand and the milk is is taken in coolers to a nearby cow dairy for packaging. According to co-founder Sultan Al-Oteibi, a computer expert, "The hardest part of the business was convincing our relatives that we should enter this business. Traditionally, it is a shame to sell camel milk, and you should give it away free. But we said that this is the only way we can help preserve the camel and our heritage, so they finally agreed."

Saudi farmers and nomads traditionally raised livestock. The Kingdom contains an estimated 2.2 million goats, 2.9 million sheep, 399,000 cattle and 164,000 camels. These animals are seriously over-grazing the desert and ruining what is already marginal rangeland. Camels are still raised for their tastey meat, which is sold in supermarkets.

Although Saudis eat camel, they prefer sheep, particularly the more expensive Nejdi fat-tailed variety. Several of the public firms are building sheep pens for scientific breeding of this species. In the meantime, the Kingdom is the world's biggest importer of live sheep. This became a problem after the oil crunch made Saudis more price-conscious.

The government's response was to cripple imports from the world's lowest cost sheep producer: Australia. In 1989, inspectors turned back several shiploads of Australian sheep, claiming the animals were "diseased." The Australians noted that the alleged infections no longer occur in Australia, and that Kuwait bought the supposedly diseased sheep immediately afterwards. The Saudis refused to admit they faked disease papers, and put pressure on other GCC countries to follow their lead in rejecting Australian sheep.

Saudis obtain fish from the Red Sea and the Gulf. Gulf shrimp are exported throughout the world. The government has built small ports and cooperatives for traditional fishermen, but most exports come from one or two big firms employing foreigners.

COMPETITION

The government responded to rising domestic production, increased foreign competition, and lower oil revenues with protective duties. The private sector began forming cooperatives. The largest Agriculture companies banded together to form the National Company for Agricultural Marketing (Thimar) to build bulk sales outlets at the vegetable souks of the larger cities. Other cooperative ventures include the National Seed Company, established to provide seed for the Kingdom's wheat and barley crops. It has since been bypassed as a seed source by the big firms that created it, but is planning a joint venture under the Offset Investment Program. Conversely, the Kingdom's supermarkets have founded the National United Supermarkets to buy items in bulk. This forms an automatic counterweight to Saudi producers, but is more concerned with foreign purchases.

Meanwhile, SIDF-funded food processors are beginning to use some of the Kingdom's harvests. Companies include date packing plants, slaughterhouses, cookie, candy, and frozen pizza manufacturers.

THE FARMS AND HOW THEY WORK

Most major farms are located far from the amenities of civilization. The workers are invariably expatriates. Saudi Masstock, a joint venture between a prince and the Masstock brothers of Northern Ireland, has developed arid farming expertise. Masstock officials boast of the development of these techniques as "technology transfer" to the kingdom. However, all this knowhow is possessed by the farm workers who take it with them when their contracts expire.

Omar Al-Hoshan is a Saudi who takes a personal interest in his farm. He imports California date varieties, and has developed new cost-effective hydroponic techniques to raise lettuce in greenhouses. Sometimes, a Saudi's personal attention on a farm spells disaster. Australian farm hands in remote Wadi Dewassir met their new Saudi manager, who immediately asserted himself by changing every farm procedure. This was bad enough, but the injury was compounded when he marched to the yard where the men kept their pet dogs. The new manager rid the farm of such Islamically filthy animals by blowing their brains out with a pistol, and the Australians quit en masse.

Rod Walker, of Australia, was nearly killed after becoming involved in one of many arguments between farmers and bedouin over water and grazing rights. The bedouin lost his temper, drew his AK-47, and sprayed Walker's pickup truck with a burst of automatic fire. The pickup absorbed most of the rounds, but one entered and shattered Walker's elbow, partially crippling his arm.

Saudi farming is a triumph of technology over the environment. The center-pivot irrigation systems create circles of green in barren desert. Farms located near the red sands, seem like outposts on the deserts of Mars. One farmer said Saudi farming is similar to outdoor hydroponics.

The nearly worthless soil holds few nutrients, and serves only to hold the roots in place. Thus, sand is preferred to dirt because it is easier to plow. Sand raises water consumption by over 15 percent and fertilizer use by 10 percent, but these are subsidized, so it is no big deal. One ton of wheat requires 3 tons of irreplaceable water, and this is the most destructive aspect of the entire subsidized agriculture program.

WATER SUPPLIES

"Do not waste water, even if you are standing by a river," said the Prophet Mohammed. The Kingdom is not following his advice. Despite predictions that the Kingdom's underground water reserves are being depleted, the Ministry of Agriculture and Water Resources pursues wasteful water policies.

"We have enough water to last us 500 years at current rates of use," Al-Sheik confidently says, citing a King Fahad University of Petroleum and Minerals study. He either doesn't know about, or chooses to ignore a classified American report which predicts the Kingdom will run out of ground water by the year 2000. His optimism, which is shared by many countrymen, is part willful refusal to recognize the problem, and part belief in a flawed study which includes water that is impossible to recover because of salinity or depth. The study also ignores polluted groundwater and overestimates the ability of Saudi aquifers to recharge. Most Saudi underground water was deposited 10,000 years ago when rain fell and the peninsula was green. This "Fossil water" is not replaced. The Arabian Peninsula is an extension of the Sahara Belt and only gets an average of 100 mm (3.9 inches) rain per year.

The Ministry of Agriculture has refused to consider the following bits of information: well water levels at the NADEC farm in Tabouk fell 150 meters in its fist year of operation. Water levels in Al-Khobar, in the Eastern province, fell 90 meters in the last nine years, 60 meters of which were in the last two. A large rechargeable aquifer under Jordan reaches under the Hail region, but stops at a fault line near Buraidah. South of that town, the water table has fallen 70-80 meters a year.

The Ministry tried to arrest the declines by issuing drilling permits. In 1985, the number of government wells stood at 4,457, a slight but steady increase over the previous years. Privately drilled farm wells rose from 26,000 in 1982 to 45,000 in 1984 when the Ministry imposed a moratorium. The ban has been enforced on smaller farmers, but not the big companies. In 1985, the number of wells fell to 37,000, due in part to many wells silting or drying up and being taken out of service.[11] One Masstock expert says the shallower aquifers will be exhausted within 2 years, and the deeper aquifers could be suffering within 10.

Agriculture consumes more water than any other sector. Farmers used 7.4 billion cubic meters of water, or 84 percent of the 8.8 billion cubic meters used in 1406 (Oct. 14, 1985 - Oct. 4, 1986), according to the 1406 SAMA Annual Report. Urban, industrial, and other uses account for the remainder. Agriculture's share roughly corresponds to the percentage of water produced by wells. Desalination plants can meet most of the country's urban water needs even though waste takes place in cities, too. Riyadh, which is one of the world's heaviest per capita water users, sucked up 916,243 cmd in 1988. The Eastern Province and Jeddah consumed 423,000 cmd and 323,039 cmd respectively.[12]

Water in the major cities flows to home holding tanks. Many of these are old, and buried near leaky septic tanks and sewer lines. Almost every home has a rooftop storage tank filled by a pump. Families often leave water pumps running until the overflow cascades into the streets. After the oil glut made this practice too expensive, the Municipalities sent inspectors to fine people who waste water in this fashion.

The inspectors have made little headway against water wastage. The multitude of fountains is not only a testimony to the fascination the Saudis have with water, but also to its abundance and low cost. The Ministry estimates 1.6 percent of water use in the year 2000 will be for fountains, swimming pools, and parks. Saudis would resume water thrifty ways if they had to pay more for their H_2O, but even a modest rate hike in 1987 was dropped in the face of stiff opposition.

The best hope for increasing water use efficiency is the construction of sewage treatment plants. Without a sewage treatment plant, each gallon of desalinated water is used only once, barring the widespread but unhygienic practice of using raw sewage effluent for watering plants on highway dividers. A sewage treatment plant can recycle water several times, for less than it costs to build and operate desalination plants. Consequently, the Ministry of Agriculture is pushing ahead with water treatment plant construction. By the year 2000, the Ministry is aiming to have the capacity to recycle 40 percent of water used for domestic purposes. This depends upon the Ministry of Municipalities and Urban Affairs constructing enough sewage lines to connect the consumers. By the year 2,000, some 96 percent of the Kingdom's settled population (it estimates that at that time, 90 percent of the population will be settled) will be connected to sewers and running water.

Saudi water production efforts will be complicated by increasing salinity and pollution. Aquifers along the coasts are being invaded by salt water while water from lower depths is increasingly saline. Pollution is invading some of the shallower aquifers, including those of Mecca. Aramco frequently pumped drilling mud, a concoction containing heavy metals, down old wells where it percolated into water supplies. Industrial wastes have been haphazardly dumped; construction of a hazardous waste disposal facility was announced only in 1988. Leaky septic tanks and sewer pipes pollute shallower city wells.

Riyadh's natural drainage is so bad, that building foundations are threatened by water and hydrostatic pressure, a problem that is shared by other cities. Interestingly, the run-off of treated water has created a small river south of Riyadh, near the little town of Al-Hair. The treated water has created a freshwater river running perhaps 30 kilometers. The water is nutritious and supports huge goldfish and tilapia, as well as over 100 species of birds. The desert is truly blooming. The only other places were Saudis can glimpse standing water are 17 pond-sized lakes fed by springs, or water behind catchment dams. There are no natural year-round rivers or streams in the entire Kingdom.[13]

Catchment dams are built in the Wadis to prevent flash flooding after storms and to retain the water so it has time to sink into the ground instead of spreading thin across the land where it evaporates quickly. Catchment dams are not a new idea. The Sadd Ma'rib Dam of Yemen was built in the mid-seventh century B.C., and was known throughout Arabia.[14] The 1408 SAMA report says that by the end of 1988, 180 dams had been built, at a cost of over SR9 billion ($2.5 billion). The largest dam is the Wadi Najran Dam, with a storage capacity of 86 million cubic meters. It will be capable of irrigating 10,000 hectares of land. The Kingdom's dams hold a combined 655 million cubic meters of water, which is only that of a small dam elsewhere. Sediment threatens the dams. Wadi Jizan dam has already lost one-quarter of its capacity to silt.[15]

After a particularly heavy rain filled two catchment dams in Riyadh's Wadi Hanifah, the Mecca bridge high above the Wadi, was full of curious Saudis. One man drove his Land Rover so far into the water, the engine quit. Black clad women waded gingerly into the water. Families picnicked beside the incredible rarity: standing water. By the end of the ensuing summer, the lake had nearly dried up, leaving heavily cracked clay. But the job was done: the water had soaked into the aquifer, and serious flooding was averted.

SAUDI WATER TECHNOLOGY

Early Saudi water technology consisted of two types of wells: the Birr, a simple stone-lined well, and the Haddaj, a camel-powered well. Camels, heads held high, pull ropes slung over pulleys that are fastened to leather buckets. The largest Haddaj known still exists in Taima, 250 Kms south of Tabouk in the Northern part of Saudi Arabia. Historians say 99 camels paced back and forth to provide water for Taima in its heyday.[16]

In more modern times, donkeys pulled small tankers through Jeddah neighborhoods, and "Healthy Water" companies dispensed water through gasoline pump nozzles into large plastic jerry cans. The water is filtered and treated by these companies, but Riyadh banned them altogether. That forced choosier consumers to depend upon bottled water. The Kingdom probably sells more bottled water per capita than any other country. Around 12 plants produce water in plastic bottles that compose the most durable and ubiquitous litter across the Arabian peninsula.

Saudi water technology culminates in the removal of salt from seawater to provide drinking water. Jeddah's Corniche seaside drive contains statues ranging from stainless steel sunflowers to patrolboats on pedestals. One of its avant-garde sculptures is actually an old heat exchanger from the Kandensah, "Condenser," Jeddah's first salt water desalinator. This machine, built in 1928, marked the first Saudi attempt to derive potable water from the sea.

Not far from the Kandensah are the towering smokestacks of Jeddah I and Jeddah II, the city's massive desalination plants. Built at the cost of over a billion dollars, these giants supply millions of gallons of fresh water to the city each day. The Kingdom has more desalination capacity than the rest of the world put together. Both technologies have a harder job in the Kingdom than elsewhere. The world's seas have an average of 35,000 ppm salinity. The Red Sea has a level of 42,000 ppm, while the Gulf has a level of 56,000 ppm.

Two different technologies separate salt from water. The older technology depends upon a thermal process called Multi-Stage Flash (MSF) distillation. MSF heats water, and then runs it through low-pressure units where the water "flashes" into vapor. This is more efficient than simply boiling water, but still requires a lot of energy. The big MSF desalination units use their excess heat to generate electricity.

Reverse Osmosis depends upon more subtle processes. If salty and fresh water are separated by a semi-permeable membrane, the fresh water tends to migrate through the membrane until the average salinity of the two solutions is the same. That is osmosis. Reverse Osmosis exerts pressure on the salty water to "strain" it through membrane and reverse the process. MSF was formerly dominant, but improvements in Reverse Osmosis membranes have narrowed the gap.

Most Saudi desalination plants are built by the Saline Water Conversion Corporation (SWCC), based in Riyadh. SWCC's Chairman is the Minister of Agriculture and Water. By the end of 1988, the government had built 22 desalination plants with a capacity of more than 1.8 million cubic meters per day. Two were built by the Royal Commission for Jubail and Yanbu. The rest were built by SWCC. Two thirds of production is in the East, and one-third in the West. Seventeen new projects are planned. The MSF plants generated 20.1 million Megawatts in 1988, and new projects should add over 400 MW per day capacity. These plants cost tens of billions of dollars. Operating them is also expensive. The Turks estimate that a cubic meter of Saudi water costs $2.50-$3.00, even when using cheap natural gas in the Eastern Province.

Other technologies are on the horizon, including a solar unit built as part of the Saudi-American Joint Committee on Economic Cooperation's Soleras program. The Yanbu plant uses the sun to drive a compressor which freezes water. When the water begins to freeze, the salt crystals form on the outside of the ice. This salt slurry is washed off. The ice is then extracted. The unit uses much less energy than other desalination techniques, but is still experimental. It produces 55,000 gallons of fresh water per day.

Other proposals have been made to help alleviate the Kingdom's water shortage. One prince suggested towing icebergs to the Kingdom. His science advisor said the idea was feasible except for the fact that icebergs, which are pure water, drew too much water to enter a Saudi port. Melting it at a controlled rate would have presented other difficulties. The idea was finally killed, he claimed, because it was not secure against blockade or foreign interference. Another idea floated by the Japanese was to fill their supertankers with water, the one resource of which Japan has an abundance. The tankers would discharge water in the Kingdom, then load up with oil to take to Japan. The idea never got anywhere.

The most recent proposal was Turkish Prime Minister Turgut Ozal's "Peace Pipeline." The 1987 proposal, which was not accepted by the Kingdom, was for two $10 billion pipelines running form Eastern Turkey through Syria, Jordan, and Saudi Arabia. One would end near Mecca, while the other would terminate at the United Arab Emirates. Project consultant Brown and Root said another pipeline would carry 500,000 bpd of crude back to Turkey where it presumably would help pay the cost of the massive project. The cost is many times that of desalination plants, although the Turks say that piping would be one-fifth as expensive as desalination. Saudi officials privately say they fear the pipeline would be cut off.

Something must be done to meet new demand, since new SWCC plants will not be capable of meeting projected needs. Planners estimate that total demand will rise 12 billion cmd in 1990 and 20 billion cmd in 2010.[17] This implies that greater reliance will be placed on the fossil ground water.

CONCLUSION

The Koran has an account of the Biblical Haggar, the slave-woman of Abraham. After being expelled from Abraham's tents, she took her son Ishmael, the eventual father of the Arab nations, to the site of present-day Mecca. There, the miraculous appearance of the Zam-Zam spring rescued the two from dying of thirst. If the Saudis continue squandering their fossil water growing unneeded wheat, they will require yet another miracle. They cannot afford to run their agriculture program on desalinated water. They will find that, while substitutes for oil can be found, there is no replacement for water.

CHAPTER One - History

1. Hitti, Philip, *History of the Arabs* p. 46
2. Hitti, *History of the Arabs*, p. 25
3. Al-Yassini, Ayman, *Religion and State in the Kingdom of Saudi Arabia*, p. 26
4. Rashid and Shaheen, *King Fahd and Saudi Arabia's Glorious Evolution.* p. 48
5. Ibid. p. 49
6. Holden and Johns, *The House of Saudi,* p. 120
7. Rashid and Shaheen, *King Fahd and Saudi Arabia's Glorious Evolution,* p. 41.
8. Holden and Johns, *House of Saud.,* p. 142
9. Ibid.., 319-320
10. Ibid.., p. 390.
11. Saudi Gazette, 5/7/84.
12. Arab News, 4/9/84
13. Riyadh Development Study No. 5.0.

Chapter Two - Politics

1. Middle East Travel, July-August, 1986
2. Huyette, Summer Scott, *Political Adaptation in Sa'udi Arabia.* p. 134
3. Ibid p. 101
4. Holden and Johns, *The House of Saud.* p.412-414
5. Translated in the Wall Street Journal. 4/25/84.
6. Bligh, Alexander. *From Prince to King: Royal Succession in the House of Saud in the Twentieth Century.* pp. 33-36 and 51-52.
7. Buchan, Jamie. *Secular and Religious Opposition,* Niblock, Ed. *Society, and Economy in Saudi Arabia.* pp. 114-116
8. Helms, Christine Moss, *The Cohesion of Saudi Arabia.* p. 112
9. Helms, p. 112.
10. Cole, Donald Powell. *Nomads of the Nomads: The Al Murrah Bedouin of the Empty Quarter.* p. 54.
11. Cole, D. *The enmeshment of Nomads in Sa'udi Arabian Society: the case of the Al-Murrah' in Nelson (ed.) The Desert and the Sown p. 121.*
12. Muerhing, Kevin, "*The Ordeal of Hamad Al-Sayyari*" Institutional Investor, November,1984.

Chapter 3 Foriegn Policy

1. Saudi Gazette, 7/27/88
2. New York Times, 8/16/90.
3. Ibrahim, Youssef. New York Times, 8/25/90.
4. Mackey, Sandra. *The Saudis: Inside the Desert Kingdom,* pp. 324-324.
5. Ibrahim, Youssef. 8/26/90
6. Ottaway, David. Washington Post, 9/6/90.
7. Saudi officials denied Egyptian troops assisted in providing security for the Hajj, but an Egyptian co-worker's cousin happened to be one of the Egyptians providing security, and told us about it.
8. New York Times, 8/22/90.

Chapter 4 Military and Security

1. Safran, Nadav. *Saudi Arabia: Ceaseless Search for Security,* p. 114.
2. Mackey, Sandra. *The Saudis.* p. 283.
3. Safran, Nadav, *Saudi Arabia.*, p. 55
4. Ibid.., p. 444
5. Sampson, Anthony, *The Arms Bazaar,* pp. 163-163
6. Saudi officials claimed the explosion was caused by a faulty power transformer.
7. New York Times, 5/29/81
8. Safran, Nadav, *Saudi Arabia,* p. 68
9. Hameed, Mazher. *Arabia Imperilled,* p. 136
10. Ibid.. 159
11. Safran, Nadav, *Saudi Arabia.* p. 444.
12. Ibid.., 128
13. Holden and Johns, *House of Saud.* p. 244
14. Hameed, Mazher, *Arabia Imperilled.* p. 142
15. Ibid., p. 143
16. Safran, Nadav, *Saudi Arabia* p. 130.
17. Arab News, 4/26/87.

Chapter 5 - Religion

1. Saudi Gazette, 8/27/87.
2. Taken from the Jeddah report, January 1930, from the British Consulate of Jeddah, quoted by Derek Hopwood. *The Ideological Basis: Ibn Abd Al-Wahhab's Muslim Revivalism* in *State, Society and Economy in Saudi Arabia,* edited by Tim Niblock, p. 41.
3. This was extracted from a letter sent by a member of the group raided by the officials. Most spent several months in prison and were then deported.
4. Saudi Gazette, 12/8/86.
5. Saudi Gazette 8/9/87.
6. Al-Yassini, Ayman. *Religion and State in the Kingdom of Saudi Arabia*, p. 60.
7. Ibid., p. 67.
8. Ibid., p. 71.
9. Helms, Christine Moss. *The Cohesion of Saudi Arabia.* p. 129.
10. Al-Medina, 7/8/89.
11. New York Times 8/25/90.

Chapter 6 - Social

1. Al-Bilad, 6/3/88.
2. Arab News 12/12/88.
3. Ibid.
4. Okaz, 6/22/89.
5. Ibid.
6. Saudi Gazette, 1/18/88.
7. Arab News, 3/18/89.
8. Cole, Donald Powell. *Nomads of the Nomads: The Al Murrah Bedouin of the Empty Quarter.* p. 53.
9. Ibid., p. 17.

Chapter 7 - Women

1. Washington Post, 9/6/90.
2. Saudi Gazette, 6/4/87.
3. Arab News, 2/16/89.
4. Cincinnati Enquirer, 9/16/90.
5. Saudi Gazette, 1/29/87.
6. Saudi Gazette 2/24/86.
7. Saudi Gazette 7/2/86.
8. Arab News, 6/2/89.
9. SCB Annual Report 1989.
10. Arab News, 8/20/87.
11. Al-Riyadh, 1/29/88.
12. Cole, Donald. *Nomads of the Nomads: The Al Murrah Bedouin of the Empty Quarte*r, p. 75.

Chapter 8 - Labor

1. Saudi Gazette 3/11/88.
2. Okaz 2/2/87.
3. This data came from a source in the Ministry of Planning.
4. Saudi Gazette, 9/25/85.
5. Al-Riyadh, 8/1/86.
6. Arab News, 6/8/87.
7. Associated Press, 4/14/85.

Chapter 9 - Petroleum

1. Arab News, 5/29/85.
2. Platt's Oilgram, 11/12/87.
3. International Construction Week, 7/6/87.
4. Financial Times, 6/17/88.

Chapter 10 - Industry

1. Chemical Week, 12/9/87.
2. SIDF 1988 Annual Report.

3. Al-Yassini, *Religon and State in the Kingdom of Saudi Arabia,* pp. 61-63.

4. SIDF 1988 Annual Report.

Chapter 11 - Infrastructure

1. The London Economist. 6/27/87.

2. Saudi Press Agency 11/16/89.

3. Saline Water Conversion Corp. 1988 Annual Yearbook.

4. Derived from Huyette's *Political Adaptation in Sa'udi Arabia.*

5. Rashid and Shaheen, *King Fahd and Saudi Arabia's Glorious Evolution,* pp. 50-51.

6. Al-Yassini, *Religon and State in the Kingdom of Saudi Arabia,* p. 75.

7. Solaim, Soliman, pp. 159-160.

8. Solaim, Soliman, Op. Cit. p. 123.

9. Ibid. p. 127.

10. Ibid. p. 118.

11. Ibid. p. 84.

12. Ibid. p. 140.

Chapter 12 - Finance

1. Wilson, Peter. Saudi Gazette. 10/30/85.

2. Wall Street Journal.

3. SAMA Statistical Review. Spring 1986

4. Financial Times, 6/27/88.

5. Arab News 6/6/87.

6. Al-Jazira 1987 Annual Report.

7. SAMA Annual Report.

8. Field, Michael. "*The Richest Man in the World.*" Euromoney Magazine. May, 1983.

9. Niblock, Tim Ed. *State, Society, and Economy in Saudi Arabia,* pp. 283-285.

10. Institutional Investor, 6/12/87, p. 15.

11. Muerhing, Kevin, "*The Ordeal of Hamad Al-Sayyari*" Institutional Investor, November, 1984.

12. Institutional Investor, 6/7/82, p. 15

Chapter 13 - Agriculture and Water

1. Saudi Business Magazine, 5/21/83.

2. Arab News 11/25/85.

3. Arab News 3/29/89.

4. Annual Bulletin of Current Agricultural Statistics.

5. SAMA Quarterly statistics 4th Qtr. 1986.

6. SIDF Annual Report 1988.

7. Saudi Business Magazine, Vol. VII No. 4.

8. Annual Bulletin of Current Agricultural Statistics.

9. Ibid.

10. Arab News 9/18/85.

11. Annual Bulletin of Current Agricultural Statistics.

12. Saudi Press Agency 5/16/87.

13. Al-Medina 2/6/87.

14. Al-Riyadh 4/20/86.

15. Arab News 3/19/87.

16. SAMA 1406 Report pp. 106-108.

THE SAUDI ROYAL FAMILY

Abdulaziz, founder of Saudi Arabia, fathered at least 45 sons from some 22 mothers, and an unverified number of daughters. He was born in Riyadh, Jan. 15, 1902, was declared King of Saudi Arabia in 1932, and died in 1953. Many of his sons died either in childbirth or during the worldwide Influenza epidemic of 1919. Sons are numbered according to the order of their birth. Note the mothers, for they are important. Abdullah has no full-brothers. The Al-Fahad are incorrectly called the "Sudairy Seven" because other princes, such as Badr, have Sudairy mothers as well.

2. Saud b. Jan 12, 1902. (son of Wadha bint Hazzam) He became King in 1953, and was deposed in 1964. He died in Greece, in 1969.

4. Faisal b. in 1904-1905 (Tarfa bint Abdullah). He became King in 1964, and was assassinated in 1975. One son, Abdullah, is prominent businessman, involved in SAADCO dairy. Turki Bin Faisal is head of the Intelligence Bureau. Saud Al-Faisal is the Minister of Foreign Affairs. Khaled bin Faisal is the popular governor of the Asir Province.

6. Muhammed (known as Father of the Twin Evils) b. 1910 (son of Jauharah bint Musaid) and died in 1987. He ordered the executionof Princess Mishal.

7. Khaled b. 1912-1913 (son of Jauharah bint Musaid). Died 1981. Became King in 1975. He died of heart attack in 1982.

11. Fahad b. 1921 (son of Hassa bint Ahmed Al-Sudairi). He became King in 1982. His eldest son, Faisal, is head of the General Presidency of Youth Welfare. Mohammed is Governor of the Eastern Province. Abdulaziz, the youngest, is a source of bitter envy of his brothers.

12. Abdullah b. 1923 (son of Bint Asi Al-Shuraim of the Shammar). He is Crown Prince and Commander of the National Guard. His son, Miteb, is head of the military academy and the Kingdom's Ford agent in the Central Province.

16. Sultan b. 1924 (son of Hassa). Deputy Prime Minister and Minister of Defense and Aviation. His sons include Bandar, Ambassador to the United States.

19. Abdul Rahman b. 1926-27 (son of Hassa) Deputy Minister of Defense and Aviation.

22. Badr b. 1931 (son of Haya bint Saad Al-Sudairi) He and his sons are famous horse breeders and racers.

23. Talal b. 1931 (son of Munaiyer) Former Minister, former liberal free-prince and present philanthropist. Son Walid is a tough-minded businessman, andhcairman of USCB.

26. Naif b. 1933 (son of Hassa) Minister of Interior. Son Saud is deputy to Turki bin Faisal in the Intelligence Bureau.

28. Turki b. 1934 (son of Hassa) married to one of the Al-Fassis and holds no positions.

29. Fawwaz b. 1934 (son of Munaiyer) Erstwhile liberal Prince.

32. Salman b. 1936 (sonof Hassa) Governor of Riyadh. Son Abdulaziz serves under Hisham Nazer in the Ministry of Petroleum, while Sultan went into space on the Space Shuttle.

34. Thamir b. 1937 (son of Bint al Shalan of hte Ruwala) Wanted a sex-change operation, and died after committing suicide in 1969. He drenched his clothes with gasoline and immolated himself.

41. Sattam b. 1943 (son of Mudhi) Deputy Governor of Riyadh.

42. Miqrin b. 1943 (son of Baraka al Yamaniya) Governor of Hail.
(Condensed from *The House of Saud*)

BIBLIOGRAPHY

Ali, A. Yusuf (translator) *The Holy Quran. Translation and Commentary.* Brentwood, Maryland: Amana Corp. 1983

Bligh, Alexander. *From Prince to King: Royal Succession in the House of Saud in the Twentieth Century.* New York: New York University Press, 1984

Chapra, M. Umer. *Towards a Just Monetary System.* Leicester: The Islamic Foundation, 1985.

Cole, Donald Powell. *Nomads of the Nomads: The Al Murrah Bedouin of the Empty Quarter.* Cambridge, Mass.: AHD Publishing Co. 1975

Cole, D.P. 'The Enmeshment of Nomads in Sa'udi Arabia Society: the case of the Al Murrah' *The Desert and the Sown.* Cynthia Nelson,Berkely, Calif. Ed. U. Of Cal. International Studies. 1975

Field, Michael, *The Merchants: The Big Business Families of Saudi Arabia & the Gulf.* New York: Overlook Press, 1985.

Golub, David. *When Oil and Politics Mix: Saudi Oil Policy, 1975- 1985.* Cambridge, Mass.: Harvard Center for Middle Eastern Studies. 1985.

Hafiz, Faisal, and Murshid Samir, eds. *Who's WHo in Saudi Arabia 1983-84.* Jeddah: Tihama For Advertising, Public and Marketing Research. 1984.

Hameed, Mazher A.*Arabia Imperilled: The Security Imperatives of the Arab Gulf States.* Washington, D.C.: Middle East Assesments Group, 1986.

Helms, Christine Moss. *The Cohesion of Saudi Arabia: Evolution of Political Identity.* London: Croom Helm, 1981.

Hitti, Philip. *History of the Arabs: From the Earliest Times to the Present.* 7th Ed. New York: St. Martin's Press, 1960.

Holden, David and Richard Johns. *The House of Saud.* London: Holt Rinehart and Winston, 1981

Huyette, Summer Scott, *Political Adaptation in Sa'udi Arabia: A Study of the Council of Ministers.* Boulder, Colo.: Westview Press, 1985.

Kingdom of Saudi Arabia. General Presidency of Youth Welfare Dept. of Planning. Projects and Programes Accomplished by the General Presidency of Youth Welfare, 1983-1984.

Kingdom of Saudi Arabia. Ministry of Interior. Tenth Statistical Book of the Ministry of Interior for 1984. Riyadh: Dar Al-Hillal Printing Press, 1985

Kingdom of Saudi Arabia. Ministry of Labour and Social Affairs. Labor and Workmen Law and Attached Procedures. Jeddah: Vocational Training Center Press.

Kingdom of Saudi Arabia. Ministry of Agriculture and Water Resources. Annual Agriculture Reports. Riyadh.

Kingdom of Saudi Arabia. Ministry of Planning. 4th and 5th five year plans. Riyadh

Kingdom of Saudi Arabia: SAMA Reports. Riyadh. 1399-1409

Kingdom of Saudi Arabia. Saline Water Conversion Corporation 1988 Annual Report. Riyadh.

Lacey, Robert. *The Kingdom: Arabia and the House of Saud.* New York: Harcourt Brace Jovanovich, 1981.

Mackey, Sandra. *The Saudis: Inside the Desert Kingdom.* Boston: Houghton Mifflin Co., 1987.

Mattione, Richard P. *OPEC's Investment & The International Financial System.* Washington, D.C.: The Brookings Institution, 1985.

Mauger, Thierry and Danielle Mauger. *In The Shadow of the Black Tents.* Jeddah: Tihama, 1985.

Munif Abdelrahman. Peter Theroux (Translator) *Cities of Salt.* New York: Random House, 1988.

Niblock, Tim Ed. *State, Society, and Economy in Saudi Arabia.* New York: St. Martin's Press, 1982.

Rashid, Dr. Nasser Ibrahim and Dr. Esber Igrahim Shaheen. *King Fahd and Saudi Arabia's Great Evolution.* Joplin, Mo: International Institute of Technology, 1987.

Safran, Nadav. *Saudi Arabia: The Ceaseless Quest for Security.* Cambridge, Mass: Belknap Press of Harvard University Press, 1985

Sampson, Anthony, *The Arms Bazaar.* London: Hodder and Stoughton Ltd., 1977.

Sampson, Anthony, *The Seven Sisters,* London, Hodder and Stoughton, Ltd., 1975.

Solaim,Soliman, Doctoral Thesis, Johns Hopkins University, 1975.

Thesiger, Wilfred. *Arabian Sands.* New York: E.P. Dutton, 1959

Al-Yassini Ayman. *Religion and State in the Kingdom of Saudi Arabia.* Boulder, Colo.: Westview Press, 1985.

Zwemmer, Rev. S.M. Arabia *The Cradle of Islam.* London: Darf Publishers Ltd. 1900

INDEX

ABDULAZIZ Bin Saud, King 7-9, 17-18, 28, 81, 82, 129, 133, 134-193
ABDULLAH Bin Abdulaziz 18, 19, 24, 25, 27,   45.
AGRICULTURE 2, 8, 13, 149-154
ACC, SEE IRAQ
AIR FORCE 11, 16, 24, 26, 34, 39-42
AIRCRAFT 11, 16, 21, 34, 37-42, 54, 58, 125, 128-129
ALCOHOL 73, 76, 80, 114
AL-FAHAD AND SONS 9, 19, 23, 34, 51
AL-RAJHI 84-85, 143-145
AL-SHEIKH, SEE WAHHAB, DESCENDENTS OF
ARAB LEAGUE 31, 32
ARAMCO 8-9, 79, 84, 112, 113-114, 119
ARMS DEALS 11, 16, 34, 38, 40-41, 42, 48-49, 117-118
ARMS INDUSTRIES 35, 47-48
ARMY 25, 33, 34, 42-43, 95
ASIR 3, 29, 33, 95
AWACS 16, 39-40, 41, 58
BAD LOANS 2, 16, 20, 139-141, 153
BAHRAIN 3, 12, 85
BAKSHEESH, SEE COMMISSIONS
BANKS 2, 16, 60, 84-85, 94, 122, 139-141, 145-146
BEDOUIN 3-4, 25, 28-29, 45-46, 76-77, 81, 82, 89, 90
BIN BAZ, ABDULAZIZ 57, 60-61, 65, 141
BRITAIN 7, 102, 118
BUDGET 1, 9, 11, 13, 17, 94-95
CAMELS 4, 46, 82, 127, 153
CHINA, PEOPLE'S REPUBLIC OF 31, 36.
CHRISTIANS, DISLIKE OF, OPPRRESSION OF, 54, 56-57, 64, 66, 74, 78
COMMITTEE FOR BANKING DISPUTES 137, 142
COMMISSIONS 11, 18-20, 23, 27, 127, 137
CORRUPTION, SEE COMMISSIONS
COUNCIL OF MINISTERS 9, 21, 22-24, 133-134
CONSTITUTION, PROPOSED, SEE DEMOCRACY
DEMOCRACY 2, 9, 26, 28, 135
DIPLOMACY 2, 16, 33-37, 59-60
DIPLOMATS KILLED 36
DIPLOMATIC QUARTER 72-73, 92
DOMESTIC SERVANTS, SEE MAIDS AND DRIVERS
DRUGS 76, 135, 152
EASTERN PROVINCE 1, 6, 8, 19, 29
EDUCATION 11, 24, 43, 46, 51, 75, 81, 86-87, 96-97, 132-133
EGYPT 6, 7, 9, 10, 19, 35, 47, 99
EXECUTIONS 59, 67, 68-69, 136
EXPATRIATES 8-9, 18, 59, 75, 78-79, 79-81, 90, 99-108, 119
FAHAD BIN ABDULAZIZ, KING 1, 9, 12, 17, 18, 19, 20-21, 25, 26, 27, 32-33, 34, 45, 54, 61, 84, 92, 95, 109
FAISAL BIN ABDULAZIZ, KING 9-11, 35
FIVE-YEAR PLANS 96
FOREIGN AID 1-2, 35-36, 59-60, 105
FRANCE 11
GULF COOPERATION COUNCIL (GCC) 12, 31-32, 33, 46-47, 120
HEJAZ 7, 8, 27, 29
HIGHWAYS 125, 126-127
HOUSING 15, 72-73, 97, 125-126
IKHWAN 6, 7, 17, 28, 137
INDUSTRY 2, 84, 117-124, 126, 130
INTEREST CONFLICT 2, 60, 139, 141-142

IRAN 11-12, 35, 36, 58-60, 62
IRAQ 1, 3, 7, 16, 18, 19, 25, 31-32, 33, 36, 38, 39, 94, 95
ISLAM, THE RELIGION 5-7, 10, 17, 35, 53-69, 135
ISLAMIC BANKING 139, 142-143
ISLAMIC FUNDAMENTALISTS, SE ALSO POLICE, RELIGIOUS 2, 24-25, 35, 54-55, 61, 63-64, 65, 137
ISLAMIC MOVEMENT 17, 35, 36, 56, 59-60, 62, 64, 135
ISRAEL 8, 10, 19, 32, 35, 43, 78
JORDAN 3, 7, 39, 45
KHALED BIN ABDULAZIZ, KING 9, 11-12, 17, 65
KHASHOGGI, ADNAN 11, 48-49, 73, 126
KORAN 5, 9, 60, 66, 92
KUWAIT 1, 3, 12, 16, 18, 19, 31-32, 33, 95, 125
LABOR, EXPATRIATE 2, 12, 15, 16, 33, 80-81, 94-95, 99-102, 102-108, 114, 119, 128, 132 SEE ALSO MAIDS
AND DRIVERS
LABOR, SAUDI 2, 13, 15, 17, 38-39, 84, 86, 95-99, 119, 128, 133, 152
MAIDS AND DRIVERS 74, 84, 107-108
MAJLIS SYSTEM 11, 25-27, 50-51, 71
MASTER GAS COLLECTION SYSTEM 115
MECCA 3, 5-6, 8, 9, 20, 39, 53, 57-58, 61-62, 66, 68
MECCA DISTURBANCES 35, 36, 47, 55, 58-60, 62
MECCA MOSQUE, 1979 SEIZURE 11-12, 24, 43, 60, 65
MEDICAL SYSTEM 10, 17, 20, 22-23, 54, 82, 86, 90, 94, 131-132
MERCENARIES 2, 47
MILITARY 1-2, 11, 13, 24, 31, 33, 38-48 SEE ALSO AIR FORCE, ARMS DEALS, ARMS FACTORIES, ARMY,
AND NAVY
MINING 4, 115-116
MISSILES 31, 36, 38
MOHAMMED, THE PROPHET 5-6, 66, 72, 82
MONEY EXCHANGERS 84-85, 143-145
MUTAWWA, SEE POLICE, RELIGIOUS
NAIF, PR. MINISTER OF INTERIOR 19, 22, 49, 52, 59, 60
NATIONAL GUARD 11-12, 24, 25, 38, 44-46, 59, 77
NAVY 11, 43-44
OFFSET INVESTMENT PROGRAM 97, 117-118, 122
OIC, SEE ISLAMIC MOVEMENT
OIL GLUT 1-2, 11, 31, 109-111
OMAN 3, 12, 23, 32
OPEC 2, 10-11, 109-112
OPPOSITION 24-26, 38-39, 64-65
PALESTINIAN LIBERATION ORGANIZATION (PLO) 32, 33, 45
PAN-ISLAMIC MOVEMENTS, SEE ISLAMIC MOVEMENT
PAYMENTS, TOTAL AND DELAYED 11, 12-13, 16, 57-58, 78, 101-102
PETROLEUM 1-2, 3, 10, 12, 31, 33, 34, 44, 109-111, 121
PETROMIN 112, 119, 120, 121
PIPELINE, IRAQI 113
PEACE SHIELD, SEE OFFSET INVESTMENT
PETROCHEMICALS, SEE SABIC
POLICE, SECRET AND OTHER 25-26, 49-52, 59, 89, 136
POLICE, RELIGIOUS 15, 54, 55-56, 63-64, 81, 91-92
PROSTITUTION 73, 75
QATAR 3, 12
RAILROAD 127-128
REFINERIES 39, 112, 119-120
REVENUES 1-2, 9. 10-11, 12, 109
ROYAL FAMILY 3, 6-8, 9, 18-21, 22-25, 26-28, 92, 138, 153
SABIC 39, 112, 115, 119, 120-122
SALMAN, PR. GOVERNOR OF RIYADH 18, 20, 22, 32, 52, 80, 127
SAMA 29, 60, 137, 139, 142, 143, 146-148

SAUD BIN ABDULAZIZ, KING 9-10, 21, 74
SHIA 4, 6, 8, 11, 22, 29, 61, 65, 95, 114
SIDF 97, 117, 121, 123
SLAVERY 10, 27, 95-96, 103-104
STOCK MARKET 118, 121, 145
SUBSIDIES 1, 13, 17, 78, 89, 117, 129, 150-151, 152
SUBSIDIES, ATTEMPTS TO CUT 13-14, 149-150, 155
SUDAIRY SEVEN, SEE AL-FAHADSHIA 4, 11, 22, 29, 56, 65, 95, 114
SULTAN PR. MINISTER OF DEFENSE 19, 22, 38
TALAL, PR. 9, 27-28
TARIFFS, PROTECTIVE 117, 122-23, 153
TAXES 14-15, 17, 94-95, 117, 119
TEXACO DEAL 113-114
TURKI, PR. 22
ULEMA9, 10, 11, 54, 60-63, 103, 135-136
UNION OF SOCIET SOCIALIST SOVIET REPUBLICS (USSR) 8, 36-37
UNITED ARAB EMIRATES (UAE) 3, 12, 32
UNITED STATES 8, 18, 34-35, 38, 102, 110, 114, 117-118, 120
UNIVERSITIES 9-10, 12, 24, 65, 86-87, 133
WAHHABI, ISLAM 6-7, 29
WAHHAB, MUHAMMED AND DESCENDANTS 19, 22, 63
WATER 1, 4, 13, 39, 130, 154-158
WHEAT 13, 149-151
WOMEN 11, 20, 24, 25, 34, 57, 72, 73, 75, 80, 81, 83, 84-93, 98-99, 133
YAMANI 10-11, 24, 109-110
YEMEN 3, 4, 9, 10, 33-34, 35, 39, 43, 107-108
YOUTH 30, 65, 69, 71, 74-76, 87-88, 92, 97-98, 133
ZOO 15, 79, 82, 91-92